M000095706

You're Pregnant? You're Fired!

Protecting Mothers, Fathers, and Other Caregivers in the Workplace

Tom Spiggle

Published by Morgan and Dawson Publishing
www.MorganandDawson.com

Copyright © 2014 by Tom Spiggle

All rights reserved. Copying or reproducing this publication in any form, selling or reselling its content, or storing it in a retrieval system for the purposes of commercial gain constitutes a breach of copyright.

The publisher of *You're Pregnant? You're Fired! Protecting Mothers, Fathers, and Other Caregivers in the Workplace* has exercised the utmost care in the composition of this publication; however, the Spiggle Law Firm cannot be held responsible for errors, inaccuracies, or omissions resulting from the nature of the information provided or previously published, or through typographical compilation.

This book is designed to introduce readers to important information about their rights as caregivers. Reading this book does not establish an attorney-client relationship between readers and the Spiggle Law Firm. Nothing in this book should be construed as legal advice.

ISBN 10: 0989370127
ISBN 13: 9780989370127

Library of Congress Control Number: 2014905095
Morgan and Dawson Publishing,
Raleigh, NC

Acknowledgments

I wish to thank my wife, Anne Spiggle, and our four rug rats: Harrison, Jonah, Julia, and Lucy; you are my rock and my guiding lights. Also, much appreciation goes to Jacob Small and Krista Goelz, the attorneys in my firm who contributed sections to this book. Finally, I want to express my gratitude for my colleagues in the National Employment Lawyers Association and its District of Columbia chapter, the Metropolitan Washington Employment Lawyers Association. They are a constant source of inspiration.

Contents

Preface

I wrote this book for employees in a bad place at work—or fired—just because they tried to care for themselves, a child, or a sick parent.

Our country has little in the way of a social safety net. Even if you are not a paycheck or two away from ending up on the streets, if you're like most people, you couldn't go without income for long. Workers who are sick, who are pregnant, or who have to care for a loved one are particularly vulnerable. But there are protections, and you should know about them. That's why I wrote this book: to give you the answers you need, and maybe just a bit of hope.

How should you use this book? Though you can certainly read it front to back, you need not do so to get ideas about how to handle your situation. Look through the table of contents for sections that seem to apply to you. Laws that protect a pregnant worker may not help a person suffering from a disability. That said, there is a fair amount of overlap in federal antidiscrimination law, and the examples I have provided in one section may have useful points that could be used in another. So, pick and choose the chapters you find most useful.

Keep in mind that employment law is very, very complicated. Each chapter could be a separate book. Many resources explain in greater detail the ins and outs of the laws discussed. The Center for WorkLife Law (http://worklifelaw.org) is a particularly good one. As I write this, Cynthia Calvert with the center is preparing to publish a lengthy treatise on laws, including local and state laws, that protect caregivers. The center also has many other helpful publications (many of them available at no cost). Other organizations do yeoman's work in this area. They include the Equal Employment Opportunity Commission (EEOC; http://www.eeoc.gov), the Families and Work Institute (http://www.familiesandwork.org/), the National Women's Law Center (http://www.nwlc.org), and A Better Balance (http://www.abetterbalance.org/web/), just to name a few.

I have not tried to cover every aspect of every law. Instead, I provide an overview and some examples so that you might be able to recognize a situation similar to yours. But each employment problem is different. A simple twist in your particular case could mean you have more—or fewer—legal protections than what I describe. So, you need to see a lawyer to get the best idea of how the law might apply to you. After reading this book, I want you to know that surgery is possible; I don't intend for you to know how to wield the scalpel.

As a practitioner in the trenches, what I have attempted to do in this book (which is different from what you might find in books solely on the law) is to give you a real-world sense of what litigation is really like. Knowing whether you have a "strong" or "weak" case is important, but it is only the beginning of the process. In certain circumstances, it might make sense for an employee with a "strong" case to settle quickly and move on. Likewise, a different employee in a different situation, with a "weaker" case, might make a reasoned decision to push forward in litigation. But these decisions are largely personal ones. For example, you need to decide how long you are prepared to fight, and what it is worth to you to force a recalcitrant employer to finally sit down and give you some answers. In the examples I share in this book, I hope to give you a sense of the liabilities, and possibilities, that exist when taking action against your employer. Spoiler alert: you have more options and possibilities than you might think.

Regardless of what, if anything, you do, rest easy knowing that you took the best course of those available to protect you and your family.

A Word to Employers (and Their Lawyers)

I don't think you are the "bad guy" or that HR folks are evil. I know that running a workplace is difficult on many levels, not the least of which is complying with a bewildering array of employment laws. I know this because I run a small business. I employ people, just like you do. I have to meet payroll. I have to market my services. That's why I don't take cases that I perceive to be marginal. Employers sometimes make judgment calls. Sometimes there are bad calls. These kinds of decisions should not land you in court— at least by my hand. I do this work because outrageous violations of employment law continue to occur. Really, you would be shocked at some of the things I hear from employees who come to my office.

When I first started, even I was inclined to disbelieve some of the stories I heard—or at least that they happened in the way the employees believed they had. But thanks to the advent of the iPhone and other recording devices, many times there has been direct evidence: for instance, a recording of a sexual harasser who was charming in front of a crowd but a disgusting letch behind closed doors. I heard it from his own mouth. I have many other stories like this.

That's why I do the work I do. This isn't blackmail or whining. This is justice.

Part I: To Sue or Not to Sue

Chapter 1
Do You Have a Case?

Is It Illegal to Fire Mom?

"Here's what happened to me. Do I have a case? Is there anything I can do?"

The first reason that many people call my office is to find out whether they have a legal claim. Something has happened at work. Maybe they have been fired. They know that what happened was not right, but was it illegal? (The follow-up question is usually "What is my case worth?" I will discuss that in the next section.)

In employment law, this question can be surprisingly difficult to answer, especially when compared to other areas of the law. For example, if you are married and you want a divorce, you have a case. The family lawyer can skip directly to considering the strength of your position. Likewise, if you get arrested, like it or not, you have a case that a criminal lawyer can help with. Not so with employment law.

Just because you have been treated badly at work or fired does not mean you have a case. In fact, most people who have been mistreated at work or fired were not treated illegally. This is worth repeating: **most of the time, bad behavior by your boss is not illegal.** Stated another way: **dysfunctional workplaces are not illegal (even if they are bad business).**

That said, many laws apply to the workplace, even in a right-to-work state (as most states are). It is not uncommon for people who talk to me to be surprised (and relieved) to learn that their legal rights may have been violated.

There's yet a third variation. An employee comes to me believing that her rights have been violated. After talking to me, she realizes her rights have been violated—just not the ones she thought. For instance, the person who believes she has been subjected to a "hostile work environment" learns that having to put up with a boss who yells is not a hostile work environment. But after talking to this employee, I learn that her employer has not paid her for overtime, even though it routinely required her to work more than forty hours per week. So this is also worth repeating: **you might have a case against your employer, even if it is not obvious to you that you do.**

So, the answer to the question "Do I have a case?" is very likely "It depends." One way to explore this question is to call a lawyer. If you do nothing else, do that. I am routinely surprised when I hear stories of people whose rights were blatantly violated at work who never did anything about it or who waited too long to file a claim. Don't be one of those people. You may not want to bring a lawsuit, but at least find out—if only for your own peace of mind—what your rights are.

Now, to get the most effective use out of the call to your lawyer, do what you are doing now. Or if you are advising a friend, tell him or her to do this. Educate yourself. Certainly, you are not going to be able to learn a complex body of law by consulting a few online resources or even by reading this book. But with a bit of effort, you can get a sense of (1) whether what happened to you is possibly illegal, and (2) if so, which facts of your situation are important.

Let's take a simple one. Many discrimination cases are enforced under Title VII of the Civil Rights Act of 1964. This act applies only to employers with fifteen or more employees. That's an easy question for you to answer. But before you did some reading, you likely had no idea that the number of employees was important. Knowing that will help maximize your time with a lawyer. Right up front you can say, "I work for Construction Contractors. It has only ten employees, so I know I am not protected by some discrimination laws." You get bonus points if you say, "I think this means Title VII does not apply." This does two things. First, it saves time with your lawyer. Second, it telegraphs to your lawyer that you have taken the time to educate yourself. For most lawyers, this makes you a more attractive candidate for representation.

Here's a word of caution, however. Don't be a know-it-all or pretend you are. Most attorneys welcome a client who has taken the time to try to educate herself. But most attorneys are wary of employees who have discovered their inner lawyer and now want to play that part. Lawyers want a client who can be a productive participant in the case, not one who tries to drive the case from the back seat.

What Are Your Chances of Success?

This is the most obvious question, and it is impossible to answer with certainty, even for experienced lawyers. However, it is possible to make an educated guess. Here are some factors that an attorney will consider:

- *Did your employer do something unlawful?* Sometimes it is difficult to determine whether your employer actually violated the law. (As you know, your employer can behave badly without crossing the line. So, although you may have been mistreated, you don't have a case to bring to court.)

- *Do you have an employment contract?* The next thing to determine is whether you have an employment contract. If so, you need to see whether the contract provides you with any protection. For instance, the contract may state that you can be fired only "for cause." The contract may also control other matters that will affect whether you can get a severance agreement and what type.

  If you are like most employees, you do not have a contract. You are what is known as an "at-will" employee: that is, your employer can fire you for any reason—for example, it doesn't like your attitude, your work, or the color of your shirt—as long as the reason does not violate federal or state law. But it is worth emphasizing: **even at-will employees have workplace rights**. I often hear from people who think that, because they are at will, they have no recourse if their employer mistreats them. Wrong! If you employer violates anti-discrimination law, for instance, it is liable. It does not matter if you are an at-will employee.

- *Does the employer fall within the guidelines set forth in the law?* Another initial issue to determine is whether your employer is covered by federal and/or state law. Many federal laws—for instance, ones that protect against race and sex discrimination—require

5

that an employer have a minimum of fifteen employees before they even apply. So, if your employer has fourteen employees, federal antidiscrimination law does not protect you.

However, the state you live in may provide additional protections. For instance, while generally no additional protections are provided to employees in Virginia, both the District of Columbia and Maryland have laws that protect employees subjected to discrimination. Note that in states with laws that protect employees, you can bring a lawsuit under both federal and state law.

- *Did you file your claim within the applicable deadline?* Employment law is full of arbitrary time limits that can knock out even the best of claims. Below are some limitations periods for common employment law statutes.

TYPE OF CLAIM	TIME LIMIT
DISCRIMINATION CLAIMS	
These claims, which must be filed with the EEOC, include the following types of issues: • Race discrimination • Sex discrimination (including stereotypes based on caregiving status) • Pregnancy discrimination • Age discrimination • Discrimination based on disability under the Americans with Disabilities Act (ADA)	• 45 days (government employees to report to EEO) • 180 days to report to the EEOC if there is no local agency with a work-sharing agreement with the EEOC • 300 days to report to the EEOC if there is an agency with a work-sharing agreement with the EEOC (these agencies include the District of Columbia Office of Human Rights, as well as the Arlington, Fairfax, and Alexandria Offices of Human Rights)
WAGE AND HOUR CLAIMS	
Fair Labor Standards Act (FLSA) • You can file these claims with the US Department of Labor, but it is not required.	Rolling two-year statute of limitations, meaning the limitations period reaches back two years from the date of your last paycheck

WAGE AND HOUR CLAIMS (CONTINUED)	
Equal Pay Act (EPA) • You can file these claims with the EEOC, but it is not required.	• Two-year statute of limitations for nonwillful violations • Three-year statute of limitations for willful violations In other words, you have two years to bring a lawsuit if you find out that you are being paid less than your male colleagues doing similar work. If evidence suggests that your employer instituted the unequal payment intentionally, the period is extended to three years. If you choose to file with the EEOC, this <u>does not</u> stop the statute of limitations from running, unlike other claims that you file with the EEOC. This means if you file a charge with the EEOC eighteen months after the violation, and it takes the EEOC seven months to issue a right-to-sue letter, you will have lost your ability to file in court, unless you can show that your employer intentionally violated the EPA, which can be difficult to do.
Family Medical Leave Act (FMLA) • You can file these claims with the US Department of Labor, but it is not required.	• Two-year statute of limitations for nonwillful violations • Three-year statute of limitations for willful violations The lawsuit must be filed within two years of the last action that violated the FMLA; the statute extends to three years if the employer intentionally violated the statute.
SECTION 1981 CLAIMS	
42 USC Section 1981 prohibits racial discrimination in the right to "make and enforce" contracts, including employment contracts. These claims are not handled by an administrative agency and so must be pursued in a lawsuit	Four years

EMPLOYEE RETIREMENT INCOME SECURITY ACT (ERISA) CLAIMS	
If you file a claim with your insurance company and it denies the claim, you can appeal the decision to the insurance company. If the insurance company again denies your claim, you can file a second appeal with the US Department of Labor or in federal court. ERISA claims can also be brought against a defendant for denying benefits for a discriminatory reason.	Three years from the date of a proof of loss under the plan
ASSAULT AND BATTERY CLAIMS	
Threats of physical battery and unwanted touching are illegal in most states.	Varies by state: • District of Columbia: one year • Virginia: two years
TITLE VI & IX CLAIMS	
Title VI makes it unlawful for an educational institution to discriminate on the basis of race. Title IX makes it unlawful to discriminate on the basis of sex. These claims can be filed in federal court or with the US Department of Education, Office of Civil Rights.	• US Department of Education: 180 days • Federal court: varies, but is most often two years (as is the case in Virginia)

To successfully prosecute your case, you need not know the ins and outs of employment law, but you do need to know about limitations periods. So, for instance, if you are a federal employee who has suffered from discrimination, you have forty-five days—forty-five days!—from the date you were affected by the discrimination to report it to your agency's EEO officer. Private sector employees have at most three hundred days to file a charge with the EEOC after they have been affected by discrimination. (See chapter 17 to learn how to file a charge with the EEOC.) If you fail to meet this deadline, you lose your right to sue.

Note that you <u>must</u> file most federal discrimination claims with the EEOC before you can bring them in court. To confuse matters, some types of claims—those involving wage and hour and family medical leave—may be filed with the US Department of

Labor, but you need not do so before filing in federal court. You should also consider (or better yet, talk to your attorney about) state law claims that may apply. State laws may have limitations periods that differ from those under federal law.

Because these limitations periods can be short and confusing, it is better to act quickly and see an attorney as soon as you can. If you are unsure about what time limits your claim has or whether you need to file a charge with the EEOC (an easy and generally low-cost option), see a lawyer or contact the EEOC. Remember, talking to an attorney does not mean that you have to sue your employer. It's simply a good way to find out what your options are.

> **Note:**
> This book is designed to give you an overview of the main employment-related laws that affect women and caregivers. Keep in mind that many of these laws apply in many other contexts. For example, while Title VII makes it illegal for an employer to treat a woman differently because she is pregnant, it also makes it illegal for an employer to treat someone differently just because she is African American. This book is written for those experiencing problems because they have child care or other caregiving responsibilities, so those are the examples I've used here.

Chapter 2
What Is Your Case Worth?

To many, it is distasteful to take what happened and reduce it to a dollar figure. How can you put a price on your dignity or reputation? You can't. But money is the primary yardstick courts use to evaluation a violation of employment (and other) laws. They almost never force your employer to admit wrongdoing. A court won't even make your boss apologize. A court can require that your employer write you a check in an effort to give you something for what you have suffered. Of course, through the process of bringing a lawsuit, you can achieve many of your own nonmonetary goals, like regaining some self-respect.

The vast majority of cases settle well before trial. But the potential award at trial is what lawyers look at. When a demand letter lands on the desk of the company's attorney, the first thing she will do (after cursing) is start to think about what your case is worth. To do that, she will consider what categories of damages you are eligible to win, and these can vary from case to case depending on which law or laws you are proceeding under. Think of these categories as fishing holes. If you go fishing, you may or may not catch a fish, but you cannot catch any fish if you are not allowed to at least cast your line in the water.

Let's talk about the different fishing holes.

Lost Wages

This is money you would win to replace lost income as the result of your unlawful termination. If you are wrongfully fired and it takes you a year to find another job, you are entitled to the money you would have received had you kept working. This also includes the value of benefits, like health care.

Let's assume that as a result of losing your job, you lost $5,000 per month in wages and health-care benefits. Let's also say it took you a year to find a job that paid you that much. Assuming that you won at trial, you would be entitled to $5,000 times twelve months, or $60,000. Let's change this a bit and assume that after three months, you got a job that paid you as much or more than you were making at the old job. In that case, you would be entitled to $5,000 times three months, or $15,000. Let's change this again and assume that you lost your job and in six months found another one, but it paid $3,000 per month in wages and benefits. Let's further assume that your case went to trial and you won a year to the date after you lost your job (it almost always takes longer—sometimes much longer—than a year to get your case to trial, but we'll use it here for simplicity's sake). In this instance, you would be entitled to receive the amount in back wages for the time you were out of work: in this case, that's $5,000 times six months, or $30,000, plus the difference between what you made in your new job and what you were making in your old job. Here, that would be $5,000 – $3,000 = $2,000 x six months = $12,000. Thus, your total lost wages would be $30,000 plus $12,000, or $42,000.

You may wonder why you should be forced to get a lesser-paying job. What if you decided not to get another job? The law requires you to "mitigate" damages: that is, you are expected to avoid running up damages numbers on purpose. In the employment context, this means looking for other work and taking a job for which you are qualified.

Tip:
Keep track of all your efforts to find a job. This is a bit harder than it was in the "old days" when folks responded to a job application with a résumé. Then you could keep a copy of the ad and cover letter or e-mail application to show that you applied. Today, applicants may use LinkedIn or another social media tool that doesn't produce an obvious trail of applying for a specific job. So, as you look for work, keep a journal of your efforts. Defendants love to ask former employees about their efforts to find a job. They go over it in great detail in an effort to make you look less than thorough.

When you keep the journal, pretend you are doing it to demonstrate to your neighbor that you are working hard to find a job. This doesn't mean you have to apply for a job at McDonald's if you just lost a position as a senior vice president. But it does mean that you should be able to explain what efforts you used to find work, including why you did not use certain avenues. For instance, if you didn't use LinkedIn, just be prepared to explain why not. Here's one possible answer: "I work in industries that require a security clearance. Companies actually don't want applicants to have a conspicuous online profile. It might hurt my chances if I used social media."

Front Wages

These are future wages. You might be eligible to receive front wages if you win at trial. Let's assume that you made $5,000 a year in salary and benefits at your old job. At the time of trial a year later, you are still out of work. So, you are out $60,000. Now the trial is over, and you are still out of work and have no prospect of finding another job any time soon, through no fault of your own. And, for any number of reasons, reinstatement to your old job is not possible. In some cases, you will be entitled to a money payment (an "award of damages") to compensate you for wages you would have received after the date of judgment if you had not been fired.

There is obviously some guesswork in this, which is why it's advisable to have an expert witness testify on this issue. It is possible that you will find a job with the same salary a month later. But it might be three years later. The court will generally consider your efforts to find work and estimate how long it will take you to find comparable work, and it will then give you money ("award damages") based on that educated guess. If the court thinks it will take you a year to find a job, and you were making $60,000 per year, then you will win back wages plus another $60,000.

Front pay is often called an "equitable remedy" and is usually awarded by the judge, even if a jury heard your case. Any time you hear the word equitable, it usually means fair. So, if you hear someone talk about the court's "equitable powers," this essentially means courts have the power to do what is fair. The period for front wages varies, but the average range is usually in the two- to five-year range. It is rare for a court to award a long period of front wages in an employment case.

Emotional Distress

Most civil rights and discrimination laws allow for the award of damages for emotional distress. When I have clients come in with dollar signs in their heads, this is the claim they pin their hopes on. Unfortunately, they are often disappointed. It is true, however, that a plaintiff can win money for emotional distress simply by testifying about the distress the defendant's wrongful conduct caused. As a matter of common sense, the more disturbing a story, the higher the potential award.

For instance, a woman raped by her supervisor at work is likely to receive a substantial award, perhaps well in excess of $100,000. Someone who was subjected to disturbing discrimination and experienced expected distress—for example, loss of sleep, loss of appetite, and depression—can also win emotional distress damages, but not large damages. These usually range, at least in the Eastern District of Virginia, between $5,000 and $50,000. As evidence of how blasé the courts are about these kinds of damages, they refer to claims supported only by the plaintiff's testimony as "garden variety."

Emotional distress damages tend to be higher if they are supported by the testimony of a mental health professional. For instance, a jury is likely to give a larger award (and the court less likely to reduce it) if the employee's testimony of emotional distress is supported by a psychiatrist who will testify that it is some of the worst she has seen and that she had to prescribe high doses of antidepressants to combat severe depression. Note that an employee cannot win emotional distress damages caused by the litigation itself, even though litigation results in a lot of emotional distress for everyone involved.

Negligent/Intentional Infliction of Emotional Distress

When alleging emotional distress under state law, plaintiffs have a choice of two types of claims: negligent infliction of emotional distress or intentional infliction of emotional distress. They are state law claims; thus the law, while often similar, can vary from state to state. As with most tort claims, the plaintiff is entitled to be compensated for emotional distress if she wins. However, and this is certainly the case in Virginia, what courts consider sufficiently egregious conduct to satisfy this standard is unbelievably high. For instance, in Virginia, the conduct must be "outrageous and intolerable in that it offends against generally accepted standards of decency and morality." So, if your boss threatened to inflict serious bodily harm on you and then pummeled you in the parking lot, that would almost certainly count; however, being repeatedly yelled at by your boss to the point that you cried would almost certainly not count. In Virginia, to succeed on those claims, there typically has to be some touching involved. Other states may not be so exacting, but in most, the standard is still higher than many people understand.

Punitive Damages

Punitive damages are designed to punish the defendant. For years, these damages were not tied to compensatory damages. You could still win a fairly large award even if your actual damages were low. However, the US Supreme Court has held that these damages must be proportional to the underlying award. So, a jury cannot lawfully award, for instance, a $30 million punitive damages award when the plaintiff won, say, $30,000 in lost wages.

Still, these damages can be a multiple of the underlying award. Of course, this presumes that you can win such an award. The willingness of juries to award damages, and for courts to uphold damage awards, varies by jurisdiction. For instance, a jury in New Jersey may be more likely to award punitive damages than a more conservative jury in Virginia. I had a case in Virginia in which the client won damages of around $100,000. The judge (this was a bench trial) awarded another $100,000 in punitive damages. This was considered a large and unusual award for our area.

Liquidated Damages

This essentially means "times two." So, if you are awarded lost wages of $10,000, liquidated damages would double this amount, giving you $20,000. Liquidated damages are a form of punitive damages. They are available only if the statute says that a court can award them: both the FLSA and the FMLA allow for this type of damages.

Consequential Damages

This money is awarded to compensate someone for a loss that occurred as a result of the defendant's bad acts. For instance, if you are fired, you may have to go without income. As a consequence, you might lose your house. As with other damages, the statute will determine whether a judge can award them.

A Judge Can Reduce Your Damages

Shocking to most people is that a judge can reduce a damages award given by a jury. Let's suppose that the jury in your case thought your employer acted reprehensibly. They want to sock it to the employer for damages of a cool $10 million. Two weeks later, the judge issues an opinion essentially saying that's nice, but how about $300,000? She then gives you the option of taking that amount or having a whole new trial on the issue of damages. Judges (usually) don't do this to be mean; they are worried about the court of appeals that reviews their decisions. In Virginia, the court of appeals has issued rulings disfavoring large damages awards, particularly punitive damages.

Caps

Some states cap emotional distress damages. And Title VII explicitly limits the money you can win in certain categories: the highest is $300,000 for a large company, but that figure drops to $50,000 for a company with fifteen to fifty employees. That's right; go to trial on a sex-discrimination claim and win, and the best you can do is $300,000 if your main claim is for emotional distress. You also get your attorney's fees paid, and front and back wages. So, how much money you are entitled to depends on which categories of damages you qualify for. If you were fired illegally and suffered severe emotional distress but got a job right away, the award you can win at trial is limited by Title VII caps.

Attorney's Fees

I will talk about this later in the book, but want to address it briefly here, given that we're talking about money that may end up in your pocket. Many discrimination statutes—including Title VII, FLSA, and FMLA—have what are called "fee-shifting provisions." This means that, if you win, the defendant must pay your attorney's fees and costs. Depending on the retainer agreement you sign with your attorney, this money may or may not have actually come out of your pocket. The advantage of these provisions is that, unless you have a contingency fee arrangement with your attorney, you get to keep the entire award.

Taxes

First, I am not a tax attorney, so I can talk only generally about this subject. But you should know that your award will likely be taxable, particularly if it includes an award of back and front wages. This amount will probably be subject to payroll taxes and income taxes. And your entire award will likely be subject to income taxes. So, if you get $100,000 at settlement or trial, a large chunk of that will go to taxes.

Chapter 3
Your Job Exit Strategy

If you are still employed or just on your way out the door, you may want to consider the following tools.

Report Discrimination

If you are the victim of discrimination or you suspect wrongdoing, let your boss know it. Telling your boss about discrimination or wrongdoing at the company may buy you more time. Courts may presume that your employer is retaliating against you if it fires you right after you complain about mistreatment. So, speak up!

Get a Severance Agreement

Employers are not required to offer you a settlement agreement, but they often will. If you have experienced or can point to discrimination or other wrongdoing at work, you have leverage to ask for severance. Your employer will want you to sign a waiver in which you give up your right to sue. Your employer should pay for it. In addition, or in the alternative, if you have been with your employer for a long time and have built up goodwill, your employer will have an incentive to treat you well on the way out the door. How much is reasonable? One to two weeks per year of employment is standard. If you have been the victim of wrongdoing, you may be able to get more.

When negotiating your severance agreement, keep the following points in mind:

- *Money:* The obvious reason for negotiating a severance agreement is to obtain money. There is no hard-and-fast rule about how much you could get. Except for very high-level positions, the general rule is one to two weeks of salary for every year of service. You can get more if your company believes it is avoiding a lawsuit.

- *Release:* All severance agreements include a broad release of any claims you might have against your employer. This, in essence, is what the employer is "buying" with the severance agreement. If you have a potential claim against the company, the value of the release increases. Of course, raising a potential claim is a delicate issue. It could get you a higher severance agreement, but it may also burn bridges with your former employer. This is another time when bringing a lawyer to the table can help. If you assert that you have claims against the company, it is more likely to take you seriously if you have counsel.

- *Be a consultant:* Some companies are reluctant to characterize any money paid to you as a "severance" agreement. One way around this is to offer to be a "consultant" to the company, essentially doing your same job, for a period corresponding to the amount of severance. In most cases, the company will not actually want you to do any work, so the payment will in effect be a settlement agreement. Of course, consider the tax consequences of any such agreement. Payments pursuant to this sort of agreement will almost certainly be considered wages, and you will have to pay taxes on them.

- *Taxes:* Watch for any provision that will require you to indemnify the company for any tax consequences of the settlement. What this means is that the company will want you to pay its lawyers if the IRS comes after it claiming that a settlement should have been characterized as wages and taxes should have been withheld. There are limited circumstances in which it may be advisable to agree to such a provision, but as a general rule, these are not a good idea and could result in a legal bill from the company that exceeds the amount of the settlement.

> **Tip:**
> Consult with a tax attorney or an accountant about the tax consequences of any settlement agreement. Tax law in this area is complicated and can result in your severance putting much less in your pocket than you expected.

File for Unemployment

Ask your employer not to oppose an application for unemployment. Some employers, even if they are not willing to offer a monetary settlement, may agree not to oppose unemployment benefits.

Go to the EEOC or State Civil Rights Agency

This applies even if you have been shown the door without a severance package. Employment and civil rights statutes often have short deadlines for filing a claim. For instance, you usually have no more than three hundred days (and 180 days in many states) to file a claim of race discrimination or you lose the right to bring even slam-dunk claims. Don't forgo the right to bring a claim. With all that goes on after you lose a job, take a few hours to visit the EEOC or your state or local government agency.

See a Lawyer

I am a bit biased in this respect, but I think it's time (and perhaps money) well spent to talk to a lawyer about any employment matter. In Virginia, you will want a lawyer with federal court experience, as that's where most employment law cases in the Commonwealth end up. Your boss wants you to sign a severance agreement? Take an hour and see a lawyer. You may have a great claim that your boss wants you to give up for pennies. But only a trained employment lawyer may be able to spot it. The same holds true for your trip to the EEOC. Visit a lawyer first. Even if you don't ultimately hire the lawyer, he or she can help you maximize the value of the claim and explain the process.

I often get questions from clients about whether they should hire a lawyer. Here are two of the most common.

"Do I need a lawyer to negotiate a new employment contract or an exit from my job?"

The short answer is no. You don't need a lawyer for any of this. You can negotiate a severance agreement or a new employment contract without a lawyer. However, having an attorney can help, and the earlier in the process you get one, the better. Employment law is complicated, and you may be able to negotiate more advantageous agreements if you have an attorney.

Remember, your employer has an attorney—or at least a human resources department—to advise it on any agreement, and the company doesn't have your best interests at heart. Also, it is possible that your employer could pay your legal fees, particularly if you are negotiating a new employment contract.

"Won't it make matters worse if I get an attorney involved in the process?"

Yes, it could, but your attorney need not announce that he or she is involved. That is a strategy call for you to make in consultation with your lawyer. Your lawyer can provide you with advice to help you in negotiations; she does not have to participate in the actual negotiation.

Chapter 4
If You've Lost Your Job

If you've lost your job, or if you're about to lose your job, here are some quick action items.

- <u>Don't sign anything</u>. Your employer may offer you a severance agreement. It will likely be three to five pages long. Here's what the gist of it will be: "If you sign this, we'll pay some money, and you will give up your right to sue us for pretty much anything." Depending on what the circumstances are, it may be advisable to take the deal.

  But it is also possible that your employer is trying to buy you out on the cheap. At the very least, with some negotiation, you may be able to get a more favorable agreement—for instance, to include a positive reference—even if the total money doesn't change.

- <u>Don't do anything stupid</u>. For instance, don't take a bunch of confidential documents or do anything that the company can use against you.

  o As for documents, it is certainly fine to print your e-mails and communications. Just don't go into areas that you are not supposed to have access to and take documents: this includes computer databases to which you are not permitted to have access. If there is evidence that you think will be important to your case, just note what and where it is. Your attorney can ask for these items in discovery.

o   Don't break things. I once had a client who, with glee, put her
     company-issued BlackBerry under her car tire and pulverized it. She
     then told some of her friends at her job about it. It took only a short
     game of telephone for this story to make it to the company's general
     counsel, who promptly called me. Luckily, we still got the settlement
     done. I say luckily because there is a nifty bit of law called the "after-
     acquired evidence doctrine," which provides that an employer will
     avoid liability if—*after it fired you*—it finds out something for which it
     would have fired you if you were still on the job. Intentionally running
     over company property is a terminable offense just about anywhere.
     Even if the company had violated the law in some other respect,
     it could say, "Okay, okay, maybe we fired her for an improper pur-
     pose, but we definitely would have fired her for running over that
     BlackBerry, which is worth all of thirty dollars." On this basis, the com-
     pany could not get completely off the hook, but it could mean that a
     court would find that you are not able to collect any back pay or front
     pay, which are often the biggest money damages in an employment
     case. So, keep your powder dry. The company may have stepped in
     it by firing you. Don't let anger lead you to do something that would
     let your boss off scot-free.

•   Do some homework. Hopefully, you have the impulse to go see an attorney
    right away. That's good. There are worse things than talking to an attorney be-
    fore the ink is even dry on your pink slip. But you likely have at least a couple of
    days before you have to do anything. I recommend you use that time to get a
    sense of what kind of case you might have—and what kind of case you don't.
    There are lots of resources you can turn to:

     o   This book, for one.

     o   There also are many good blogs and websites.

          ▪   The EEOC (at http://www.eeoc.gov) has a lot of good basic infor-
               mation written for nonlawyers about employment law.

- Nolo (http://www.nolo.com/) is a fantastic site for all kinds of non-lawyer-friendly information about your rights, including those related to employment.

- *Your Rights in the Workplace*, by Barbara Kate Repa (available through Nolo), is one of the best "Cliff's Notes" versions of the law that I have seen.

After you've scratched around a bit and have at least an overview of employment law, then go see a lawyer. Why take this step if you are going to see an attorney anyway? Because it will help you maximize your time with the lawyer. While the attorney knows the law, no one knows the facts of your case better than you do. It is possible that an attorney could miss an angle of attack that occurs to you as a possibility while you are conducting some of your own research.

- <u>Go see your doctor</u>. If you are experiencing negative health effects as a result of the stress of your termination, go see your doctor or a therapist. It can only help your case. Emotional distress damages are a part of many employment cases. You don't need a doctor to testify to get compensated for this, but you'll have a much better shot if you have someone with a PhD behind his or her name testify on your behalf. This is not the time to play it tough. Your ability to receive emotional distress damages is directly proportional to making a judge or jury understand what you went through. Your doctor can help with this. Yes, you can do this at any time in the litigation, but chances are that consulting a doctor will be most productive when everything is fresh.

- <u>Ask for plan documents</u>. If you have a benefits package, send a written request to human resources for your "plan documents." In the letter, ask human resources to let you know who the "plan administrator" is so that you can direct your request there. Why? The short answer is that your employer (or plan administrator) is likely obligated by federal law to give you those documents. Sometimes employers/administrators screw this up. If they do, it can give you another point of leverage in negotiations or litigation. But you don't get that chance if you don't ask.

- <u>Be careful who you talk to at work</u>. People make friends on the job. Some are true friends, and others will turn out to just be "friends." Think carefully before you share with a colleague potentially sensitive information, such as, "I'm going to sue these bastards for all they're worth. They want to make it about money? Well, two can play that game." I've seen it happen more than once that a work "friend" of client later showed up to testify on behalf of the company. (Hey, got to keep paying that mortgage, right?)

Chapter 5
An Overview of Employment Laws

Many federal and state laws protect employees (including at-will employees). The descriptions below merely provide you with a place to get started. I strongly advise you to consult an attorney to determine whether any of these laws apply to you.

What Is Caregiver Discrimination?

Michelle Singletary wrote an interesting article (http://www.washingtonpost.com/business/ economy/aarp-study-burden-of-long-term-care-needs-of-elderly-straining-families/2011/08/03/ gIQAT9Fdsl_story.html) in *The Washington Post* about the increasing demands that women (and some men) face as they take on the role of caregiver for aging or disabled family members. Clearly, these demands can cause strain for working caregivers who have to balance the demands of family and work.

Although not discussed in the article, many of these caregivers suffer adverse—and often illegal—actions at work: for instance, the salesperson who is not promoted because management believes she cannot take on increased responsibility due to her need to care for a parent with Alzheimer's. Other examples of caregiver discrimination include the following types of actions when they are not motivated by a valid business reason:

- Firing an employee after finding out she is pregnant
- Firing an employee when he or she returns from paternity or maternity leave
- Firing an employee for performing his or her family responsibilities

- Firing an employee who is pregnant, who has an aging parent in poor health, or who has a sick spouse, to avoid health insurance costs and to avoid expected excessive absences from work
- Refusing to hire or promote a parent in favor of a less-qualified person who does not have children
- Refusing to offer a flexible schedule to allow a caregiver to provide child care or other assistance to a family member, though some employees are granted flexible schedules for other reasons
- Providing inaccurate information to an employee about the availability of leave and benefits
- Discouraging an employee from taking maternity, paternity, or family and medical leave
- Punishing an employee who provides care or takes leave—through performance evaluations, disciplinary actions, reassignment, or transfer
- Scheduling an employee for shifts that interfere with his or her caregiving responsibilities
- Criticizing an employee for being a caregiver, including comments based on stereotypes

No single statute prohibits these acts or protects those who are subject to discrimination because they have caregiving responsibilities. But together, a number of laws do provide such protections to caregivers:

- Title VII of the Civil Rights Act disallows discrimination on the basis of any sex-based stereotype. It applies to both men and women. This means that an employer cannot deny leave to a man to care for his child because "that is something his wife should do."

- The Americans with Disabilities Act (ADA) bars discrimination against those who "associate with" disabled family members. "Associate with" includes serving as a caregiver.

- The Family and Medical Leave Act (FMLA) protects both women and men who need to take leave to care for a child or a family member.

We will explore some of these claims in more depth in the following chapters.

Additional Resource:
The Center for WorkLife Law has published some excellent information about caregiver discrimination on its website.

Employment Laws for Individual Employees

Harassment and Discrimination

Title VII of the Civil Rights Act of 1964 is a federal law that protects individuals against employment discrimination based on certain protected characteristics, such as sex, race, age, and religion. This law applies to employers with fifteen or more employees. Many states and localities have a similar statute that addresses discrimination in the workplace; sometimes these statutes offer greater protections than the federal law. In the District of Columbia, that law is the D.C. Human Rights Act of 1977; in Maryland, it is Title 20 of the state government article in the Maryland Code; and in Virginia, it is the Human Rights Act.

- ***Race***: An employer cannot take any action against you based on your race, nor can it treat a person differently than other employees based on race. For instance, an employer cannot promote only white males over black males.

- ***Sex***: An employer may not treat an employee in a different way based solely on that person's sex. For instance, an employer cannot prevent women from applying for a certain position because the employer thinks the tasks are "a man's work."

- ***Sexual orientation***: Many courts have found that sexual orientation is not protected under federal law; however, it is a protected status in some states and localities, including the District of Columbia and Maryland. The District also protects employees from discrimination based on gender identity.

- ***Pregnancy***: Pregnancy discrimination is a form of sex discrimination and is prohibited by the federal Pregnancy Discrimination Act (PDA). Under this act, an employer cannot make an employment decision based on a stereotype of the capabilities of pregnant women. For instance, an employer cannot refuse to promote an otherwise qualified pregnant woman based on a belief that she will not return to work because all mothers want to stay home with their kids. District of Columbia law prohibits discrimination based on pregnancy, childbirth, medical conditions related to pregnancy and childbirth, parenthood, and breast-feeding. Maryland law prohibits discrimination based on pregnancy, childbirth, and related medical conditions.

- ***Marital and family status***

  Family status and marital status are generally not protected under federal law. However, District of Columbia law protects both; it even covers family responsibilities. Maryland and Virginia include marital status as a protected characteristic, though the ability to win a monetary award under Virginia law is limited.

- ***Disability***

  The Americans with Disabilities Act (ADA) protects those with disabilities from discrimination at work. Just because you are sick or have a medical problem does not mean that you are covered by the ADA. Instead, you must have a disability that interferes with a "major life activity," like working, walking, breathing, or seeing. If so, the law requires your employer to provide an "accommodation" to you so that you can continue to do your job.

This is a very complicated area of law. If you believe you may be covered by the ADA and need your employer to make changes to your job duties, write a letter to your superior requesting a "reasonable accommodation" and be specific about the changes you need. Then make an appointment to see a lawyer. Better yet, see the lawyer first.

In the caregiver context, the ADA prohibits discrimination based on "association with" an individual with a disability, which includes relationships between caregivers and their children, parents, or spouse. Employers cannot treat employees less favorably based on stereotypical assumptions about their ability to perform their job duties while also providing care to a relative or other individual with a disability.

Hostile Work Environment

I often receive calls from people who have heard the phrase "hostile work environment" and believe they have been subjected to one. It is undoubtedly true that many people are. But it is important to know that a "hostile work environment" is illegal only when it is based on something called "protected status," which can mean any protected characteristic, such as sex, race, or religion. Thus, if you are an African American woman and your boss and colleagues repeatedly make racist jokes, that is a hostile environment based on race. On the other hand, if you are an African American female whose boss yells and screams every time you make a mistake—and if the boss also yells at your Caucasian colleagues when they make a mistake—this is no doubt a "hostile work environment," but it is not based on race and therefore is not illegal.

Wrongful Termination

Just because a termination is unfair doesn't make it illegal. Below are examples of some legal terminations from employment. Even if your dismissal is legal, keep in mind that you might still have a case if the reason for termination offered by your employer is a lie.

Example 1

> You work in a sales position for your company that involves managing five junior sales executives. You have no employment contract with your company and are an at-will employee. Your numbers are consistently good, but you have experienced a few problems with underperforming junior sales executives. However, this is not your fault because you cannot hire or fire, even though you have management authority. That decision is left up to your boss.

> At your year-end review, you are told you are being let go because, although you are a great salesperson, you lack management potential. You later learn that you were replaced by a junior salesperson with inferior numbers, and he happens to be a golfing buddy of your boss.

You go to a lawyer wondering whether this is wrongful termination.

Answer: While this termination is certainly "wrongful," it is not illegal. Employers are entitled to be wrong about your abilities and to make (within reason) dumb employment decisions.

However...

Now, take the same situation as above, but assume that you had just returned from maternity leave when your boss fired you. He later told a co-worker that you were a great salesperson but "a new mother really needs to be home with her kids, not putting in forty hours a week here. Plus, I know she's married. The man of the house should be the one to bring home the bacon."

This is a different situation. Here the employer's real reason for firing you—stereotypes based on gender—is illegal.

Example 2

You work as an administrative assistant in a large nonprofit organization and are paid an hourly rate. Your boss is, well, strange. You have no written contract with the company and are thus an at-will employee.

On Monday, you come to work wearing a blue shirt. Your boss calls you in and says that he is uncomfortable with you and for that reason you are fired.

Is this illegal? Strangely, no. In an at-will relationship, an employer can fire you for any reason, so long as the reason is not unlawful.

However...

Assume the same facts, but when talking to your lawyer, it comes out that you were paid for forty hours of work per week, but your boss often required you to work fifty hours or more a week, while instructing you to put only forty hours on your time sheet. Because you loved your work and wanted to keep your job, you complied.

Is this illegal? Yes. It is not illegal for your boss to fire you for wearing a blue shirt, but it is illegal to require you to work without pay.

Example 3

Your boss is a blowhard. He constantly complains and yells. You find this unprofessional and tell him so. Although your boss doesn't say anything, next week you find your workload doubled. You complain to the boss, but nothing happens. This continues for weeks. Unable to keep up with the increased workload, you miss some deadlines. Your boss calls you into his office, puts his feet up on his desk, and fires you, with a big grin on his face.

Is this illegal harassment? Unfortunately, no. Your boss is a jerk, but that is not illegal.

However...

Assume the same facts, but this time you have an employment contract with the company stating that you can be fired only for gross misconduct, including fraud.

Is it illegal now? Maybe. It could be under this situation that you have a case for breach of contract because you were not really fired for cause.

Medical Leave

The federal Family and Medical Leave Act (FMLA) applies to any employer with at least fifty employees within a seventy-five-mile radius (see why you need an attorney!). Under this law, employees who have worked a minimum of 1,250 hours over the past year must be allowed at least twelve weeks of unpaid leave to take care of their own or a family member's medical needs. (Note that even if the employee is not covered by the FMLA, she may still be entitled to take leave under the ADA, provided that her employer has at least fifteen employees.)

In addition, employees may be covered by other state and local laws—for instance, the D.C. Human Rights Act. To complicate matters further, an employee may be entitled to paid leave under the employer's short- or long-term disability policy. An employee should be careful, however. A statement on an application for long-term disability indicating an inability to work could result in the loss of rights under the ADA. So, if you are having difficulty with your employer over leave, contact a law firm that handles leave discrimination cases.

Retaliation

For many of the claims discussed above, an employer violates the law if it takes action (retaliates) against you for attempting to assert your rights. Often it is easier to prove a retaliation claim than it is to prove the underlying violation. For instance, if you report pregnancy discrimination to your HR department and the company fires you as a result of that complaint, that is illegal retaliation. You can win a case on this even if you are unable to actually prove the pregnancy discrimination.

Overtime

Establishing an employer's failure to pay overtime is straightforward compared to discrimination law. If you are an hourly employee, you may be covered by the FLSA, which requires that your employer pay you for any amount of overtime. Failure to do so can result in your employer having to pay **double** the amount owed to you.

Defamation

This claim occasionally comes up in the employment context. It can occur if your boss or a co-worker says something false that damages your reputation and causes you harm. These cases are difficult. You should consider filing this claim only if (1) the statements against you are particularly damaging—for example, someone falsely accuses you of sexual misconduct or theft—and (2) you suffered damages, meaning that you lost your job or suffered other financial harm as a result of the statement. Truth is an absolute defense to defamation, so it doesn't matter how embarrassing or hurtful the statements are. If they are true—or even arguably true—it isn't defamation.

Be careful, because defamation claims are sometimes also brought by employers against employees, sometimes as a counterclaim (that is, to harass) an employee who has sued.

Chapter 6

Why Start the Legal Process?

Why Money May Not Be the Answer

What strikes me about the cases my firm handles is that the emotional issues involved are often the primary consideration, and the money is just a nice side benefit. Of course, there are exceptional cases that involve a whole lot of money, but large awards are rare, particularly in employment cases.

That's not to say that the money isn't important. Of course it is. By the nature of our practice, many clients have just found themselves without a job. Certainly, a pressing need is being able to pay the mortgage.

But the driving force for many people is the need for an apology, justice, or, at the very least, answers. Money would be nice, but it is less important than the first three. I often find that the less of the first three someone can get, the higher the price tag for settlement. If, after you filed a complaint, your CEO called you, offered a sincere apology and evidence that she was going to change the company culture, and offered $10,000, you might very well take it (okay, let's bump it up to $30,000) and, with just a bit of effort, put the whole thing behind you.

But that almost never happens. The litigation process rarely produces an apology. The company doesn't want to expose itself to legal liability, it doesn't believe that anything wrong happened, or the executives just don't care. They have third-quarter numbers to worry about! Or some combination of the three.

Litigation can sometimes deliver some version of justice, just often not the one people hope for. Litigation can deliver justice in that it can force the company—through the process of litigation—to answer for its conduct. You can force your boss to sit for a deposition. The company's lawyer will have to double-check the company policy on, for instance, reporting sick leave. But there is no guarantee of systemic change. The best way to achieve this is to go to trial and win a public verdict. That is rare, unfortunately. Even then, for a large company, it may have little effect. If the company had insurance for your claim, the insurance company will handle the litigation. Any payout will likely be within the policy's limits. If you win, the CEO will most likely get a call or an e-mail version of "aw, shucks" and then quickly forget about it. That's not to say winning a trial isn't cathartic. There is virtually nothing like it for an employee. A colleague recently told me about a client who stopped him on the courthouse steps after winning a jury trial that involved claims of sexual harassment. She said, "I appreciate the money. But I mostly want to thank you for getting my dignity back." Priceless, indeed.

Justice short of trial also exists. I once represented a man fired from a company after delivering top sales numbers for more than twenty years. The real reason the company fired him was because his multiple sclerosis was getting worse. But the reason the company offered was that my client was not performing as well as others on his sales team. During discovery, the company produced a chart that the vice president of human resources said she used to rate the salespeople. The vice president, who was twenty years younger than my client, had been at the company for less than five years. During the litigation, the vice president sat in on all the depositions as the company representative. We also got to depose the vice president for the better part of a day. I questioned her extensively. She admitted that she had made the chart *after* the company fired my client. Huh? The case settled before we got to trial, not for make-your-eyes-pop-out money, but not bad. (Our legal argument had weaknesses that made it possible to lose on some of the bigger claims.) Shortly after we settled, my client learned that the vice president got fired. There is no doubt that my client liked the settlement, but he got even more satisfaction knowing that the vice president had received her just desserts.

Litigation always produces answers. They may not be the answers you want, but you'll get them. In most states, an employer is not required to give you any reason for firing you.

Your HR department can literally hand you the proverbial cardboard box and walk you to the door without so much as an "I'm sorry to do this, but..." If you sue and get past a motion to dismiss (and most cases do), your employer will have to explain in great detail why it fired you. And your boss is likely to have to answer in person when he or she is deposed. But you should be prepared for what your boss is going to say. The most common defenses raised by corporations are that you weren't doing your job well enough and, even worse, you couldn't get along with others, were abrasive, couldn't spell, and on and on. The company may even produce as witnesses people you considered friends. It can be a lot of fun to watch your attorney poke holes in these stories, but they are still hard to hear.

That leaves money. It is important, but only in relation to how important the other factors are to you. Before you sally forth into active litigation, have a frank talk with your attorney about the strength of your claims and the art of the possible. Sure, it probably would take $550,000 to make up for the lost work, missed mortgage payments, and credit card interest, not to mention the sleepless nights. But can you get that? How far would you have to push? For that amount of money, you're likely going to need to push deep into litigation, probably all the way to trial. What are the chances that you could lose it all? Once you have those answers, give it some thought. Would it be worth it if you could get $80,000 and the pleasure of watching your former boss squirm at a deposition? Only you can answer that question. But you should have a sense of your objective and the numbers—recognizing that these are something of a moving target—before you give your attorney the go-ahead to file the complaint.

What you want is to avoid a conversation like this one:

> ATTORNEY. (*After a six-hour mediation.*) The company has just offered $75,000, plus it will pay your attorney's fees. As we discussed—even though I understand this has caused you great pain—juries in Virginia will award back pay, but not much for emotional distress. If you went to trial and won, you might not net much more than $75,000.

> CLIENT. That just doesn't come close to what I would need to feel good about this. I lost my house after losing my job. It caused

tremendous stress on my marriage. And my creepy boss is still there. (*Pause.*) But I can't put another $50,000 into this. (*Pause.*) Fine. I'll take it. But I want my boss fired and an apology from the CEO.

ATTORNEY. I completely understand that, but you can't make the company fire your boss, even if you win at trial. And your boss is never going to apologize. In fact, all settlement agreements contain language saying that neither side admits wrongdoing. The settlement is to resolve the dispute and avoid future litigation. We can ask to exclude that language, but—having done this for a while now—I can tell you that will be a nonstarter.

CLIENT. Really? This is pathetic… Fine. I'll take the company's money and start a blog about the truth about that place and how things work there. See how they like that.

ATTORNEY. (*Shaking head.*) I wish you could, but the company is going to require a nondisparagement agreement, which will virtually bar you from even talking about this case, much less starting a blog. I might be able to get the company to tone down that language, but you won't be able to blog about the company if you accept the agreement.

CLIENT. This is bullshit! Forget it. They can keep their damn money. I want my day in court. I'll sign anything they want, but it will cost them $2 million. Minimum.

ATTORNEY. Look, I get it. I'd be mad, too. But if you take this to trial and knock it out of the park, the most you can recover is around $100,000. There are statutory caps on compensatory damages of $50,000, which would include emotional distress. And you have about $45,000 in lost wages. You have a new job, so that number is not going up. Plus, as we discussed, you have a good chance of losing this at summary judgment. The judge could come down with her opinion any day. Some of the depositions did not go well for us. Even if you win the motion, we could easily lose at trial. Then you not only walk away with nothing, but you will also owe me about $125,000 in attorney's fees *and* you will have to pay costs to the defendant. Those would probably be between $7,000 and $10,000. I know this seems unfair. And it is. But this is a very good settlement offer, given the possibilities here.

CLIENT. Can't you just waive your fees if we lose? We've come so far together. This can't all be about money.

ATTORNEY. If I had a trust fund, sure. But I don't. This is how I pay my mortgage. Going to trial will mean that I have to work on this case exclusively for weeks at a time. I'd go out of business if I did this without getting paid for my time. Look, this is ultimately your decision, but if it were me, knowing what I know about this process, I'd take that money and run.

CLIENT. I know, but it's not you. I'd rather take my shot at trial. I want the chance to tell my side to someone. I mean, I haven't even been able to say one word to the judge. All she knows is what was said in the papers everyone has filed. And those are all damn lies by the company. You believe me, right? All damn lies. (*Crying now.*)

ATTORNEY. Of course, I know it's true. But proving it at trial is a much different thing. I just think we have a good chance of losing at trial. That's due to the vagaries of the litigation process, not because we don't have the truth on our side.

CLIENT. I get it. But I want to sue. Tell the company to pound sand. We'll see them in court.

ATTORNEY. (*Long pause.*) I want to see you get the most you can out of this case. And I think this offer is it. I hate to bring this up, but there is no way around it. You have forgotten that in our contract for legal services, there is a part that says I can withdraw from your case if you refuse to accept what I deem to be a reasonable offer. If I do that, under the contract, you owe me for attorney's fees up to this point, which are about $78,000. I can cut that some, and would, if we end up there. But I don't want to end up there. Let's do this. Let me see if the company will keep the offer on the table for twenty-four hours. If it will, and I bet it will, go home. Get a good night's rest. Talk to your husband. Then decide what to do. We've been at this a long time now. I can tell you're tired. Hell, I know I am. Now is not the time to make this decision.

How do you think this person feels about the litigation process? You got it. Not very good. She has been through a long, sometimes painful process, only to find out that all she's likely to get out of her case is money, and not nearly enough to make it worth the pain.

It's much better to feel like this person in the e-mail below does. This is an unedited e-mail that I received from a client.

Dear Tom,

First, I want to thank you for your professional courtesy and kindness during a time that was so difficult and stressful for me. I am finally coming out of the haze of shock and disappointment that I was engulfed in for the last three months. My last day in the office was in August. I received the severance that I wanted with full benefits until the final payment has been made, and I was paid all my accrued vacation in a lump sum. That wasn't bad considering they originally offered me best wishes and a luncheon. :-) I gained some courage through all of this. I asked and it was given. I've never been good about asking for money, raises, etc. And I didn't take the lunch.

For some people, going full tilt into trial is worth draining the 401(k). Having carefully weighed the options with their lawyer and family, they rest easy knowing what they're after. Others just want a few months' severance and the pleasure of telling their guilty boss where he can stick his "going-away lunch." Either one can be a perfectly rational choice. But make sure it's a conscious choice that you make after careful consultation with your conscience and your lawyer. You have to make that decision at some point, regardless. Better to do it at the outset of your case (and at various points throughout the process) than wait until you're forced to make a choice at the mediation table.

The Emotional Aspects of Litigation

Few sane people equate a lawsuit with happiness, but there are upsides. Here are some positives that I've seen my clients experience.

Standing Up for Yourself Is Empowering

By the time people end up in my office, they often have been kicked around at work. For instance, they've put up with an abusive boss or had the indignity of being fired simply because they got pregnant. When a high-performing professional gets invited to a surprise meeting where she sits across a table from the vice president of human resources and a soon-to-be-former supervisor and hears that "things just aren't working," she is left with a lifetime mental scar.

It feels good to do something about that. Who's waking up at night now, boss? Enjoying that deposition prep where you get to explain to your lawyer what you meant in that e-mail where you said you wanted to "replace that accountant with someone not quite so pregnant"? You must have felt like a badass when you sent it—like a kingmaker. I'm guessing not so much now.

Even for clients who lose a lawsuit, standing up to fight can be a cathartic experience. As this article by Emily Esfahani Smith in *The Atlantic* discusses, sometimes meaning in life comes from the struggle. "There's more to life than being happy." Writing about the famous psychiatrist Viktor Frankl, Smith notes:

> As he saw in the camps, those who found meaning even in the most horrendous circumstances were far more resilient to suffering than those who did not. "Everything can be taken from a man but one thing," Frankl wrote in *Man's Search for Meaning*, "the last of the human freedoms—to choose one's attitude in any given set of circumstances, to choose one's own way."

Of course, being discriminated against in no way compares to the atrocities that occurred in concentration camps, but the same principle applies. The experience of discrimination—especially when it results in job loss—can be devastating. Taking legal action is one way to take meaning from that situation. It is your opportunity to choose a course of action to deal with a bad situation not of your creation.

Getting Answers

A company that fires you is generally under no obligation to give you any reason for your termination. Let's suppose that you were fired a month after requesting medical leave to care for a child. You are replaced by a man with no children. You're fairly certain this guy had twice been reprimanded for submitting improper expense reports. In contrast, your record is without so much as a blemish. When the director of HR meets with you in an effort to get you to sign a severance agreement waiving your right to sue, you raise this issue. She looks at you blankly and eventually moves on, not even responding to the question. Perturbed, you raise the issue again. The HR director says, "That's just not right. He has a clean file." You say, "Well, let's settle this. Go get his personnel file." How do you think this request will go over? Do you think you'll get that personnel file? No. You're more likely to get walked out of the building by security.

But if you file a lawsuit, you'll get that personnel file and more. The company will have to give it to you under the rules of discovery. If the company refuses or hides information, it will have to face a very angry judge. Remember President Clinton and the Paula

Jones litigation? In that case, a sitting president was required to participate in a deposition under oath. Powerful people are not exempt from the legal system. If David sues Goliath, Goliath has to answer, no matter how fearsome he is. Those involved in your case will likewise have to sit for a deposition. If the CEO of your company knows something about what happened to you, he too will have to sit down at a deposition table and answer your questions (or your lawyer's questions) under oath. Powerful stuff. The only way to get that satisfaction is by going to court.

Receiving Money

Most people who come into my office are not motivated primarily by money, contrary to what the Chamber of Commerce would have you believe about individuals who choose to enforce their rights. I would never recommend to a client that she sue only in the hope of achieving a substantial award. The risks involved in any litigation, particularly employment litigation, do not make suing an efficient moneymaking endeavor. It is certainly not uncommon for an employee to lose in court. That said, money can be a very nice result. I have had the privilege of handing to clients the largest one-time payment they have ever received.

Are You a Whiner?

I ran across a post on *You're the Boss*, the *New York Times* blog on small business issues, titled "How Do You Handle Employee Litigation?" The article reports on a small business owner who had settled several employee lawsuits (not sure what's going on there!), but decided once to push a case to trial. When he did, not only did the employee fold and take a low offer of $10,000, but he and his lawyer also issued a letter of apology for bringing the lawsuit. The article links to a number of others, all of which have the same basic underlying theme: employee lawsuits are brought by whiners who are merely seeking a handout.

What about you? Are you a whiner? Of the many people who have come into the firm over the years to file a lawsuit, none thought it would be fun or a good way to get a payday. The truth is that most people want to work and would rather do things other than go to court. Sure, some people bring lawsuits without justification, but these lawsuits are rare, and the ones that are brought are weeded out early in the legal process by motions to dismiss or motions for summary judgment. Every lawsuit that I have brought was on behalf of people who were discriminated against, often in truly shocking ways. My clients are not whiners. I'm guessing that you are not a whiner either.

In fact, sometimes businesses fire employees even if they don't complain about anything. For instance, the US EEOC recently settled a lawsuit against an employer for firing a food server because she had the temerity to get pregnant. This woman did not complain about a thing but still lost her job. This is illegal under the Pregnancy Discrimination Act, which prevents employers from discriminating against employees solely based on a pregnancy.

And before you start feeling sorry for the burden placed on "small businesses," consider that many federal laws, including the PDA, do not even apply to businesses with fewer than fifteen employees. That's right: in most states, if you work for an employer with anywhere from one to fourteen employees, your boss can fire you simply because you get pregnant, or even if your spouse gets pregnant.

Consider the story told by this woman describing a friend who was harassed at her job only because she became pregnant. For instance, after she told her boss that she was pregnant, he later asked whether he now had to "open a friggin' day care." He then had his wife come to work with the pregnant employee because she would need help in "her condition," even though the worker had not requested help. Because this was a small business with fewer than fifteen employees, there was nothing the pregnant employee could do.

Look, I get it. Running a small business is difficult. Making payroll is stressful, and having an employee out of commission can cause problems. But this doesn't justify outrageous treatment from the boss (or his wife).

The irony of the *New York Times* blog post is that the lawsuits it complains about are brought by attorneys who are small business owners themselves. If the lawyer can't pay the rent, she can't maintain a private law practice. This is perhaps the best check against "frivolous" lawsuits. They are expensive and time-consuming for both the attorney and the client. No attorney wants to bring a bad case. It hurts the client, and the lawyer will lose money.

If you are thinking of seeing a lawyer about discrimination at work, you'll have to endure some of this misguided thinking. But you'll know the truth, and so will your lawyer. Standing up for justice and proper treatment does not make you a whiner, no matter what your boss or his well-paid defense lawyer may say.

Keeping Perspective

A key practice for attorneys and clients to use in litigation is to keep the perspective of how *other people* will view your case.

Here's a hint: other people will spend only a fraction of the time that you do thinking about your case. That's probably not a shock to you, but it's easy to forget. This event is a big deal for you. You know the ins and outs of each meeting, e-mail, slight, performance review, and so on. Of course you do; you lived it. During litigation, it's easy—for both attorney and client—not to see the forest for the trees. You'll want to get *everything* into that brief. At trial, you'll want the court and jury to hear from as many witnesses as possible.

But in litigation, there is such a thing as too much. Even a judge or jurors who are trying to do the right thing have a limited amount of attention for your case. (Let's put aside those who are lazy and may give the case only a quick review, making snap judgments on the basis of a few facts or what the witnesses look like. Believe me, it happens.) And they will likely make up their minds quickly based on which person they think is the "bad guy" in the story. At trial, even complicated cases often come down to a few key witnesses and five or fewer exhibits.

I once had a case in which the employer got the court to exclude from evidence a document that we wanted to enter into the record. It was a good document, and we wanted to use it at trial. But it wasn't a key document. My client was beside himself that the court excluded the document. He insisted that we file a motion to try to get the document back before the court. This was at the same time we were trying to get subpoenas out so that we could have witnesses at trial—clearly something of key importance. I spent far too much time on the phone with the client about this issue when we should have been tracking down witnesses. Eventually, in an attempt to get the document back into evidence, I filed a motion to reconsider—at considerable time and expense. The court granted the motion. At trial, we used the document. We won the case. Do you know how much that document ended up mattering? None. The judge indicated that in his opinion (this was a bench trial) he found it to be of no importance. All that time and energy for nothing.

At the summary judgment stage, the time constraints are even greater. I think there is a perception among some that federal judges are wise and all-knowing, and that they will spend hours poring over your filings, legal tomes spread out around them while they ponder justice. Not so much. Most (though not all) judges are diligent and hardworking. Your judge will do the best she can to do the right thing in your case. But she has limited time for any one case. If you are lucky, she will read the brief that you (or your attorney) submit and spend an hour or so considering it. Sometimes, though, particularly at the state level, judges won't give a brief more than a cursory review. This isn't because the judge is not interested. It's because she has other cases to consider, trials going on, and administrative duties to handle. Even judges have to report to someone. It is for this reason that judges often complain to lawyers that they write too much and send the court too much paper. They want advocates to present the best argument in support of the case—not the best three. Even if the judge in your case is really paying attention, she will likely never know your case as well as you do.

So, keep the big picture of your case in mind. If you had five minutes to tell someone about your case, what would you say? If you were limited to three documents, which ones would you show them? It's worth fighting to keep those in front of the court and jury. The rest? Don't sweat it.

Focus on the highlights. Your best evidence will win the case. All the rest is a distraction.

Chapter 7
Lawyers

Do You Need a Lawyer?

Litigants representing themselves are said by the legal system to be acting *pro se*, or "for one's self." It is certainly possible to bring a discrimination claim without an attorney. Indeed, I once took over a case for a *pro se* litigant after she had handled the case alone in federal court for more than a year. But she was a retired lawyer and able to devote herself full time to the litigation. The better course of action is to hire an attorney with experience in discrimination cases, even if you have to file on your own at first.

The Risks of Self-Representation
The EEOC often deals with individuals representing themselves. Individuals can also represent themselves in any court, though given the procedural rules, this can be difficult. If you find yourself in a pinch—for instance, if the statute of limitations is about to run out—you can file a lawsuit on your own and then try to find a lawyer. But proceeding on a case without a lawyer is perilous, as indicated by the result in *Balas v. Huntington Ingalls Industries, Inc.*, 711 F.3d 401 (4th Cir. 2013).

The employee in *Balas* claimed that her employer:

> "subject[ed] her to an ongoing sexually hostile work environment that included unwanted requests from her supervisor for sex, numerous sexual comments, sexually explicit posters knowingly being

allowed in [her] workplace, employees massaging one another, sexually offensive pictures, and unwanted touching...." Her complaint centers on the actions of her supervisor, Brad Price, who, she alleges, "frequently and repeatedly commented to [her] about how much he liked her attire and physical appearance"; "referred to [her] as a 'good woman'"; "frequently and repeatedly entered [her] small workspace and her personal space"; and "frequently talked about his sex life to [her]." According to Balas's complaint, "[i]n or around April 2009, Mr. Price solicited sex from [her]." Balas also claimed that Price forcibly hugged her, though she admitted that it was just after she had given him some cookies for Christmas.

Balas filed a charge with the EEOC. The EEOC, as it does in all cases, shared the charge with the employer. The charge did not include all the details that Balas shared with the EEOC: for instance, it did not include the time Balas's boss asked her for sex. The Fourth Circuit upheld the trial court's ruling that it could not consider anything other than the allegations in the EEOC charge. Thus, Balas was out of luck, even if it was true that her boss had asked her for sex.

For those who go to the EEOC, the lesson here is to make sure that the EEOC charge contains all the key allegations. Also, send the employer (by certified mail or other return-receipt method) everything that you share with the EEOC. In this case, Balas had sent the EEOC a letter and had shared more detail during the intake process. However, this information was not shared with the employer. As a result, she was not able to rely on this information for her lawsuit.

The moral of this story: it can be difficult to find an attorney to handle a discrimination case, but keep at it. If you need to file with the EEOC before you are able to retain an attorney, make sure that your charge is as complete as possible. If you have been subjected to a continuing course of discrimination, make sure your charge reflects that. There should be a box to check for continuing discrimination. In addition, if you send material to the EEOC, copy your company's human resources department so the company cannot argue that it was not notified of everything that happened to you.

The Cost of Representation

I'm certain you've thought about the costs of hiring an attorney to represent you. But you may not have considered that you can make much more by taking action than you will spend on your lawyer.

I know, I know. An attorney telling you that it's good for you to pay an attorney? Right. You still with me? Good. Because it's true. In fact, I rarely take a case unless it makes financial sense for the client. Most of my clients usually make more money than they pay me. For instance, I took a case on behalf of a woman who suffered terrible discrimination at her work and was eventually forced out, partly because she told the chief executive she planned to have another child.

She settled the case before trial for $100,000. She paid me approximately $25,000. I don't want to say that she popped out the bubbly when the deal was done. The $75,000 she netted was not nearly enough to compensate her for what she went through, but it was certainly better than the zero dollars her employer was initially willing to offer. Plus, she had the satisfaction of standing up for herself and causing significant discomfort for the CEO who pushed her out.

Here are some steps to help you come out in the black.

- *Spend some time early on developing a settlement plan with your attorney.* The plan should take into account the strength of your case and your litigation objectives: for example, do you just want to maximize your severance, stay in your job, or "swing for the fences" and go to trial if that's what it takes? As you might imagine, it takes a lot longer and represents greater costs—both emotional and financial—to take a case to trial than to get one or two extra months tacked on to your severance agreement. Creating a settlement strategy may not be something your attorney will suggest up front, so you might have to push for it. If you need to pay hourly for it, do it. It may not feel like it initially, but it will pay off later.

- *Be realistic in your settlement objectives.* I understand that you might prefer a trial in which your jerk of a boss is publicly humiliated and you win seven figures.

That rarely happens, and pushing for it may very well result in many months of disappointment, a damaged relationship with your attorney, and minimal financial return. Listen to your attorney about the art of the possible. It's fine to litigate for reasons other than money. The time, stress, and money might be worth it if, after careful consideration, you decide the fight alone is worth the cost. But to feel good about that course of action, you need to make it a conscious choice early on.

- *Do the background work for your attorney.* No one knows your case like you do. Over time, your attorney (hopefully) will learn it, but it will take time. You can shorten the learning curve by drafting a timeline and a list of key names. If you have supporting documents, organize them and make copies.

- *Be an active participant in your litigation.* Even diligent attorneys will occasionally miss facts and arguments. Don't be afraid to ask your lawyer questions and offer suggestions and corrections, especially as to the facts of your case. However, don't overdo it. Discovering your inner lawyer may be counterproductive and costly. Talking to your lawyer about key facts in your case can be helpful; talking to your lawyer about your latest legal theory will likely only slow down your case and irritate her.

- *Produce evidence that supports your case.* Certainly, your testimony about your own case is strong evidence. But your lawyer (not to mention courts and jurors) will want to know whether there is evidence that supports your story. If there are e-mails, performance reviews, and other written documents, find them and give them to your lawyer in an organized fashion. You can even highlight important portions. Also, think about who can support important facts about your case. For instance, did your assistant see your boss stroke your hair in a weirdly inappropriate way? Is there anyone who can talk about the emotional distress? A good friend? Spouse? Doorman? But be careful. Resist the urge to turn into a gumshoe. There is certainly nothing wrong with combing through your e-mail for relevant documents. But speaking to co-workers to convert them into witnesses or accessing workplace databases without authorization could result in your employer suing you. Let your attorney know who could be witnesses and where evidence might be. She can use an investigator and the federal rules of discovery to get this information legally.

- *See a doctor.* If you suffer from mental distress as a result of your employer's actions, go see a psychologist or psychiatrist. You do not need medical testimony to be eligible to receive damages for pain and suffering. But your claim will have more value if someone with an MD behind his or her name can tell the jury about the effect the discrimination has had on you.

Finding (and Paying for) a Lawyer

There are a number of good resources for finding an employment lawyer. I recommend starting with the National Employment Lawyers Association (NELA), an association of attorneys who represent individuals in employment matters. The website (www.nela.org) has a "find a lawyer" function that will allow you to search for a lawyer in your area. Note, however, that lawyers must pay to be on this list. So, it is not a comprehensive list of attorneys.

For employment attorneys in the Washington, DC, metropolitan area, a great resource is the Metropolitan Washington Employment Lawyers Association (MWELA). Like NELA, MWELA provides an attorney search function, which you can find at www.mwela.org. Any attorney you find here focuses on representing individuals in employment disputes. Again, like NELA, the list is not comprehensive; that is, not all good employment lawyers are on it. But it's a great place to start your search.

Tip:
Most employment lawyers who represent individuals work solo or in small firms. Larger firms generally represent employers.

Some other good resources for finding an attorney include the following websites:

- *Avvo.com:* This website includes a comprehensive list of attorneys searchable by specialty and geographic location. You will notice that some profiles are complete, while others are not. This is because attorneys can "claim" their profiles and add information. Avvo gets the rest of its information about listed lawyers from public resources. The rating system (one through ten) is a bit arbitrary, but does give you some indication of your lawyer's areas of expertise. Just remember that the lawyer's rating is based, in part, on his or her participation on Avvo, so one with a perfect ten rating is not necessarily better than one with a lower score.

- *Nolo.com:* Nolo is a legal publisher that puts out some very good educational information on all areas of law, including employment law. I highly recommend this site. Nolo also has a list of attorneys, and you can search by geography and specialty. Attorneys pay a fee to be listed and are not screened by Nolo.

- *Justia.com:* Justia is another good resource for locating attorneys. As with the other two, attorneys pay to be listed on this site. One interesting thing about Justia is that it allows attorneys to post filings from other cases so that you can see samples of their work.

- *Google:* Of course, you can also do a blind Internet search for employment law attorneys. Make sure you search for attorneys who represent employees, known in employment actions as the "plaintiff." You will undoubtedly pull up a number of attorney pages. This is not a bad way to research, but recall that a prominent placement in search engine results does not mean the attorney is the best one for your case.

Tip:
The Internet is a terrific resource for researching lawyers, but it is a "buyer beware" system. Lawyers can, within reason, advertise for any type of case that they want, and a slick website does not necessarily mean the lawyer behind it is the best one for you.

Choosing a Lawyer

Employment law is highly technical. Winning an employment law case requires knowledge of case law, statutory law, constitutional law, and regulatory law. There are rarely simple employment cases. You need someone who knows what he or she is doing.

Here are some ways to find the right lawyer for your case:

- Look for a lawyer who advertises as a lawyer that represents employees, as opposed to, for instance, an attorney who describes himself as a general litigator.
- He should put his advertising dollars where his mouth is: that is, the attorney should do more than simply say he practices employment law. He should have written about the topic and have information to give you about employment law.
- He should be able to tell you about employment cases that he has successfully litigated in the recent past. Ideally, he should have experience in the particular area in which you need help. A breach of contract case in Virginia is very different from a race discrimination case in the District of Columbia.
- Ideally, the lawyer should have trial experience. Defendants are more likely to offer favorable settlements if they believe your attorney will take your case to trial, if necessary. However, extensive trial experience is not required. Civil cases, like employment cases, most often settle before trial. I would choose the experienced employment lawyer over a seasoned trial lawyer without employment law experience.

What Your Lawyer Is Thinking from the Beginning

If you're a cynic, you may think that the first thing a lawyer considers is "How much money can I make off this case?" Okay, the secret is out (not that it is much of a secret). Any lawyer in private practice has to pay the bills and thus must, on average, make a profit from the cases he or she takes. Involved in that question for the lawyer is whether he or she can win.

For that reason, from the moment you start taking to your lawyer, he is thinking about what might happen if you were to go all the way through trial and win. What is the best possible outcome in dollar terms? (As I discussed in an earlier section on money, the civil legal system is, at bottom, a system for transferring money from one party to another.) For this reason, all legal disputes—from the tragic death of a baby to which party is in the wrong when an apartment floods—are reduced to money. That is, what amount of money is the party who is suing entitled to get? So, lawyers thinking about taking a case are considering—and changing throughout the course of litigation—the amount of money the dispute will generate.

This may be why you would be excused for thinking that your lawyer is planning to run off to the courthouse from day one. He or she may start out talking about "damages" and trial while knowing that your case will resolve before you get to trial. Your lawyer is also thinking this way because the lawyer for your employer will think this way. As soon as your company's lawyer becomes aware that you might sue, he or she is thinking about the possibility that you might win, and if you did, how much money would be on the line. Lawyers often refer to the amount of money on the line as the company's "exposure."

For instance, before a lawsuit begins, your lawyer might say to the company's lawyer, "Look, John, if your company pushes this to trial and loses, you're looking at back wages of at least fifty thousand dollars, an award of front wages of possibly the same amount, not to mention my attorney's fees and a possible award of punitive damages. You saw that recent case where the jury awarded one hundred thousand dollars in damages. If you add that up, your client has significant exposure here, maybe in the range of three hundred thousand dollars or more." The company's lawyer will then respond with why she thinks your claims are worthless because the judge will kick the case out before trial. This scenario describes how 90 percent of all employment cases start. But, to my point, these conversations often begin, and sometimes end, before the complaint is drafted.

That's why you may be confused to hear your lawyer talk to you about your case as if you'd already filed a complaint and were on the way to a trial.

Paying Your Lawyer's Fees

Employment lawyers charge their clients in various ways. Here are just some examples.

Hourly: The most traditional way lawyers bill in any practice is by the hour. Rates in this area vary, but can range anywhere from $250 to $500 per hour. The advantage of this type of system is that you pay the lawyer only for the time he works on your case. The disadvantage is that the bill for any particular month will be unpredictable.

Retainer payments: Many lawyers who bill hourly require what is called a *retainer.* This is a down payment by a client toward future fees. Here, you give the lawyer a sum of money that the lawyer deposits into a trust account. These funds still belong to you.

The lawyer will deduct funds from the trust account, according to an agreement with you, as he works on your case. An "evergreen" trust account is one that, by agreement, you must replenish when the balance of the account drops below a certain amount. The lawyer decides the amount you put in the trust account. Generally, the more complicated the matter (for instance, matters in active litigation), the bigger the retainer.

Contingency: Contingency fee agreements are those in which the lawyer collects fees only if you win: that is, his fees are "contingent" upon your success either in settlement or at trial. Generally, a lawyer in these situations gets one-third of the money you win. So, if you settle your case for $10,000, the lawyer would get $3,330, regardless of how much work he or she has put into the case. These fee agreements are the norm in physical injury cases.

The advantage to the clients for these fee arrangements is clear: you don't have to pay your attorney unless you win. The disadvantage is that you may end up paying the lawyer more than you would have if you paid hourly. For instance, let's use the example above and assume you win $10,000. Let's also assume that your lawyer spent five hours total on the case and charges an hourly rate of $300 per hour. Under a contingency fee arrangement, you would pay $3,300, but if you paid hourly, you'd pay less than half of that amount: $1,500 (five times $300).

Another disadvantage to contingency fee arrangements is that lawyers who use them are (understandably) very careful to take only those cases that have a good chance of success. Thus, a lawyer who bills on contingency may not take your case simply because it has a good, but not great, chance of success. Some employment lawyers bill on contingency, though many do not, given the uncertain nature of employment litigation.

Contingent hourly billing: This is a variation of the straight contingency fee case. In these cases, like straight contingency cases, a client does not pay the attorney unless he or she wins at trial or receives a settlement. Unlike a straight contingency fee case, the lawyer keeps track of his hours and bases his fee on an hourly rate rather than on the percentage of the win. Thus, if you win $10,000 and the lawyer has billed five hours at $300 per hour, he gets $1,500. But if he has billed two hundred, he gets $60,000.

These arrangements apply only when there is a "fee-shifting" statute. This is a law that allows a court to award attorney's fees to the winner. In an employment context, this means that if you sue your employer and win, the employer must pay its attorney's fees *and* yours. Discrimination and civil rights statutes often have fee-shifting provisions. Fee-shifting does not apply other employment law claims like breach of contract and defamation. Thus, if you win one of these cases, you must pay your own attorney's fees.

Mixed hourly/contingent: This is an arrangement in which the client pays a portion of the hourly rate, with the rest to be recovered only if the case settles or if there is a victory at trial. For instance, if your attorney's hourly rate is $300, a mixed contingency arrangement might be an agreement in which you pay $200 per hour, with the attorney collecting the remaining $100 at settlement or trial, plus a percentage of the winnings, though less than the one-third that is typical in a full contingency case.

Your attorney will generally choose the arrangement that will work best after reviewing your case and paying close attention to the likelihood of achieving settlement or victory at trial. Cases are expensive to litigate, both in terms of cost and attorney time. An attorney will not take a case on full contingency—and bear all the risk of loss—if you have a marginal case. However, an attorney may take such a case if the client is willing to bear all the risk by paying a straight hourly rate.

Part II: Law

Chapter 8
State Law

This book is primarily about the protections that caregivers have under federal law. Unfortunately, in many states, like Virginia, these laws are the only practical protections you have. But some states and local jurisdictions have parallel and even additional protections. This book does not specifically address state law claims, so be sure to do your research and, ideally, talk to an employment law attorney about protections you may have in your state. If you are researching your local area, try looking for the term "office of human rights." For instance, Virginia has offices of human rights in some counties, like Arlington. If you were to search for "Arlington County Office of Human Rights," you would find information about protections provided by Arlington.

It is particularly important that you research state and local laws if you are facing discrimination and work for an employer with fewer than fifteen employees, which means your boss is not covered by most federal antidiscrimination laws, except the Fair Labor Standards Act, which applies in most aspects to employers regardless of size. When you are looking at local laws, pay particular attention to any remedies provided by the law. By that, I mean what happens if your employer is found in violation. Can you win back pay? Reinstatement? This is important. Virginia, for instance, has a human rights law, but there are very few penalties for employers found in violation. The same is true for counties with separate human rights laws on the books. It sounds good on paper, and I guess reporting a violation not covered under federal law to, for instance, the Fairfax Office of Human Rights, beats doing nothing. But it is not likely to provide you significant relief.

The Center for WorkLife Law (http://worklifelaw.org) has some terrific resources on this, including a complete list of state laws and local ordinances that provide protections to caregivers. I suggest that you look at the Center's free report *Caregivers As a Protected Class?: The Growth of State and Local Laws Prohibiting Family Responsibilities Discrimination* (http://worklifelaw.org/pubs/LocalFRDLawsReport.pdf).

Here is a partial list of states and cities that provide additional protections to caregivers:

- Arkansas
- California
- Connecticut
- District of Columbia
- Hawaii
- Illinois
- Louisiana
- Maryland
- New York City
- Oregon
- Texas

And the list is growing. As I write this, legislation is pending in New Jersey to provide protections to pregnant workers. Also, keep your eye on federal legislation. Currently, the Pregnant Workers Fairness Act is pending in Congress. It would allow pregnant women protection if they require accommodations at work, even if they are not covered by the ADA. Sadly, it has little chance of passing in this Congress, but there is always hope for the future.

Contractual Protection and Collective Bargaining Agreements

This book also does not cover protections you may have under an employment contract or a union bargaining agreement. It is quite rare for an employee to have an employment contract that provides for leave and caregiver rights. But they do exist, particularly for high-level employees. If you have such a contract, dig it out and have an attorney review it. Also, some workers are protected by union collective bargaining rights that provide for leave from work. If you belong to a union, ask your union representative about any such rights.

Workers' Compensation

If you are injured on the job, you may be entitled to receive payment under your state's workers' compensation law. Workers' compensation laws can be complicated, and it pays to find an attorney to help you with this. Many attorneys who handle personal injury cases also handle worker's compensation cases. Most do not require up-front payment. It is important to explore this option because you may not be protected by, for instance, an assault that occurs at work if that violation is also covered by your state's workers' compensation law.

Chapter 9
Federal Laws That Protect You While at Work

The Law Does Not Require Work-Life Balance

There has been a spirited debate in this country about the role of women in the workplace.

Whether it's Sheryl Sandberg's best-selling book, "Lean In," or the uproar over Yahoo's decision to end telecommuting, the balance between family and work remains a hot button topic.

But it is important to remember that these debates are, in large part, not legal ones.

To the contrary, in most places in this country, it is perfectly legal for a company to pay an employee less, or even fire her, if she made no secret about the fact that she planned to prioritize her family and work fewer hours. The catch? The company has to apply that same policy equally to both men and women regardless of the reason for the leave.

For instance, it would be legal for a company to decline to promote Stan when he starts to take significant time off from work to take care of his two daughters, as long as the company did the same thing to Stacy, who chose to take significant time off to learn how to sail. However, it is important to note that it would likely be illegal for the company to continue to penalize Stan after he returns from leave based on a stereotypical assumption that employees with family responsibilities who take extended leave are *always* less effective workers.

But assuming no stereotypes are in play, companies are allowed to reward those who prioritize work over family.

How This Plays Out in Court

There was a laudable effort by the Equal Employment Opportunity Commission (EEOC) to use sophisticated statistical analysis in a case against Bloomberg Media. The Commission claimed that Bloomberg had a "pattern and practice" of discriminating against pregnant women and those with children. The EEOC claimed that Bloomberg routinely discriminated against those taking extended leave by reducing their pay and responsibilities based on illegal stereotypes about productivity following leave.

The case was assigned to Judge Loretta Preska -- who herself climbed through the ranks of elite law firms that likely placed more emphasis on work than life -- before being appointed to the bench. As law professor Joan Williams, a national authority on worklife law, noted in her article, "Jumpstarting the Stalled Gender Revolution," Judge Preska dismissed the bulk of the EEOC's case after ruling inadmissible the EEOC's statistical evidence, while allowing the statistical evidence deployed by Bloomberg. Judge Preska also disallowed evidence of alleged statements by Bloomberg management. For instance, according the EEOC allegations, one senior executive demanded that managers "get rid of these pregnant bitches." Addressing a complaint about his statement, the executive exclaimed, "[W]ell, is every f---ing woman in the company having a baby or going to have a baby?" He also said that unless mother or child has a health issue, "there's absolutely no reason for someone to take paternity leave." Shorn of these telling statements and statistical evidence, there was little left of the EEOC's case.

Having set up a straw man to knock down, Judge Preska's opinion became a polemic on law and work-life balance. As Professor Williams rightly notes, it is a "sermon" not connected to the claims raised by the women in the Bloomberg. Still, the opinion is effective to the extent that it artfully expresses the view of many in upper management and the law, as evidenced by this heavily quoted passage:

There is considerable social debate and concern about this issue. Former General Electric CEO Jack Welch stated, "There's no such thing as work-life balance. There are work-life choices, and you make them, and they have consequences." Looking at it purely from a career- or compensation-focused point of view, Mr. Welch's view reflects the free-market employment system we embrace in the United States, particularly for competitive, highly paid managerial posts such as those at issue here. But it is not the Court's role to engage in policy debates or choose the outcome it thinks is best. It is to apply the law. The law does not mandate "work-life balance." It does not require companies to ignore employees' work-family tradeoffs--and they are tradeoffs--when deciding about employee pay and promotions. It does not require that companies treat pregnant women and mothers better or more leniently than others. All of these things may be desirable, they may make business sense, and they may be forward thinking. But they are not required by law. The law simply requires fair treatment of all employees. It requires holding employees to the same standards.

In a company like Bloomberg, which explicitly makes all-out dedication its expectation, making a decision that preferences family over work comes with consequences. But those consequences occur for anyone who takes significant time away from Bloomberg, not just for pregnant women and mothers. To be sure, women need to take leave to bear a child. And, perhaps unfortunately, women tend to choose to attend to family obligations thereafter over work obligations more often than men in our society. Work-related consequences follow. Likewise, men tend to choose work obligations over family obligations, and family consequences follow. Whether one thinks those consequences are intrinsically fair, whether one agrees with the roles traditionally assumed by the different genders in raising children in the United States, or whether one agrees with the monetary value society places on working versus childrearing is not at issue here. Neither is whether Bloomberg is the most "family-friendly" company. The fact remains that the law requires only equal treatment in the workplace.

Like this excerpt, the court's opinion is more important as commentary than as law. Judge Preska is a federal trial court judge. As a well- known and experienced jurist, her opinions carry persuasive weight beyond that of most trial court opinions, but as a matter of law, this opinion is not binding on other courts.

That Judge Preska eviscerated the EEOC's case, and then used it as a platform to hold forth on issues of work-life balance was, in my view, unfair to the women bringing the lawsuit. They were not – as Judge Preska suggests – asking the court to mandate a family-friendly work environment. They wanted what Judge Preska herself notes was legally required - equal treatment at work.

Nevertheless, Judge Preska's opinion is correct – and something to keep in mind when thinking about the intersection between the law and the workplace – there is no legal requirement that companies enact family-friendly policies. To do so is good business, but it is not the law.

Stereotypes Against Caregivers

Title VII of the Civil Rights Act of 1964
Title VII is a broad statute that prevents discrimination against employees or applicants for employment based on race, color, religion, sex (including pregnancy), or national origin. It also prohibits employers from retaliating against employees who oppose discrimination, file a claim of discrimination, or participate in a discrimination investigation or lawsuit. You can find Title VII in volume 42, chapter 21 of the US Code.

The most relevant language for those facing caregiver discrimination is at section 2000e-2. It states:

It shall be an unlawful employment practice for an employer—

> (1) to fail or refuse to hire or to discharge any individual, or otherwise to discriminate against any individual with respect to his compensation, terms, conditions, or privileges of employment, because of such individual's race, color, religion, sex, or national origin; or

> (2) to limit, segregate, or classify his employees or applicants for employment in any way which would deprive or tend to deprive any individual of employment opportunities or otherwise adversely affect his status as an employee, because of such individual's race, color, religion, sex, or national origin.

You may have noticed that the statute doesn't say anything about caregiver discrimination. But the US Supreme Court has found that Title VII makes discrimination based on sex stereotypes illegal. See *Phillips v. Martin Marietta*, 400 U.S. 542 (1971), and *Price Waterhouse v. Hopkins*, 490 U.S. 228 (1989).

Note:
It would be illegal for an employer to discriminate against a man because he asked for time off to care for a newborn simply because the boss believes that taking care of children is "women's work." But, given that women still bear the burden of child care and elder care responsibilities, I most often see these stereotypes used against women.

Sample Scenario

Cathy is a high-level executive at a nonprofit. The executive director has been explicitly grooming her to take over his position. He is in his sixties and ready to retire. Cathy has a two-year-old daughter.

Once, when on a business trip, the executive director asked her whether she planned to have more children. Momentarily caught off guard, she responded, "I don't know. Maybe. I've been too busy to think about it." The executive director looked at her for a moment, paused, and said, "You know, this executive director position is not really for someone with young kids. If you plan to have more children, you should plan to stay at home. Young children need their mother." Cathy said nothing.

As she thought about this exchange over the next several days, it troubled her more and more. Eventually, she decided that she needed to say something to the HR department. She did. Shortly after that, she noticed a change in the way the executive director acted around her. He was stiff and seemed defensive.

Two weeks later, the executive director called an important staff meeting. At the meeting, he announced a "restructuring." He also declared that he planned to push off retirement and that Cathy would become the communications director. She would keep the same salary and benefits, but the new position would allow her to "stop traveling so much." Feeling like she had been punched in the stomach, Cathy sat numb and did not respond. Believing that she could no longer trust people in the organization—a place where she had invested the past seven years of her life—Cathy felt isolated, alone, and angry.

Is the executive director's behavior illegal? What options does Cathy have?

The scenario above describes something that falls under the banner of **caregiver discrimination**.

Cathy's situation is considered sex stereotyping. That is, the executive director is making an assumption about how Cathy should live her life solely on the basis of a stereotype of how women should perform in the workplace. Here, he is trying to enforce his belief that women should be at home with their children. While he is certainly able to hold those beliefs, he cannot use his position in the workplace to enforce them. This is illegal discrimination under Title VII of the Civil Rights Act. Of course, one important issue is how many employees work for the non-profit. .

Moreover, Cathy is likely the victim of unlawful retaliation. She complaind to HR about the director's statements. He found out and took action against her by essentially demoting her. Thus, she has two separate claims: one for violation of Title VII and another for retaliation after she raised an objection to his discriminatory statements.

The first thing Cathy should do is decide whether she wants to stay with the organization or leave with an appropriate severance. She should talk to an attorney to decide how best to accomplish her objective. Regardless, if she wants to preserve her option to go to court, Cathy must file a charge with the EEOC within 180 days from the day she was demoted. (In some states, she may have 300 days.)

Title VII Applies to Men, Too!
Antidiscrimination laws like the FMLA and Title VII of the Civil Rights Act protect both women and men from caregiver and gender-based discrimination. I wonder how many men know that. I'm guessing that much discrimination against men of this nature goes unaddressed. The failure to address discrimination against male caregivers likely stems from societal bias, as detailed in two recent studies.

The Boston College Center for Work & Family published a paper (https://www.bc.edu/content/dam/files/centers/cwf/pdf/BCCWF_Fatherhood_Study_The_New_Dad.pdf) about the experience of today's working fathers. The study debunks perception by some that the birth of a child will not influence the father in the same way as the mother, and thus the man's work performance will not be affected.

In February 2013, the EEOC held a hearing (http://www.eeoc.gov/eeoc/meetings/2-15-12/index.cfm) on the issue of family responsibilities and pregnancy discrimination. Sociologist Dr. Stephen Benard discussed his findings regarding discrimination against male caregivers. You can read his testimony (http://www.eeoc.gov/eeoc/meetings/2-15-12/benard.cfm) for yourself. In his research, he found that employers reviewing job applicants generally considered men with children in a favorable light, in contrast to women with children. However, other studies cited indicated that this advantage disappeared if the men asked for time off to care for a child or parent.

Below is an excerpt from Dr. Benard's study.

> Discrimination faced by men: An important frontier in work on the motherhood penalty is whether fathers also face discrimination. Our work found that fathers tended to be evaluated as positively or more positively than men without children. However, the evaluators in our studies may have assumed that the male applicants—but not the female applicants—had a partner serving as the primary caregiver for the children. This raises the question of whether men experience discrimination when they engage in caregiving activities. Increasingly, research has begun to explore this possibility. One study (Wayne and Cordeiro 2003) finds that men who took leave to care for a child or an elder parent were seen as worse "organizational citizens" than those who did not take leave. In addition, a study by Rudman and Mescher (forthcoming) finds that men who requested family leave were perceived as weaker, less masculine, and at greater risk for being demoted or downsized. This suggests that the motherhood penalty may be more accurately described as a caregiver penalty. This question is closely related to another issue: perceptions of individuals who use flexible work options.

Mad Men and the Workplace

The Huffington Post published an interesting blog post (http://www.huffingtonpost.com/sherri-snelling/creating-company-culture-for-caregivers_b_3034670.html) by Sherri Snelling about creating a corporate culture supportive of caregivers. Ms. Snelling talks about the increasing number of workers with caregiver responsibilities, sometimes multiple ones for people with both children and an elderly parent or relative to care for. Ms. Snelling advocates for a change in corporate culture so that these needs are recognized and addressed.

I wholeheartedly support that goal. But until that happens—and it has in some places, at least for educated workers—sometimes the best you can do is talk to a lawyer who handles caregiver discrimination about your rights and, if necessary, assert them.

What caught my eye, though, was that Ms. Snelling uses *Mad Men* as an example of how the workplace was beginning to change in the 1960s and 1970s. For instance, Joan became a partner at her firm at a time when she was raising a child alone. Interesting point. But what this article made me think of was the vanishing archetype of Don Draper. (I started to say vanishing Don Draper, then thought better of it. He is still out there—not so much in sense of the womanizing and drinking, though that still happens—but in the sense of the lone male breadwinner who has a wife at home to do all the heavy lifting with house, kids, school projects, etc. But those men—some women, but mostly men— are not rare. Many of the male partners I know at law firms have a work-at-home wife.)

Case Study

In 2014, it is certainly more common for men to work and have real caregiver responsibilities. These men, either by choice or necessity, have to get home to put dinner on the table, go to the science fair, and so on. These men are increasingly found in the ranks of the corporate world. Sometimes this doesn't work out so well for them.

Consider what happened to attorney Ariel Ayanna. Mr. Ayanna's employer, a prestigious law firm, fired him. In 2010, Mr. Ayanna sued the firm in federal district court in Massachusetts. The case is *Ayanna v. Dechert, LLP*, 914 F. Supp. 2d 51 (D. Mass. 2012). Lawyers suing lawyers: there's got to be a good joke about that somewhere.

Here are the facts as described in court filings. Mr. Ayanna was an associate in a big law firm from 2006 to 2008, when he was fired. When Mr. Ayanna started with the firm, he had one child and a wife with a chronic mental illness. During his first year, he performed well and received a bonus. The following year, his wife became pregnant with their second child, and her mental health deteriorated. She even tried to commit suicide. Mr. Ayanna took family medical leave to care for his wife. After their child was born, Mr. Ayanna took four weeks off as paternity leave. When he wife's condition improved, Mr. Ayanna returned to work, even though he had four weeks of FMLA leave remaining.

When Mr. Ayanna returned to work, he continued to have significant caregiver responsibilities at home for both his children and his wife. After he returned from leave, Mr. Ayanna's supervising partner began to monitor his work more closely than that of other associates. After Mr. Ayanna's wife was hospitalized in September 2008, the partner began assigning most of his work to other associates. Later in 2008, Mr. Ayanna received a performance appraisal of "fair." In December 2008, the firm fired him.

Mr. Ayanna first filed a claim of discrimination with the EEOC and its state counterpart, the Massachusetts Commission Against Discrimination. He later withdrew those claims and requested a right-to-sue letter. (For many discrimination claims, employees are first required to file with the EEOC. If the EEOC fails to resolve the matter within 180 days, which the agency rarely does, the employee can request a letter giving him permission to go to federal court.) Unfortunately, Mr. Ayanna failed to file a lawsuit within the ninety days after receiving his letter, as required under federal law, and thus lost the right to bring some of his claims.

> **Tip:**
> Don't let those ninety days slip by. If you do, you are out of luck, no matter how strong your case is. If you are having trouble finding a lawyer, go to the courthouse and file a complaint yourself. This will stop that ninety-day clock.

His case went forward in federal court on claims of FMLA retaliation and sex discrimination under a Massachusetts law, Chapter 151B. Mr. Ayanna was lucky in that he had a state law to rely on. (Most states, including Virginia, do not have such laws. Fortunately, for employees in the District of Columbia, the D.C. Human Rights Act offers similar protections.) Mr. Ayanna's FMLA theory was that the partner he worked for routed work away from him and downgraded his performance only after finding out about his wife's condition, and expected that Mr. Ayanna would need leave. The court found that Mr. Ayanna had produced enough evidence for this claim to go forward.

Mr. Ayanna did not fare so well on his 151B claim. His theory there was that the firm fired him because he did not fit in with firm culture "which he assert[ed] is dominated by a traditional male 'macho' stereotype that promotes relegating family responsibilities to women." Interestingly, the court found that the firm could legally fire Mr. Ayanna because he had caregiver responsibilities. Huh? Isn't that the point, a company cannot discriminate against someone just because he has a sick child and a spouse with a mental illness? Actually, that's exactly right. The only thing that is illegal—assuming we are not talking about denial of leave under the FMLA—is if a company treats men and women differently. This firm treated men and women the same. That is, as the court noted, the firm fired both men and women who had caregiver responsibilities. Here's what the judge said:

> At most, the record suggests that [the partner] may have disfavored him because Ayanna prioritized his family over his employment responsibilities. While those facts suggest Ayanna may have been terminated because of the time he allotted to his caregiving duties, Chapter 151B does not provide protection for employees based on their caregiver status alone. Because Ayanna has proffered no evidence that his termination was based on his gender, Dechert is entitled to summary judgment on this count.

So, an employer is entitled to favor employees who prioritize work over family. The employer just cannot make the decision based on gender. This case might have turned out differently if the firm had **not** fired women associates with caregiver responsibilities. Those facts would have supported the notion that the firm was making a decision based on a gender stereotype—that is, that women can take time off for caregiving, but men should not—rather than simply preferring those who prioritize work over family. Welcome, Don Draper. You are our kind of man! Actually, we mean: Welcome, Don Draper and Peggy Olson. You are our kind of people!

Note, however, that the firm would have run into trouble if it denied FMLA leave to both men and women just because they had caregiver responsibilities. The FMLA expressly prohibits that kind of discrimination. See, I told you that you needed a lawyer.

Americans with Disabilities Act—Association Clause
The ADA not only protects those with disabilities, but it also protects those who have a relationship with someone known to have a disability. 42 U.S.C. § 12112(b)(4). Consider the following case study.

Case Study

Emily took a job as an auditor with a bank soon after graduating from college. After seven years, the bank promoted her to vice president of Operations and Informations Systems. Three years of solid work performance later, Emily got pregnant. Shortly before her due date, she took leave under the FMLA. While she was on leave, the bank hired a consultant to restructure senior management positions. Emily gave birth to a baby girl with Down syndrome. Emily called the bank president, with whom she had a close working relationship. She told him about her daughter's condition and said that she would need two more weeks of leave to recover fully from the delivery. During the conversation, Emily said she was afraid that the bank might eliminate her job because of the restructuring. The president assured her that she would always have a job with the bank, given that she was a star employee. That turned out not to be true.

The next day, the president attended a meeting with his leadership team and the outside consultant. The consultant recommended eliminating Emily's position and combining it with another position that was currently not filled. Participants in the meeting agreed and decided they would post the position internally first. The president said Emily would be well qualified for the new position. At this point, a brash new vice president of finance said a female employee who reported to Emily would be good in the position. He added that she was younger and without children, and thus "cheaper." The president said he was reluctant to let Emily go, given her strong work record. He also felt bad about firing someone who had just given birth to a child with Down syndrome. The young VP jumped in, saying, "Oh, man. She had a disabled child? Do you know how much that will distract her from work? I mean, I feel for her. But we have a bank to run." The president thought for a bit and said, almost to himself, "Yes, I bet she will need a lot of time off in the coming years. Okay, but someone else has to take care of this. I can't do it. And make sure we offer a good severance."

The new vice president called Emily in the next day. He told her that her position was being eliminated due to the restructuring. Emily, stunned, asked whether she could apply for a different position in the bank. The VP said there was a new VP slot being created and she was welcome to apply, but she probably wouldn't be a good fit, adding that the schedule would be inflexible and therefore incompatible with her need to take leave to care for her child. Emily responded that she didn't know where he had gotten that idea; she had arranged child care and would not require any additional leave just because she had a child with special needs. The VP again said Emily could apply, but if she agreed not to, the bank was prepared to offer her severance, to include one year's salary. Fighting to hold back tears, Emily said, "I don't want severance. I want my job. I love what I do." The VP, showing no emotion, said, "Right. Well, the deal's on the table for forty-eight hours. No extensions. I suggest you take some time to think about your options."

So, what were Emily's options? Did the bank do anything illegal?

Yes, it did. The situation described above closely tracks what happened in the case *Strate v. Midwest Bankcentre*, 398 F.3d 1011 (8th Cir. 2005).

Essentially, the ADA association clause protects employees from illegal stereotypes (e.g., that an employee with a disabled family member cannot be an effective worker.) In Emily's case, that is precisely what happened. The bank essentially fired her because senior management believed she would need time off to care for her daughter with Down syndrome. Yet, Emily had not said that she would need time off. In fact, she expressly told the brash young VP that she had arranged for child care and would not need time off. Thus, the only explanation for the bank's action was that senior management believed otherwise. That is illegal under the ADA association clause.

What could Emily get if she sued and won? She could receive back wages to include the time that she was fired until she obtained a new job. She could ask for front wages, extending from the time that she won her case to some point in the future. This is assuming that she had been actively seeking work and had been unable to find a comparable job. Emily also could ask for emotional distress damages for the emotional pain that she experienced for being unlawfully fired. Given the bank's particularly brazen behavior here, she might even win some punitive damages. If she won at trial, the bank would be on the hook to pay her attorney's fees as well. Emily has a strong case and likely would win many of these damages.

Change some very important facts, and the situation becomes very different. Assuming the same facts but that, when Emily calls the bank president, she says, "You know, with my daughter's condition, I'm going to need some time off during the day for doctors' appointments. I'll try to minimize the time away from the office and make up the work in the evening. It's just something I'm going to have to do." The next week, she's fired. Does Emily still have a case?

Not under the ADA (though she might under the FMLA). This is an important distinction to make about the ADA. Under the ADA, an employer is required to *consider* making reasonable accommodations to an employee to allow her to do her job. This could include providing flexible work hours, as Emily suggests here. In contrast, the ADA does not require an employer to provide an accommodation to someone who is protected under the association clause, which protects those associated with a disabled person only from improper stereotyping on the basis of that association.

But here's an issue for Emily: she won't know for some time what her actual damages will be. Suppose that three months later, Emily finds another position that actually pays better than her previous job. Now she is not eligible to receive front wages, and she could win only three months of back wages. Sure, she could win emotional distress damages, but that may not translate into a significant sum unless she can show lasting emotional distress due to her firing. Let's suppose that she spent a week feeling "down" and for two weeks would often cry for no apparent reason. But after two weeks, she resolved not to let the bank "win," and, with renewed energy, set out to make a new life, which she did. This is great for Emily, but not so good for her emotional distress claim. She likely would win something for it, but probably less than $10,000. That leaves punitive damages. Emily might well win punitive damages in this case, but these are often hard to win in employment cases, particularly in more conservative areas of the country. Still, she might hit it big if the jury is sufficiently angered. Even then, a court probably would reduce a large punitive damages award to make it proportional to her damages award. So, it is entirely possible that a year's severance is more money than she would receive if she filed a lawsuit and won. Plus, she would get the severance immediately. Getting to a jury trial in most federal courts would take well over a year and would involve the considerable inconvenience of slogging through a lawsuit. But a severance agreement would require Emily to sign a contract including language that the bank was admitting no wrongdoing, and it probably would require that Emily not disclose the terms of the severance. These provisions are the reason that defendants settle. It allows the defendant to buy security and peace of mind, and, in this case, Emily's silence. That's tough medicine to swallow.

If she goes to trial and wins, there would be no restrictions on Emily. She could say what she wanted, plus she would have the pleasure of seeing a jury punish the bank and its brash young VP for breaking the law.

So, Emily has a tough choice: fight for principle and the possibility of an award that would exceed the year's severance, or take a sure thing that would provide immediate security for her family. No choice is wrong. It really comes down to what Emily wants out of the situation.

The Americans with Disabilities Act (ADA)

The ADA is a powerful tool available in some circumstances to protect caregivers directly (see the prior section on the ADA's association clause) and to address the effect of caregiving: that is, intense stress and physical manifestations.

What Does It Mean to Have a "Disability"?

First, many people are reluctant to call themselves "disabled," particularly if they suffer from depression or anxiety. For some, it seems wrong to claim disability status because the iconic image of someone with a disability is a person suffering from a physical one: for instance, a person in a wheelchair. Some don't think of themselves as disabled if the condition is temporary, as with some types of depression or anxiety. If this describes you, I urge you to let go of your reluctance to seek protection under this statute. It doesn't mean you are weak or a charlatan for claiming protection under the ADA. This law is there precisely to help people in your position. Moreover, depending on your situation, the ADA may be the only legal remedy you have to protect yourself from wrongdoing in the workplace. And it is important that you seek the protections *before* you are fired, because you can request accommodations only while you are employed. The sad truth is that legal problems in the workplace can devolve into brutal hand-to-hand combat. To protect yourself, you need to use all the tools you have.

Under the ADA, a person suffers from a disability if she has "(A) a physical or mental impairment that <u>substantially limits</u> one or more <u>major life activities</u> of such individual; (B) a record of such an impairment; or (C) being regarded as having such an impairment." 42 U.S.C. § 12102(1). (The underlining is mine.)

Prior to 2009, it was more difficult to be qualified as a person with a disability because of the language regarding "substantial limitations." The US Supreme Court and other courts had narrowed the definition of disability, primarily by finding that the "substantially limits" prong required that an impairment last for a significant amount of time. So, if you had an impairment that affected you only occasionally—like asthma, for instance—you would not be protected by the ADA, even though asthma affects the "major life activity" of breathing.

No more. Congress amended the law instructing courts to back off. In 2009, Congress added provisions that make it very difficult for an employer to challenge an employee's claim of disability. The amendments are called the Americans with Disabilities Act Amendment Act of 2008 (ADAAA). Indeed, the law now specifically provides that under the ADA, the emphasis "should be whether covered entities have complied with their obligations and whether discrimination has occurred, not whether the individual meets the definition of disability." 29 C.F.R. § 1630.1(c)(4). Moreover, Congress expanded the definition of disability, explaining that "[a]n impairment need not prevent, or significantly or severely restrict, the individual from performing a major life activity to be considered substantially limiting." The law goes on to provide that the term disability should be interpreted by courts to "favor a broad coverage of individuals." Thus, under the new law, it is much more difficult for an employer to shirk its responsibilities by claiming a health problem does count as a disability. Of particular relevance for pregnant workers, a condition that lasts fewer than six months—gestational diabetes, for instance—can qualify as a disability.

The other underlined prong above is major life activity. The law provides examples of major life activities, which are listed below. But note that this list does not include everything. So, don't despair if what you are experiencing is not listed.

- caring for oneself
- performing manual tasks
- seeing
- hearing
- eating
- sleeping
- walking
- standing
- communicating
- working
- sitting
- lifting
- bending
- speaking
- breathing
- learning
- reading
- concentrating
- thinking
- reaching
- interacting with others

But check this out. The ADAAA provides that "major life activities" also include the operation of major bodily functions, including, but not limited to, normal functioning of the following systems:

- immune
- cell growth
- digestive
- bowel
- bladder
- neurological
- brain
- respiratory
- circulatory

- endocrine
- reproductive organs
- special sense organs
- skin
- genitourinary
- cardiovascular
- hemic
- lymphatic
- musculoskeletal

The importance of this second list is that what constitutes a normal function of these systems is the province of a medical professional, not your HR department, or even a judge. That's why it is key in these cases to have a thorough medical diagnosis of any issues you may be facing and have a doctor who will explain in writing to your employer why changes at work are required as part of any treatment.

Because of the ADAAA, many employers today will not put up a fight as to whether you are disabled. However, particularly for mental disabilities, sometimes an employer will request follow-up information from your doctor. In some circumstances, your employer may even ask you to take what is called an independent medical exam (IME), which is an exam conducted by a doctor chosen by the company. Regardless of whether your employer requests such information, it is important that you stay in close communication with your doctor and that he or she understands what kind of information your employer needs. This is crucial if your disability is an anxiety disorder. In that instance, you'll need your doctor to tie your anxiety disorder to physical or mental impairments: for example, that you have significant trouble sleeping, a loss of appetite, or difficulty concentrating.

Think about it. Let's suppose that since you became pregnant, you've started experiencing really bad headaches. You've even had to go to one of those emergency after-hours care places ("doc in a box") for treatment—twice. It's been so bad that you haven't been able to concentrate at work. But you want to get that big report out. All you need is the ability to work at home for a month or so—a place where you control the lighting, and where it is not nearly as noisy as the office. You've asked your curmudgeonly boss, but he's an old-time butt-in-the-seat-at-the-office kind of guy and rejected your request outright. "You get headaches? So what? Join the crowd, *at work*" was what he said when you asked. Human resources has been little help. You know about the ADA and plan to make a request.

Which of these do you think has the greater likelihood of success?

Choice A

You draft a letter for your doctor to sign. It says:

> Ms. So-and-So has really bad headaches because she is pregnant. They interfere with her ability to work. It is my opinion that she needs to work from home for a month to treat the migraines.
>
> Sincerely,
> Overworked Doctor Who Barely Read This Letter Before Signing It

Choice B

You skip the doc in the box and go to a specialist. You explain what is happening. After having read some publications by WorkLife Law and meeting with a lawyer, you even are able to explain some challenges and possibilities under the new law. After the discussion, your MD/PhD doctor writes a letter stating:

> Dear Mr. Curmudgeonly Boss and Nonresponsive Vice President of HR:
>
> Ms. Patient suffers from chronic and sometimes debilitating migraines. As I believe you are aware, she has twice had to seek

emergency medical care to treat severe episodes. After thoroughly examining Ms. Patient, I have determined that these chronic migraines are interfering with her neurological systems in the same way migraines that occur as the result of a concussion would. Ms. Patient must, for the next month, limit her exposure to bright lights and noise. The ideal way to accomplish this is for her to work from home, where she can control these variables. Please let me know if you require any more information from me.

Signed,

Look-At-All-These-Degrees-and-Tell-Me-I-Don't-Know-What-I'm-Talking-About

Of course, the right choice is obvious. But let's talk about why. Choice A might be enough to trigger the ADA process. So, that's at least something. It identifies an impairment of "really bad headaches." If you sent this in yourself, you might get some opposition on whether headaches are an impairment that constitutes a disability. But it is from a doctor, so that lends some credibility. Upon receiving it, your employer likely will at least talk to you about possibilities of making a change at work. Great. You've saved yourself a trip to a lawyer and a specialist. The problem is this: if your employer, after some weak and *pro forma* efforts to help you, decides to push back, you don't have strong grounds to fight back. Little in the letter suggests that your employer—or a court—needs expertise to evaluate your inability to work. Everyone has some familiarity with headaches, even really bad ones. But where you really fell through the trap door is in putting "ability to work" as the major life activity. Yes, it is listed in the law as one, but that doesn't matter. Courts hate this one. Why? A lot of people work despite interferences. You don't need an expert to tell a court what work is about. Your employer will know that, or at least the company's lawyer will.

Choice B is more powerful in a number of ways.

- First, a "really bad headache" becomes a chronic, sometimes debilitating migraine.

- Second, and most important, it moves the battlefield from an area in the bailiwick of your employer—what constitutes a substantial limit on your ability to work—to one where your doctor rules—what constitutes a substantial limit on the normal functioning neurological system. Is the vice president of HR, or even a judge, going to be able to tell the doctor she is wrong? Nope. Of course, the employer can require a second opinion. But it is likely to grant a temporary accommodation before going to the trouble. Even if it does ask for the second opinion, you have a real disability. So, bring it on.

- Third, this letter goes the extra mile by not even mentioning pregnancy and instead comparing your disability to one suffered by someone recovering from a concussion. Why should this matter? Some courts have concocted a bizarre doctrine under which impairments that are incident to a "normal pregnancy" cannot be considered a disability. In many instances, this is wrong under the law, particularly after 2009. But you might save yourself some trouble and a fair amount of legal fees if you don't point your employer down that path in the first place. We sidestep that here by omitting the fact that you are pregnant and comparing what you have to the same disability that many athletes have experienced. Have a Neanderthal judge who thinks pregnant "ladies" shouldn't have a job "if it hurts to work," but remembers that time playing college football that he got his bell rung after which he couldn't get out of bed for week due to migraines? Yeah, well, he's going to be much more likely to rule in your favor now that someone with an advanced medical degree has told him that you suffer from something he can relate to.

Let's be clear. I am not asking you to scam the system. Have you seen those news reports where a detective takes video of someone out on disability cutting down a tree with a chain saw or roughhousing with the kids? This is not that situation.

What I'm recommending that you put forward is the simple truth written in a way that helps you get the protection you need. Employment law is stacked against the employee. The law is full of strange pitfalls that prevent those who have been truly wronged from getting any kind of justice. Employees brave enough to stand up to wrongful employment actions in the workplace should be protected to the full extent possible.

In the ADA context, this means explaining to your doctor the nature of your symptoms and your circumstances at work. For instance, as discussed, one relevant factor in ADA matters is how long your condition will last. The longer you will have to put up with the impairment, the more likely you are to be covered under the ADA. We're not talking about getting a payday here—just about keeping a job that you probably need very much.

So, if you ask the doctor how long your condition will last and she responds, "Well, let's hope that it's cleared up in a month or so," follow up by explaining your difficulties at work and that you could be entitled to small changes in your work environment, but probably not if this goes away in a month or so. And you can't keep on for a month or so. Maybe your doctor responds, "Oh, of course. I do hope that it clears up in a month or so, but in over half of my patients, it can take several courses of treatment. It's not uncommon for your condition to continue for up to a year." That makes a big difference in whether you get relief under the ADA—relief that many times will cost your employer next to nothing to provide. Let's face it, the real reason your employer may not be making the changes (e.g., letting you bring a water bottle, go to bathroom more frequently, etc.) is that your boss doesn't want you around anymore. Babies are time-consuming. People without kids are more available. Let's go hire one of them. That's why this is happening. It's not right. Protect yourself with the best, most accurate information you can get.

Here's the bottom line if you need changes to your work due to pregnancy. Remember that your employer is not required by law to change your work routine because you are pregnant. To get the relief you need, you need a doctor with a full understanding of your condition who can explain it to your employer. Your doctor should describe the medical reason underlying the need for changes in your workplace and should not rely on your pregnancy. If you can, find a lawyer with knowledge of this area before you approach your employer.

Making Sure That You Are a "Qualified" Individual
Consider the following example.

Janice is chief financial officer for a government contractor. She has been with the company for five years, during which time she has been given strong performance reviews.

In 2013, Janice got pregnant with twins at the age of thirty-eight. The pregnancy took its toll on her. A CrossFit enthusiast, Janice took pride in her level of physical fitness, but she was unable to keep up her training as the pregnancy progressed. To make matters worse, Janice began to have trouble sleeping for the first time in her life. Despite these difficulties, she performed well at work. In the summer of 2013, Janice gave birth to healthy girls. It was a difficult labor, however, that ended in an emergency cesarean delivery.

Janice stayed out of work on FMLA leave for eight weeks. She was glad to have the time off, but was ready to get back to work. But she just couldn't get back to her old self. She had multiple difficulties recovering from the cesarean, and her sleep problems became worse, as the babies were up multiple times a night for diaper changes and feedings. Even though her husband often handled the diaper changes, Janice awoke any time the babies cried and then couldn't go back to sleep. She kept performing at work only by drinking coffee throughout the day. Determined to "excel" at motherhood like she did at work, Janice continued to breast-feed (pumping at work), made her children's baby food, and planned activities for the nanny to do with the children during the day.

Although Janice tried to will her body to perform, it couldn't keep up. She began to lose weight and experience days of depression, shutting her door at work to cry. Eventually, she went to her ob-gyn because her milk supply began to dwindle. When in the exam, Janice broke down in tears. Reluctantly, she told her doctor about the difficulties she was experiencing at home and work. Alarmed, her doctor arranged for Janice to see a psychiatrist located in the building that same day. The psychiatrist diagnosed Janice with generalized anxiety disorder, depression, and insomnia. She prescribed antidepressants and told Janice that she would need to take some time off and make changes at work to reduce her stress. Janice was despondent. She had always considered herself something of a superwoman, able to thrive in her male-dominated workplace. Her doctor reassured Janice that she would be back to her fighting self in a few months, but only if she took the time to heal.

Janice's difficulties had not gone unnoticed at work. Known for being always on her A-game and insufferably perky, colleagues began to notice that Janice spent most of her time in her office, which was right beside the printer, the busiest—and noisiest—place in the building. Since returning to work, Janice kept the door closed and her shades drawn. Given that she usually left her door open because, as she often said, "I thrive on the chaos," colleagues noticed the shift in her behavior.

Janice's boss, Brenda, the vice president of Operations, was a single woman in her early forties. Brenda began to notice that Janice was making errors in some of her work. These were not significant errors, but they were out of character for Janice. Brenda did see Janice as something of a competitor, but she did not wish her ill. Her primary concern was that the company was gearing up to bid on a significant government grant. Brenda was under tremendous pressure to produce and was afraid that Janice, as she told a co-worker, was "going off the deep end." She remarked, "This was a really bad time to come down with postpartum depression."

Janice took the antidepressants and sleep medication prescribed by her doctor. However, she was reluctant to ask for changes at work. She knew this was a busy time and wanted to do her part. But she found it difficult to concentrate, especially given that her office was at the printer, the office social hub. Normally Janice, an extrovert, loved this. Not now. She found that if she could work in a quiet place, she could get the tasks she needed to done. It just wasn't going to happen in her office.

One day, Brenda came into Janice's office and shut the door. She asked Janice whether she was okay. Janice took a deep breath and said she was trying, but that things were "difficult," and suggested obliquely that it might help if she could make some changes in her work environment. Brenda said she understood, but that it was an "important time" for the company and she needed her A-team, which included Janice, with her.

Brenda left Janice's office and immediately called the company's lawyer. She told him that she might need to replace a key employee who was "coming apart at the seams after having a damn baby." When the lawyer responded that there might be ADA issues to consider, Brenda, as overheard by a secretary, exploded, "I don't care about the damn ADA! None of us are going to have a job much longer if we don't win this bid."

When Janice went back for a follow-up, she told the psychiatrist what had happened. The doctor told Janice in no uncertain terms that she could not recover fully unless she got work under control. The doctor suggested that Janice ask for a regular eight-hour workday and a quiet place to work—perhaps in a different office or at home. Janice said she didn't think Brenda "would go for that" and she couldn't afford to be without the job and health insurance now. The doctor said she didn't think the company had any choice. She offered to write a letter requesting that Janice be allowed to work in a different office space and for no more than eight hours a day for the next two months. Janice gave her the fax number for the human resources department. The doctor faxed a letter indicating that Janice suffered from generalized anxiety disorder that affected her ability to sleep and work. The doctor also noted that Janice suffered from insomnia and depression, and that, in her professional opinion, Janice required a quiet working environment and, for the next month, could not work more than regular eight-hour days.

The next morning, Janice received an e-mail from the director of human resources instructing her to stay at home until further notice. Janice protested, noting that she could work in an empty office down the hall from her current office. She received no response. That afternoon, Janice received a letter from the company's attorney saying that the letter from her doctor provided insufficient information for the company to determine whether she was, in fact, disabled. Janice contacted her doctor, who sent a follow-up letter to human resources noting that Janice had suffered from persistent depression and anxiety that had resulted in long-term insomnia. The doctor further noted that her anxiety had caused a loss of appetite and that Janice now weighed twenty pounds less than her prepregnancy weight. The doctor stressed that Janice's mental condition made it difficult for her to work in a noisy office environment.

The following morning, the company's attorney sent Janice a follow-up letter indicating that the company "took no position" on whether she was disabled, but would consider her request for an accommodation. It declined to allow her to work in a different office, claiming that no "sufficient office space was available." It also refused to "guarantee" that she would not be required to work more than eight hours a day, but would make every effort to ensure that she worked no more than ten hours a day.

Janice responded via e-mail, requesting an in-person meeting with Brenda so that she could explore what tasks the company had in mind in the coming weeks, to determine whether she could complete them in eight hours or less and, if not, whether some tasks could be assigned to someone else until the bid was complete. She also noted that there were several empty offices in the building that could give her a quiet place to work.

Two hours later, the company, through its lawyer, said that it was not able to "act on" her suggestions. Janice did not respond, but she continued to work on company business at home. The next day, Janice received an e-mail requesting that she report directly to human resources. She did, and was told it appeared that "things aren't going to work out." The HR rep took her access key and gave her a severance agreement offering three months' salary with no benefits.

Does Janice have a case? Before we get there, let's review the law under the ADA.

In situations like the one Janice experienced, it is important to be strategic and use the ADA to your advantage. To that extent, you don't want to disable yourself out of a job. Under the ADA, an employer is required to offer reasonable accommodations only to a qualified individual, which is "an individual with a disability who, with or without reasonable accommodation, can perform the essential functions of the employment position." 42 U.S.C. § 12111(8). There is no bright-line rule for determining the essential functions of your position. Courts will look at these four factors:

1. A written job description,
2. The amount of time on the job performing the function (e.g., lifting heavy boxes),
3. The consequences of not requiring you to do the function, and
4. What other people with your job are doing.

The first thing for you to do is to see whether you have a job description. Courts generally defer to the employer to determine what the essential functions of a position are, and a job description is good evidence of the employer's intent. In Janice's case, she primarily does knowledge work (e.g., synthesizing complex information, writing reports, etc.). These would be essential functions of her job. By claiming a disability, she is not making herself an unqualified person. She is not claiming that she can no longer synthesize complex information or write reports; she is just asking for a quiet office where she can conduct those functions. The only potential issue is the requirement that she work only an eight-hour day. Her employer could try to argue that during this crunch time, it is essential that she work more than that. But this would be a tough argument to win. It is unlikely that her job description contains that requirement, and even if it did, the company probably has not always required executive staff to work overtime.

The qualified individual issue often comes most starkly into play when doctors require lifting restrictions for an employee in a manufacturing or delivery position. For instance, if a doctor says that, due to a back injury, you can no longer lift more than twenty-five pounds, and you work for a next-day delivery service that requires employees in your job to be able to lift seventy-five pounds, then you are no longer a qualified individual for your job, even if you are disabled under the ADA. This does not mean that you automatically lose your job; a reasonable accommodation could be to move you to an open available position with such a restriction. But you should communicate closely with your doctor about what restrictions your disability really requires.

A good example of how courts analyze the qualified individual requirement can be found in *Feldman v. Olin Corp.*, 692 F.3d 748 (7th Cir. 2012), a case the Seventh Circuit decided in 2012.

The Reasonable Accommodation Process

Under the ADA, an employer must offer a qualified person with a disability a "reasonable accommodation" that will provide an equal employment opportunity, including an opportunity to attain the same level of performance, benefits, and privileges available to similarly situated employees who are not disabled. Reasonable accommodations may include "job restructuring, part-time or modified work schedules, reassignment to a vacant position, acquisition or modification of equipment or devices, appropriate adjustment or modifications of examinations, training materials or policies, the provision of qualified readers or interpreters, and other similar accommodations for individuals with disabilities." 42 U.S.C. § 12111(9).

In most instances, an accommodation request must *come from the employee*. It is not the employer's responsibility to suggest an accommodation if, for instance, your boss suspects you suffer from depression. Indeed, the employer could face liability if it suggested that you have a disability when, in fact, you do not. This is why it is vitally important that you tell human resources if you have a disability.

Once the employee requests an accommodation, the ADA requires that the employer engage in a good faith effort to find a reasonable accommodation that will allow you to perform the essential functions of your job. This process should not be a one-time event; instead, it should be an interactive process where the employee and employer work together to find a solution.

Reasonable Request and Undue Hardship

If you're protected under the ADA, once you make a request, the employer must make the accommodation unless the request is unreasonable or constitutes an "undue hardship." As with most things dealing with the ADA, there is no one-size-fits-all answer for any of these questions. Instead, courts conduct what lawyers call a "fact-specific" inquiry: that is, the court will look at all the variables and decide whether the ADA requires the requested accommodation.

Let's start with the first prong, reasonableness. Most requests will be considered reasonable if they will help the employee perform the essential functions of the job. I think we can all agree that a request for a quiet office space is reasonable if you are an accountant whose job it is to churn out financial reports. An example of an unreasonable request is a disabled employee who sued his employer because the employer refused to lower the sink in the kitchen so that he could reach it to pour out his cold coffee. (This is a true story.) The employee could still pour out his coffee, but had to go to the bathroom to do so. It would have cost the employer a mere $150 to lower the sink, which was not an undue hardship by any analysis. But the court ruled that it was not a violation of the ADA—not because lowering the sink represented a hardship, but because the requested change had little relationship to the essential functions of the employee's job. Thus, it was not a reasonable request for an accommodation. So, game over.

The technical definition of undue hardship is when an accommodation would result in "significant difficulty or expense incurred by a covered entity." You can read the full, mind-numbing regulation that defines undue hardship with five factors here: 29 C.F.R. § 1630.2(p). Most of the factors boil down to common sense. For example:

- How much would the accommodation cost the employer?
- How well is the employer able to absorb this cost?
- What kind of impact would the accommodation have on the employer and other employees?

Clearly, what might constitute an undue hardship for a mom-and-pop operation with sixteen employees might not be a burden for Google.

Retaliation

As with many employment and civil right statutes, the ADA makes it illegal for an employer to take action against an employee because she tries to assert her rights under the statute, even if she may be wrong about what rights she has.

What About Janice? Does She Have a Retaliation Claim?

Without a doubt, Janice has a good retaliation case. Her generalized anxiety disorder and depression clearly do interfere with the major life activities of sleeping and working. An important question for Janice is when her rights under the ADA kicked in. If Janice had suffered in silence and gone unnoticed, she would not have had rights under the ADA until she requested a reasonable accommodation, which arguably occurred when Brenda came into her office and asked her how she was doing. Her rights certainly accrued when her doctor faxed the request for accommodation.

But recall that the ADA also protects from discrimination those that an employer regards as disabled, even if the employee does not, in fact, suffer from a disability. Here, Brenda was overheard saying that Janice was "coming apart at the seams" and suffering from postpartum depression. Brenda said this in the context of talking to the company's attorney about firing Janice. This alone is a violation of the ADA because Brenda was expressly discriminating against someone that she believed had a disability.

This raises an important strategic issue with the ADA. Namely, should you tell your boss or HR that you suffer from a disability, even if you don't require an accommodation? There is no right answer to this. On the one hand, there is (usually) no requirement that you divulge private medical information to your employer. If you do, there is a risk that your employer will use it against you, though it certainly won't say that it is. For instance, let's say that you have multiple sclerosis. It is a progressive disease, but for now, with treatment, it does not affect your work. Let's further suppose that you tell HR just because you think it's important for someone at work to know. Nothing happens for several years.

One day, the company gets new management. Though your medical information is supposed to remain confidential, the VP of human resources tells the new tough-as-nails president that you have MS. The president, known for being a ruthless, bottom-line guy, decides that you will eventually be a liability. Over the next year, he finds reasons to criticize your performance in writing. At the end of the year, he fires you.

Is that illegal? Sure. Can you sue and win? Probably not. Although the president fired you because of your MS, he covered his tracks well and can now rely on a year's worth of bad reviews. Plus, there is no evidence that he even knew about your disability. That information was in your separate, and supposedly confidential, medical file. The VP of HR certainly is not going to cop to the fact that he told the president about your condition.

Now, let's change the facts a little bit. Let's suppose that, as soon as the new president joined the company, you sent an e-mail to him, in confidence, letting him know about your condition but not requesting an accommodation. All of a sudden, you start getting poor reviews after nothing but excellent ones in the past.

Do you have a case now? Yes, you do. Now you have a written record that the president knew about your condition. Yes, he will still say that he fired you because of poor performance. But that's going to be more difficult now. What else explains your performance going from great to terrible, except that now your boss knows you have a disability that might affect your work?

So, there are risks and benefits to telling. There are also risks in not telling.

Let's change the facts again and suppose that you don't tell anyone about your MS. While it remained under control, no one at work had a clue. But this year, the disease began to progress. You can still work, but you start to have some trouble walking. On rare occasions, you slur your words. In an effort to get the disease back under control, you take time off to see your doctor for treatment. Your work performance does not suffer, though. The VP of human resources doesn't say anything to you, but she notices the changes, and, because her sister has MS and suffers from some of the same symptoms, she strongly suspects that you have the disease. The VP is not heartless, but she knows the company is positioning itself to be purchased and is getting ready to go through a reduction in force (i.e., fire a bunch of people) to improve, if only temporarily, company profits. She stands to gain from eliminating your position. Though she has not planned to include you in the RIF, once she suspects that you have MS, she moves your name from the "keep" to the "pink slip" column.

Is that illegal? Yes. Do you have a case? Not really. There is no evidence that the company was on notice of your condition. But what if you had told the company about your condition and that it was getting worse. Do you have a case now? Yes, you do.

I understand that you like and are good at your job. You don't want to position yourself so that you "have a case." You're not a fan of suing for "any little thing." There is nothing wrong with that attitude. It's part of what makes you good at what you do. But remember, the workplace can be a jungle that changes at a moment's notice. Here, the VP of HR wants to throw you under the bus at a time that you cannot afford to be without work or without health insurance. This has nothing to do with your excellent work; this is because she wants to save a buck. If you have protection under the ADA, you need not file a lawsuit (though you could). But you could use the protections to which you are entitled to get the company to back down from firing you. And, even if your employer won't allow you to stay, you've got a much better chance of negotiating a good severance if you've got something to trade, which in this case would be giving up your opportunity to pursue your rights under the ADA.

Now let's turn back to our friend Janice.

How about the reasonable accommodations process that Janice attempted? Did the employer conduct the process in good faith? You got it: no, the company did not. First, it told Janice not to come into work even before it even attempted an interactive process. Then, the company's "process" involved sending only two letters from the company's counsel, and it did not bother to respond to Janice's request that she meet with Brenda to see whether they could agree on an accommodation. Combine these facts with Brenda's stated objective to get rid of Janice, and this paints a clear picture of a company with no real interest in accommodating a disabled employee.

Did Janice Handle This Situation Well? How Could She Have Done Things Differently?

For someone with no knowledge of the law, Janice handled herself well. She got medical help and eventually requested the accommodations that her doctor suggested. In hindsight, she could have gotten medical assistance more quickly, and she could have made the request for an accommodation as soon as her doctor suggested it.

The primary aspect that she could have handled differently is to get a lawyer to assist her with the accommodations process. Many people are understandably reluctant to "lawyer up" to request an accommodation. Hiring a lawyer does have the potential to ratchet things up a bit (though it need not, if the lawyer knows how to handle the situation; that is, to act calmly in an effort to help resolve the issue rather than come out of the gate with guns blazing). An employee certainly does not need a lawyer to engage in the accommodations process. With the support of a doctor and with a company acting in good faith, there's no need to show up with counsel. The problem is that the accommodations process often does not go smoothly. It is sometimes difficult to tell beforehand how the company will act, except for those cases in which you suspect that you have a target on your back even before the process starts. For instance, if Janice had known about what Brenda said to the company's lawyer immediately after leaving her office, it would have made sense to go ahead and get a lawyer to help.

ADA issues are very complicated and sometimes poorly understood by HR professionals. Hirng an attorney could result in the company's attorney getting involved. Though it didn't happen in Janice's case, getting the company's counsel involved can be a positive development. If the company is willing to accept guidance, a knowledgeable lawyer can help it understand and comply with its responsibilities.

In addition, having a lawyer weigh in on your behalf is always a good thing if the company has its sights set on getting rid of you. Even a company acting in bad faith will usually avoid blatant violations of the ADA when an employee has counsel. Your lawyer may not be able to save your job (would you really want to keep it?), but he or she can help negotiate a favorable severance that allows for a graceful exit from the company in a way that, at the very least, won't hurt your chances of finding another job.

Hiring a lawyer before you are fired can also increase the value of your severance. Sure, a lawyer can help after you are fired, but you have more leverage with your employer while you still work there. Once the employer fires you, it presumably has some reason that it is prepared to offer: for instance, you were a poor performer or your disability made you no longer qualified. If you hire a lawyer to help you before you are fired, you've likely caught the company before it could come up with some bogus reason to let you go. Now you are a significant liability, *still on the payroll*. The company wants you gone, but here you are, gumming up the works with your own lawyer, and senior management hasn't had time to sit down with the company's lawyer to figure out how to let you go without violating the law. What is the company's choice now? To buy you out.

I don't want to overemphasize this point. It's rarely, if ever, the case that hiring a lawyer will get you a million-dollar severance. However, it is often the case that a lawyer can significantly increase the company's first offer. For example, with no lawyer, you might get an offer of zero to three months' salary. With a lawyer, that number might jump from zero to six months' salary. Regardless of what the final number is, a lawyer can help structure the settlement to reduce your tax liability (e.g., by getting the employer to agree to characterize some of the settlement as payment for attorney's fees or emotional distress rather than lost wages) and to offer other nonmonetary bells and whistles, like a positive, or at least neutral, reference. Plus, defense counsel likes to load up severance agreements with a lot of employer-friendly language (that's what they get paid for, after all) that could come back to bite you later. Having your own attorney may help you avoid some of these traps.

Should Janice Take the Severance Offer or Sue?

In most cases, there are steps an employee can take before she ever has to decide whether to sue. The first is to negotiate a better severance. A severance negotiation is just like any other negotiation. That means the company's first offer is usually not its best. In this instance, I would not recommend that Janice sign the initial severance. Any severance agreement is going to involve the employee giving up any right to sue for money. Three months' salary is not enough to justify giving up her right to sue. In this case, the company stepped in it. If it wants out, it can pay for the privilege.

How much should the company pay? I would say that a good severance for this kind of violation, without having to go to court, would be one to two years of salary with continued benefits. (The amount will vary from state to state. In states with courts more friendly to employees, such as California or New Jersey, an attorney might be able to get more. In states with courts that, at least by reputation, are more pro-business, like most southern states, those numbers may be lower.)

What if Janice hires a lawyer to negotiate with the company and the company gives a final offer of six months' salary with benefits? Should Janice take that? It depends on what Janice wants. If she wants to wrap this up and move on, confident that she can find another job soon, then it might be worth taking a lower offer to avoid the aggravation of having to keep dealing with the company. On the other hand, if Janice is crushed by this experience, goes on to require months of therapy, and feels like she cannot live with herself if she took six months, then she should not take that offer. She could do better if she wins, and she has a good chance of doing just that.

This brings up a point that you should always consider when deciding whether to settle. What does your best end game look like? What are your possible damages? Sure, a $30,000 settlement offer might not sound like much if you have been seriously smacked around (figuratively speaking; if literally, we're talking different numbers) by your employer. But it might not be so bad if your attorney tells you a win at trial would net you around $50,000.

What kind of award could Janice get here? As with any case where a person is still employed or just recently fired, it's tough to say because she doesn't know when she will get a new job and what her pay will be. Let's start with the known factors.

Emotional Distress

She is without question entitled to emotional distress damages, even if she gets a job tomorrow. As a rule of thumb, "garden variety" emotional damages (e.g., those in which the employee testifies about the emotional distress) are worth anywhere from $5,000 to $30,000 if the employee wins at trial. Janice is likely to do better because she's got a psychiatrist who could testify to any emotional distress she might experience as a result of being terminated. (The employer will try to chisel that number down by arguing that the emotional distress was attributable to the difficult situation with having newborn twins, not because of her termination.) Depending on how affected Janice is by being fired and what the doctor says, I'd put a value of $50,000 to $100,000 on her emotional distress—that's if she were to win at trial. For settlement purposes, I'd reduce what a reasonable offer would be depending on where in negotiations the offer is made. The earlier in the proceedings that the employer makes the offer, the lower the figure. A $30,000 emotional distress offer is a good one if Janice hasn't yet even filed with the EEOC. If she's been to the EEOC, filed in federal court, and had to sit through a deposition, then $30,000 is not as good.

Back Wages

Without question, Janice will be entitled to some back wages. The unknown is how long she will be out of work. A very general rule of thumb is that to find a comparable position, it takes about a month of job hunting for every $10,000 in salary. Let's assume that Janice, with benefits, has a salary package worth $240,000, or about $20,000 per month. That would mean it could take her twenty-four months of looking before she finds a similar job. Of course, she could get a job in three months. Who knows? The other factor is the salary of the new job. Let's suppose she finds a job in six months, but the compensation package is worth $200,000. Janice would be entitled to $60,000 ($20,000 times six months) plus the difference between what she was making and her current salary up to the date that she won at trial. Assume that it took two years from the time that she was fired until the jury returned a verdict in her favor. A back wages award would then be $60,000 plus $60,000 ($240,000 – $200,000 = $40,000, times one and a half years, or $60,000).

I have found that a reasonable request for a strong case like this is between a year and two years of wages. Almost no employer is going to agree to two years' wages, but it's a good opening bid.

Front Wages

Front wages are the wages an employee would have received from the date <u>after</u> she wins at trial. That, of course, presumes that an employee is still unemployed or underemployed at the time she wins. It also assumes that reinstatement at the job is not possible, for any number of reasons. The amount of front wages is something the judge determines after a plaintiff wins. Jurisdictions vary on how far out they award front wages. In the Fourth Circuit, two years is a good rule of thumb. For the purpose of negotiations, however, no employer will agree to characterizing damages as front wages because it would presume that the employer lost at trial. In the negotiations phase, no employer is going to roll over and agree that it would lose in court. In a sense, Janice is lucky in that she has a fairly strong case. Not all employees are so lucky. Employers usually have some reason—sometimes a good one—why they can win at trial. It is likely that Janice would receive front wages if she won at trial and was unemployed or underemployed after making serious efforts to find comparable work.

Punitive Damages

As discussed in chapter 2, punitive damages are what they sound like: damages designed to punish the company for wrongdoing. Recent changes in the law have made it so that these damages must be proportional to the award for compensatory damages. So, for instance, an award of one million dollars in punitive damages would not be considered proportional to an award of one dollar in compensatory damages (e.g., wages and emotional distress). The way this happens is that a jury would issue a verdict and assign a damages amount, and a court would adjust the punitive damages award accordingly. As with front wages, it is rare for an employer to agree that it might get hit with an award of punitive damages. An employer usually has some argument as to why, even if its actions were arguably wrong, it didn't act with malice, so no jury would award punitive damages. An employer often has the better argument in these cases. Punitive damages are difficult to win, particularly in an area (like Virginia) where the jury pool skews conservative. This is not to say it's never worth fighting for them. If you go to trial, you should certainly argue for them. It's just that you're not going to get an employer to agree in the first instance that it is on the hook for punitive damages. Of course, there are exceptions. If you turn up that smoking-gun document or find a really honest employee who testifies in a deposition as to the company's bad intentions, then you might get opposing counsel to concede that punitive damages are in play. But this will require some litigation. For Janice, we're just considering early settlement possibilities.

Attorney's Fees

If Janice were to take this case to trial and win, the company would have to pay any costs (for instance, large copying jobs, court reporter fees for depositions, etc.) and attorney's fees that Janice incurred. This is a significant risk for an employer and why having an attorney negotiate for you provides an employee considerably more leverage.

Let's assume that Janice gets a good job one month out, so she can't win big back wages or front wages. Plus, Janice, being a resilient type, bounces back quickly after being fired. Her doctor can testify that she was despondent for a week or so, but then recovered so completely that the doctor took her off all medication within a month. So, she has no big emotional distress damages. Nevertheless, Janice decides to sue because she believes it's the right thing to do, win or lose. She wins a jury verdict, but the award is small. She gets $30,000 in back wages and compensatory damages and a $10,000 punitive award. For a sizable company, $40,000 is hardly a big hit, particularly if the company has insurance coverage. But here's the catch. The company paid its attorneys $348,000 to take the case to trial. It paid another $23,000 in costs. That brings the company's tab to $388,000 for the privilege of losing. Here comes the kicker. Now Janice's attorneys can, under the ADA, submit to the court a petition for the company to pay Janice's fees and costs. Let's assume that Janice's attorney's fees and costs come to $262,000. In real life, this would kick off a separate round of litigation about whether Janice's attorneys are entitled to receive all that they billed for. This could be an entirely separate article, but there are a number of tricks that a company's attorney can use to try to reduce the award of attorney's fees. For instance, if Janice won on one claim but not another, her employer's lawyer could argue that Janice would not be allowed to receive attorney's fees for time spent on the losing claim, and so forth. For this example, let's assume the court awarded the entire amount. This means that the company now has to fork over to Janice the entire $262,000, bringing its total tab for firing her to $650,000. Now we're talking real money, and most of it is attorney's fees. That's why having an attorney on your side gives you more leverage.

The primary cost to the company for fighting Janice's case would be paying for attorneys.

Before we go forward, let's discuss these big numbers. In considering your own case, you might reasonably say something like, "Wow, six hundred fifty thousand dollars. Why would I settle for anything less than half of that? If the company settles for that, it comes out much better. It must be running scared!" The problem is, the company isn't. A depressingly low number of employees—fewer than 2 percent of all cases filed in most federal jurisdictions—even make it to trial. As an average, employers win over half of the cases that go to trial. It does happen a few times a year, but given the number of cases filed, it is exceedingly rare for an employee to ring the bell like that. And remember, by "ringing the bell," Janice walked away with just over $20,000 in her pocket after taxes. She's not buying a beach house with that. Of course, that's not to say she might not find the fight worth it. Janice will forever remember the tears of joy that came to her when she stood and heard the jury read its verdict in her favor and watched the company president lean over his table to stop himself from collapsing. But that will have to be her payback, not the money.

There are a number of reasons why so few cases result in employee wins. First, strong cases usually settle early. In the real world, Janice's company is likely to offer her something that makes this worthwhile for her, given the alternative of risking a bigger (and perhaps more satisfying) win at trial, but only after a long slog through federal court. She might have to file suit. She might even have to push past summary judgment, but eventually the company will offer her a good settlement.

Second, many, many employment cases are lost at summary judgment. (For more on this, see chapter 20.) This means that after paying at least some money (most attorneys who take cases on contingency require clients to cover their costs), your case is unceremoniously kicked out of court before you even get to say a word to the judge. For this reason, employers will sometimes lowball an employee in the beginning. The company will do this because (a) it is calling the employee's bluff, betting the employee may never sue; and (b) the company—because it can afford attorneys who specialize in employment law—has been advised that it might win at summary judgment. Only after losing at summary judgment will the company come to the table with a serious offer.

Imagine salmon swimming upstream to spawn. Many just don't make it. They wear out before they jump past the top of the waterfall, get eaten by a bear or an eagle, or get sucked into a turbine at a damn. It's a tough gig. Civil litigation is much the same.

All of this is to say that you shouldn't look at the select few jury verdicts and assume your case will result in the same. I'm not saying you should give up the fight before you even start, but you need to be a clear-eyed realist when considering settlement options.

Bottom Line

Most pretrial settlements involve a settlement figure that is some number of months of the employee's salary. Except in really weak or strong cases, in Virginia, that number is typically between six months to a year of salary, benefits included. While employers usually won't agree that they will get dinged for punitive damages, most will concede that a winning employee would get emotional distress damages. Thus, the employer will characterize some of the severance as an award for emotional distress. Why does this matter? Taxes. Back wages are taxed just as if you were still getting your paycheck from the company, which includes payment of Social Security (and other) taxes. This is usually about 7 to 8 percent of the wages. Emotional distress damages do not have this amount deducted. It matters little to the employer. It writes the same size check; the only difference is how much goes directly from the employer to the IRS. Usually employers are willing to characterize a quarter to a half of the payment as payment for emotional distress. That's a significant benefit to the employee. Another tax benefit to the employee is characterizing some of the severance payment as payment for attorney's fees. Attorney's fees incurred as the result of pursuing a civil rights case constitute an above-the-line deduction in your taxes. So, characterizing an award of $100,000 as wages puts a lot less money in the employee's pocket than one designated as $50,000 for back wages, $35,000 for emotional distress damages, and $15,000 for attorney's fees. It's hard to get this kind of deal, though, without an attorney. Remember, part of your leverage is that the company would prefer to pay $15,000 in attorney's fees now, get a full release of claims from you, and keep this whole thing quiet (Janice will certainly have to agree to confidentiality as a term of settlement) than risk—however small that risk is—paying many multiples of $15,000 and having a public loss on the record.

If this structuring of the deal sounds like a tax cheat, it's not. As long as the wrongdoing complained of could result in an award of emotional distress damages, there is nothing wrong with private parties agreeing that a portion of the severance settles those claims. Likewise, there is nothing improper in having the company pay the employee's attorney's fees. As discussed above, the company would be on the hook for them if it lost. The only time such an arrangement becomes problematic is when the entire severance is characterized as something other than wages when clearly part of the severance was in anticipation of some lost wages.

My educated guess is that Janice's company will eventually get to around a year of salary and benefits. It will agree to characterize a big chunk as emotional distress and another chunk as attorney's fees. So the final deal might look something like this: $240,000 in severance, plus the employer pays Janice's COBRA payments for a year or until she finds other coverage. The $240,000 payment will break down as follows: $20,000 in attorney's fees; $72,600 (approximately one-third of $220,000) for emotional distress, and the remaining $147,400 as wages, with applicable taxes withheld by the employer. Janice will release all claims against the employer and will agree to keep the settlement confidential. Both parties agree not to disparage the other. The employer will provide Janice with a positive reference, and both parties will agree on the language.

This example illustrates another point. Here, I assume $20,000 in attorney's fees, which is what it might take if Janice paid an hourly rate. If she entered into a contingency fee agreement, the attorney's fees would be one-third of the total recovery, which in this case would be $79,200. Not everyone can afford to pay an hourly rate, but those who can often end up paying less in attorney's fees than under a contingency fee arrangement.

The Pregnancy Discrimination Act of 1978 (PDA)

The PDA is a part of Title VII of the Civil Rights Act. Congress enacted the law in 1978 to make it illegal for a company with fifteen or more employees to discriminate against a woman because she is pregnant. As you might imagine, this means that an employer cannot legally fire or demote a woman after learning that she is pregnant. This is true even when an employer couches action that it takes in terms of paternalistic concern for the woman: "Honey, you don't want that promotion. No pregnant woman needs to be under that kind of stress." And so on. It is important to note, however, that the law does not require employers to treat you any differently than it treats other employees. So, if, for instance, you work on an assembly line and need to take more bathroom breaks late in your pregnancy, your employer, at least under the PDA, is not to make that easy change for you. If you insist on it, your employer can legally fire you. That is, if you are not also protected under the ADA—and you may be. But we'll get to that in a bit. First, here's an example of a pregnancy discrimination case.

Big Verdicts

Pregnancy discrimination cases sometimes involve shocking facts—and big verdicts. Take the case of *The Price Is Right* model Brandi Cochran. Cochran worked as a model on the show for seven years. After years of trying, she became pregnant with twins, a boy and a girl, at the age of forty-one. While she was thrilled, her producers and co-workers were not. When Cochran told one of the producers, he said that he knew because he had noticed the weight gain. Another producer implied that he would have fired her before she announced had he known of the pregnancy. Show management reduced her workload. Co-workers began to make fun of her, calling her "wide load." Tragically, Cochran miscarried her son. She gave birth to her daughter three months prematurely. As a result, the child had severe health problems. Caring for her premature daughter was made difficult by the fact that Cochran had to struggle to lose weight to return to the show—something she wanted to do. It never happened. For months, the show refused to return Cochran's calls. Cochran first learned that she had been fired after she was removed from the show's website.

Cochran sued, and her case went to trial. The jury returned a verdict of approximately $8 million, much of it in punitive damages. You can see Cochran discuss her victory at this link: http://abcnews.go.com/Entertainment/video/price-model-wins-lawsuit-17786783.

Sadly, the California Supreme Court (this case was tried in state, not federal, court) later overturned the verdict, finding that the trial court judge had given an incorrect jury instruction. The court sent the case back down to the trial court for another trial. At the time of this writing, the case is still pending. As is often the case, Cochran will likely reach a settlement with the show on favorable terms, given how badly the show lost in the first round.

Bottom Line for Recognizing a Pregnancy Discrimination Claim

PDA cases are just like any other discrimination case. You must have evidence of discrimination. To be protected under the act, you have to have evidence that you are being treated differently than others, at least in part, because you are pregnant. Sometimes there will be direct evidence, like, "We just can't have a pregnant woman working here." Just as often, you won't have any such evidence. Things will be a bit more subtle than that. In those cases, you'll need to look for signs that you are being treated differently than you were before you announced your pregnancy and any signs that co-workers at your level are getting better treatment. If something concrete happens, like you lose out on a promotion that was rightfully yours or you get moved from a supervisory position to one with no direct reports and little room for advancement, go see a lawyer. You may be protected under the PDA.

Pregnancy Discrimination Against Low-Wage Workers

The *Bloomberg* case (read about it in chapter 9) and the *Cochran* case are examples of women with high-income jobs and career choices. This is not to minimize the discrimination against them: even high earners are often a paycheck or two away from serious financial difficulties. That said, it is important to remember that low-income families are often in even more precarious positions, and they lack the resources to fight back against discrimination. The Center for WorkLife Law issued a report titled *Lean In, Or Leaned On? Poor, Pregnant, and Fired.* You can find it here: http://worklifelaw.org/pubs/PoorPregnantAndFired.pdf.

- Low-income families are caught between extreme demands at both home and work.
- Low-income families are more likely to be headed by single parents—a reported 66 percent of low-income parents are single—and to have children with health and developmental difficulties. More than two-thirds of low-income parents in one study cared for children with learning disabilities or chronic health conditions.

- Low-income families are also likely to provide more care for elderly and ill family members than more affluent families: those living under the federal poverty level are more than twice as likely to be caring for a parent or in-law for thirty or more hours a week.
- Meanwhile, low-wage jobs typically provide little flexibility or time off, even for emergencies, and often require unpredictable schedules.
- In one survey, 60 percent of employers reported that, from week to week, hourly workers' schedules changed either "a lot" or "a fair amount." Another study reported that almost 60 percent of low-wage workers cannot choose their starting and stopping times, and one-third cannot choose their break times.

A Powerful Tool for Pregnant Workers

What about when you have not been fired but just need changes at work due to issues related to your pregnancy?

Stop! Before you go further, if you are still employed and facing pregnancy discrimination or discrimination related to childbirth and your employer has fifteen or more employees, do these things:

- Do not attempt to negotiate with your employer yourself. I am all in favor of self-help and saving on attorney's fees, but this area of the law is becoming highly technical, and a slight misstep could result in losing your job without any recourse.
- Go see an attorney who specializes in employment law ASAP. The National Employment Lawyers Association (NELA; http://www.nela.org) is a great resource for this.
    - o Tell your attorney to find this law review article, which will be hot off the presses by the time this book is published: Joan C. Williams, Robin Devaux, Danielle Fuschetti, and Carolyn Salmon, "A Sip of Cool Water: Pregnancy Accommodation after the ADA Amendments Act," which is being published in the *Yale Law & Policy Review.*
- Talk to your doctor about any health-related issues you may be facing as the result of your pregnancy. At some point, you will need to have your doctor

write you a letter, but not before you can talk with your attorney about how best to handle this. *Do not have your doctor or any other health-care provider write your employer a letter requesting light duty.* A number of courts have held that employers are not, in many instances, required to grant pregnant women light duty. You could be fired for making this request.

Many women in the workplace today are not faced with overt discrimination based on their pregnancy. Instead, they sometimes lose their jobs because they require changes (often, very minor ones) in their work schedules. Consider this extreme example:

> A Walmart employee developed a pregnancy-related urinary tract infection. To treat it, her doctor told her that she needed to frequently drink water. She asked Walmart to allow her to carry a water bottle with her while she worked. Walmart had a policy of allowing only cashiers to have water bottles. This woman was not a cashier. When she insisted on being able to carry a water bottle to treat her health condition, Walmart fired her.

Was this a violation of the PDA? No, there was no evidence that Walmart sought to discipline this employee based on her pregnancy. It fired her because the company refused to make a temporary exception to its policy to allow this employee to comply with her doctor's orders. A similar case, *Young v. UPS*, involved an employee who was not allowed to return to work just because her health-care provider said she needed light duty for a few months. Ms. Young lost her case. (See the sidebar.) This is why pregnant women who require changes at work to address health concerns should consult an attorney.

Sidebar: An Example of Pregnancy Discrimination

Some legal analysts believe that the Fourth Circuit Court of Appeals, the federal appellate court that handles appeals from federal courts in Virginia, Maryland, North Carolina, West Virginia, and South Carolina, is moving from the far right toward the middle of the ideological spectrum. That may be so, but middle of the road may be as far as it goes. At least, that's what is suggested by a recent opinion adopting a narrow view of employee rights under the PDA in *Young v. United Parcel Service Inc.*

If you are not interested in the inside baseball of the legal analysis of this case and just want to know your rights, here is the bottom line: your employer does not have to provide a pregnant employee a light-duty assignment unless those assignments are offered to employees injured "off the job." For instance, if your employer requires that employees be able to lift seventy pounds to perform the job, and your doctor says you can lift only twenty-five pounds during your pregnancy, your employer can remove you from your job, as long as it enforces this same rule for all employees who are also injured off the job. (I find it a bit strange to consider pregnancy as an "off-the-job injury." This puts pregnancy in the same category as a back injury. Certainly, an employee can injure his back on the job or off. But how many women become pregnant at their job?) This is important because many large employers only allow for light-duty job assignments for employees injured on the job. They do this primarily to save on worker's compensation costs.

Note, however, the employer must actually stick to its policy. If the employer's policy is to provide light-duty assignments only for on-the-job injuries, but in practice it provides such assignments to some employees injured off the job, then a pregnant employee is entitled to the same treatment, regardless of what the policy says.

Finding out what your employer's practice actually is may be difficult. So, as I always advise, see your friendly neighborhood employment lawyer to find out whether your employer is unlawfully discriminating against you.

Inside Baseball

Now back to the sausage making. In *Young*, UPS would not allow the employee, Peggy Young, to work because her medical providers said that she could not lift more than twenty-five pounds while pregnant. UPS claimed Ms. Young's job required her to lift at least seventy pounds. (There was some dispute about whether someone in her job had to lift that amount, but the parties did not disagree that it was the policy.) It was also UPS's policy to grant light-duty job assignments to those injured on the job. UPS characterized pregnancy as an off-the-job "injury." The parties did not dispute that UPS enforced this policy. The *Young* court had to decide whether UPS's policy was illegal under the PDA.

Applying the PDA in Young

The dispute in *Young* (at least on this issue) was how to interpret the statutory section's second clause, which states that a pregnant woman cannot be treated differently than those similar in their inability to work. Ms. Young argued that the meaning was unambiguous: the PDA prohibits treating pregnant women differently than those with short-term restrictions on the ability to work. By this argument, an employer could not provide light-duty assignments to those injured on the job while denying those assignments to pregnant women. They are both similar in their inability to work. The Sixth Circuit agreed with this argument in *Ensley-Gaines v. Runyon*, 100 F.3d 1220, 1226 (6th Cir. 1996).

UPS argued that the first clause of that section placed pregnancy discrimination within the definition of sex discrimination. The company noted that courts have long held that an employer does not violate the law just because it has a policy that negatively affects a particular woman, provided that a man would be treated similarly. That is, an employer cannot apply a policy that makes a distinction based on sex or pregnancy. But as long as the employer is making an employment decision based on a neutral factor, like an on-the-job versus an off-the-job injury, that distinction (at least on these facts) is legal, even if it happens to negatively affect a pregnant woman.

Here, the court sided with UPS, finding that the second clause made sense only when read in conjunction with the first, meaning that UPS could have a policy that denies a pregnant woman light-duty work provided that all employees injured off the job are also denied work. The court reasoned as follows:

> Interpreting the PDA in the manner Young and the ACLU urge would require employers to provide, for example, accommodation or light-duty work to a pregnant worker whose restrictions arise from her (off-the-job) pregnancy while denying any such accommodation to an employee unable to lift because of an off-the-job injury or illness. Under this interpretation, a pregnant worker who, like Young, was placed under a lifting restriction by her health-care provider and could not work could claim that the PDA requires that she receive

whatever accommodation or benefits are accorded to an individual accommodated under the ADA, because the pregnant worker and the other individual are similar in their ability or inability to work—i.e., they both cannot work. By contrast, a temporary lifting restriction placed on an employee who injured his back while picking up his infant child or on an employee whose lifting limitation arose from her off-the-job work as a volunteer firefighter would be ineligible for any accommodation. Such an interpretation does not accord with Congress's intent in enacting the PDA.

While I disagree with the court's reasoning, it is for now the law of the land in the Fourth Circuit. Ms. Young's attorneys have requested that the US Supreme Court hear the case. Stay tuned.

Bottom Line with Pregnancy Discrimination

For any woman experiencing difficulties at work (or in higher education, as discussed in chapter 12), it is important to remember that you have options. Keep these points in mind.

Talk with your doctor about any problems you may be facing in the workplace due to your pregnancy. Discuss in depth any changes you think you might need at work to ensure that you have a healthy pregnancy.

Keep in mind that the ADA protects both physical and mental disabilities. If the stress of pregnancy is causing you to experience high levels of anxiety that are affecting your sleep and eating habits, talk to your doctor about whether you might be suffering from depression or generalized anxiety disorder.

If your doctor believes that you are suffering from a disability, have her send a letter to your employer asking for changes in your work environment. Review any job descriptions to make sure that the requested accommodation does not suggest that you are unqualified for the position. Pay particular attention to any lifting restrictions.

If your company has fifty or more employees, you may be entitled to leave under the FMLA. Talk to your human resources department. FMLA requires that the company inform you of your rights.

If you have short-term disability insurance coverage through your work, you may be eligible to take time off and still receive pay. Talk to your doctor and human resources about this. Make sure that your doctor is aware of what you need to show to receive the coverage. This should be in your "plan documents." If you are not sure whether you have these, talk to human resources.

Find a lawyer to talk to, even if you ultimately do not need to hire him or her. Many lawyers offer free or low-cost consultations. If you need a contingency fee arrangement, tell the lawyer up front. There's no point in wasting your time if the lawyer does not take cases on contingency. To find a lawyer, look for someone who specializes in representing employees. The NELA website is a good resource (http://www.nela.org). The lawyer-locator function can give you the contact information for attorneys in your state.

If all else fails, call the EEOC or go to a local EEOC office and file a charge. This is easy and free (though it may take an afternoon to get done). You do not need a lawyer to do this. If you later get a lawyer, she can then take over the EEOC process for you. You can file against your employer and still keep your job. Remember that a failure to file with the EEOC within 180 days of any discrimination could mean that you lose any right to hold your employer accountable.

Retaliation

If you are still employed and someone discriminates against you, or if you are pregnant, or if you are disabled—tell human resources in writing (e-mail is fine).

Why? Putting your employer on notice of discrimination against you or any condition that is protected under federal statutes (and some state statutes) gives you more leverage. After you put your employer on notice, if it fires you or takes any other adverse action against you, then you could have a <u>separate</u> claim for retaliation.

The federal government has enacted several laws that protect employees who report wrongdoing. Several of the laws discussed in this book, including Title VII, contain anti-retaliation provisions that protect employees who come forward and report discrimination. These laws allow attorneys to comfort clients who are afraid that they'll face reprisal for asking to be treated fairly. But it's important to keep in mind that, even if retaliation is illegal, companies may still engage in it. Anti-retaliation statutes, however, award employees monetary damages when their employers retaliate for engaging in protected activity.

Sample Scenario

Let's say that you are a woman and your supervisor is a man. He's a decent guy, but sort of old school. He is nice enough to you, but spends more time with your male colleague. They talk about fantasy football. You couldn't care less.

Three times, you apply for a promotion. Each time your supervisor gives the job to a man. Two of the three men have less experience than you. The first two times, you take it in stride. By the third time, you begin to suspect that your boss has passed you over because you are a woman. Assuming that your employer has at least fifteen employees, this is potentially illegal discrimination based on sex. That's one claim.

Let's further suppose that you don't say anything to your boss, but you do share your suspicion with a female co-worker. As soon as you do, you know it was not the best call. She is the office gossip. The next week everything is fine: it's business as usual. Your boss is his friendly, if patronizing, self. But the following Monday, you come into work just as Office Gossip is walking out of your boss's office. She walks away quickly and pretends that she doesn't see you. Your boss is weird the rest of the week. He seems angry. At one point, he comments, "It's too bad that some people are not grateful for what they've got." A week later, you are called down to HR and fired. The company won't even give you a reason.

Now, you know the truth. Your ex-boss is a sexist. He's not a gross, try-to-cop-a-feel sexist; he's just a plain-vanilla kind who thinks men are better workers than women. Plus, men like sports. He was content as long as you worked under him, doing as he asked.

(And you did, and did it well.) Then Office Gossip told him about what you told her: that you knew he was a sexist. When he found that out, your boss had you fired. What he told HR is that he did not think you had long-term potential in the company. The real reason was that he didn't want an uppity woman working in his company.

As you might imagine, this is also illegal. But you don't have a claim for it. Why? Because you didn't tell him or human resources about it.

Let's change the facts a bit. Suppose that after you didn't receive the third promotion, you sent a letter to the director of human resources. It was short:

> Dear Director:
>
> I believe that my boss has failed to promote me solely because I am a woman. Please let me know if you would like to talk with me further.
>
> Sincerely,
> Me

You carbon copy your boss. The next week, you get fired. Now you have two claims: one for sex discrimination and a separate claim for retaliation.

Here's the important part. You could win the retaliation claim even if you lose the sex-discrimination case. In fact, it may be easier to do so.

Let's suppose you sue. The attorneys take a bunch of depositions. It turns out that your boss is a sexist, but mostly he's just dumb. He made bad hiring decisions using the wrong criteria. Or, at least, the company is able to tell a convincing story to that effect. The court kicks that claim out. But the retaliation claim is pretty close to a slam-dunk. When the director of human resources testifies, she says that the day before the company fired you, your boss stormed into her office, threw the letter on her desk, and said, "This is no place for a troublemaker. I want you to make sure of that no later than tomorrow."

So, you lost on what attorneys call the "underlying claim"—the discrimination—but won on retaliation. You can further imagine a scenario in which you win on both claims. That's one way to double the value of your claim.

Whistle-Blower Protection

It's one thing to be fired or disciplined at work because of who you are. But sometimes, employees are disciplined or fired because they do the right thing. When an employee comes forward and reports illegal practices by company employees to HR or company management, that employee becomes a whistle-blower. Your employer cannot legally fire you for notifying it of this wrongdoing, but sometimes, companies would prefer that their dirty laundry stay hidden.

Federal and state laws may protect and even reward an employee who learns about fraud, rule breaking, or lawbreaking by his employer, supervisors, or colleagues. Telling HR about discrimination against others can have the added bonus of giving you protection where none otherwise exists. Let's suppose that you are in management and are thus exempt from overtime. You know that your employer is not paying the overtime due to hourly workers. If you say nothing, you have no legal claim for anything. But if you tell human resources—always in writing—about what you know, and then you get fired, you have a claim for retaliation under the FLSA, which protects people who raise issues related to pay, even if the claim is not related to their own pay.

Perhaps the most important of these whistle-blower statutes is the federal False Claims Act. President Abraham Lincoln signed the False Claims Act into law during the Civil War in an effort to uncover and stamp out fraud by military contractors. Today, the False Claims Act contains two important provisions for employees (or any person who discovers fraud being committed against the US government). The first of these provisions is called the *qui tam* provision, and it allows any person with knowledge of fraud against taxpayers to file a lawsuit in the federal government's name, acting as a "citizen attorney general." If that lawsuit ultimately leads to a recovery of money damages against the defendant, then the person who filed the lawsuit, called a "relator," will receive a share of those damages of between 15 and 30 percent.

If a *qui tam* case is won at trial, those damages will likely be more than the actual fraud itself. Under the False Claims Act, a person who defrauds the government is liable for *three times* the amount of damages, plus a civil penalty. Therefore, in cases where the fraud is large, the incentives to come forward and file a *qui tam* claim can be tempting.

But the False Claims Act also has another provision important to workers, made necessary by an unfortunate truth: companies will sometimes go to great lengths to protect themselves and their income streams. That's why the False Claims Act also contains an anti-retaliation provision that makes it illegal for employers to retaliate against employees who participate in or bring *qui tam* claims against their employers. Employees who successfully prove False Claims Act retaliation cases are entitled to reinstatement, two times the amount of their back pay, interest on that back pay, special damages, costs, and attorney's fees.

However, the availability of monetary damages does not change one uncomfortable fact: being a whistle-blower is hard. *Qui tam* cases often drag on for years, and the attorneys who represent False Claims Act relators often invest significant amounts of time and resources to prepare a case for filing. An employee who is considering initiating a *qui tam* case should discuss with her attorney whether the emotional and mental costs of being a relator outweigh the potential benefits she might realize years down the road. And the employee should have that conversation with her attorney sooner rather than later.

The False Claims Act contains important provisions that limit a relator's right to bring a claim. First, no person can bring a *qui tam* case that is based upon information that has been publicly disclosed. One important exception exists: when the relator is the original source of the public disclosure, the relator's *qui tam* case can proceed. Second, a *qui tam* case is available only to the first party who files it. The "first-to-file" requirement incentivizes employees with knowledge of fraud to speak with their attorney quickly and decide whether to pursue a *qui tam* case soon after learning of the fraud.

The False Claims Act has been tremendously successful at rooting out fraud and corruption. In 2012 alone, the Department of Justice reported recovering $4.9 billion in

False Claims Act cases. In fact, the act has been so successful that more than half of the states have enacted their own version of the False Claims Act, and more are likely to follow. These acts incentivize people to file *qui tam* cases involving fraud against state governments.

It's true that the False Claims Act is an important tool for employees. It allows them to do the right thing by coming forward with knowledge of fraud. And it protects them from retaliation for doing so. But the False Claims Act is far from the only statute that protects whistle-blowers.

Some industries are subject to specific whistle-blower protection laws based on the importance of safety and oversight in those fields. For example, the Atomic Energy Act of 1954 and the Energy Reorganization Act of 1974 protect employees of nuclear power plants and others with licenses to operate a nuclear reactor. Employees in that industry are protected against retaliation for reporting safety and regulatory violations to their superiors or to governmental agencies like the Nuclear Regulatory Commission. And the Toxic Substances Control Act contains provisions that protect employees who participate in proceedings to enforce the act's requirements. Even employees of government contractors may have whistle-blower protections under the National Defense Authorization Act of 2013.

Employees who feel they've been retaliated against for reporting illegal or fraudulent behavior or safety violations should speak with their attorneys as soon as possible about the rights they may have. There are many whistle-blower statutes, and an attorney who represents employees or whistle-blowers will be able to help a retaliated-against employee learn whether her employer has violated a law.

Time limits can be short, so employees should speak with their attorneys quickly. For example, the Atomic Energy Act and the Energy Reorganization Act only protect employees who file a complaint within 180 days of the unlawful action. Other statutes have limitations as well, and a conversation with an attorney will help an employee know how much time she has to come forward with a claim.

Whistle-blower protections are an important part of a framework of laws that keep us safe, protect us against fraud, and penalize unscrupulous companies. Employees who take the risk of coming forward have special protections in some circumstances. Being a whistle-blower is difficult and can involve years of litigation. It is not for everyone. But when a whistle-blower teams up with a competent attorney, she might find herself well rewarded for her efforts, and society as a whole reaps the benefits of safer industries and less fraud.

Anonymous Complaints

Here's one more thing to think about. In the real world, many companies don't like employees who complain of illegal activity. Yes, your company may have a nice glossy website encouraging employees to report known wrongdoing. Maybe your company means it. Maybe it doesn't. If it doesn't, it means that, as soon as you report something, the clock is ticking on your job. And many human resources departments leak like a sieve.

Call your company's "anonymous" hotline to report that your colleague has been grabbing your ass, and all of a sudden, your boss stops coming by your desk. This is fine, except that she also stops sending you good sales leads, and your numbers dip. Eight months later, you are let go for poor sales. "Isn't that illegal retaliation?" you ask. Most likely, but it will be almost impossible to prove. First, you made a call to a hotline. Nothing is in writing. Second, your boss is not the one harassing you, and no one will admit that someone in human resources told your ass-grabbing colleague, who then told your boss. (It turns out he was sleeping with her.) Now the company has the excuse of eight months of dropping sales numbers as cover for its decision.

I wish I had a solution to this dilemma. If you are thinking, *I'm damned if I do and damned if I don't*, you'd be right. Welcome to the jungle of the workplace. As a lawyer, I prefer that employees always report suspected discrimination in writing. For those people who end up in my office, it gives me a lot more to work with. But blowing the whistle is rarely without risk. So, if you report wrongdoing, stay on your toes for a while, and, to the extent you can, document everything.

Chapter 10
Equal Pay and Other Wage Issues in the Workplace

The Fair Labor Standards Act (FLSA) sets the federal minimum wage and rules for overtime pay. The law applies to most employers and requires them to pay employees who are not exempt at least minimum wage and overtime pay of 1.5 times their regular rate of pay. The US Department of Labor enforces this law through its Employment Standards Administration's Wage and Hour Division.

Caregivers may experience wage discrimination in several ways. One of the most prominent is the "motherhood wage penalty." This term refers to the fact that working mothers earn less pay and fewer benefits than childless women. Some researchers have estimated the penalty as high as 5 percent per child. The root of the penalty may be employers engaging in unconscious stereotyping of the working capabilities of mothers.

The Burden of Proof

Lately, I've spent a lot of time thinking about the burdens of production and proof in FLSA overtime cases. To be more precise, I've been thinking about how the burdens stack up when an employee performs exempt and nonexempt work over a long period.

For some exemptions, like the exemption for agricultural workers contained in section 213(a)(6)(A) of the FLSA, when an employee performs both exempt and nonexempt work in a workweek, she must be paid overtime for every hour over forty that she worked during that workweek. Even if she performs one hour of nonexempt work and forty-nine hours of exempt work, she is entitled to ten hours of overtime pay.

But who has the burden of proving what type of work the employee did in a given week? Is it the employee's responsibility to show, for each week that she seeks overtime, that she performed more than forty hours of work, at least some of which was nonexempt? Or must the employer show that the employee performed no nonexempt work in any week to avoid paying overtime?

I think that the latter is likely the case, because of the way that burdens of persuasion work. In overtime exemption cases, once an employee has proven to the jury (or judge) that she worked in excess of forty hours per week without overtime, the burden of persuading the fact finder that an exemption applies falls to *the employer.* Because employers must compute overtime on a weekly basis, and because every week is a separate calculation, this formulation appears to leave the employer with the burden of proving a negative for every week the employer seeks to show that the employee was nonexempt.

Proving a negative can be difficult, particularly if the employer failed to comply with FLSA record keeping requirements or if the employer erroneously thought it was exempt from the requirements because its employees performed exempt work. And when it comes to a party shouldering the burden of proving a negative, the US Supreme Court had this to say in *United States v. Denver & Rio Grande Railroad Co.,* 191 U.S. 84 (1903): "When a negative is averred in pleading, or plaintiff's case depends upon the establishment of a negative, and the means of proving the fact are equally within the control of each party, then the burden of proof is upon the party averring the negative."

The US District Court for Minnesota applied that rule to overtime exemptions in *Snyder v. Wessner,* 55 F. Supp. 971 (D. Minn. 1944). In this case, an employer sought to escape overtime liability by claiming it was covered under the executive exemption. The employer argued that its burden should be limited to "slight proof," and, upon meeting that burden, a burden of going forward with evidence should move back to the plaintiff. But the court disagreed.

So what does this mean for employees who have been swindled out of their over-time under the guise of an exemption? Well, if the employee's lawyer convinces the court that the burden of proving the exemption belongs to the employer and must be proved weekly, then the default position is that the employee gets overtime for any given week. The employer will escape liability for a given week only by proving a nega-tive: that the employee performed no exempt work in that week.

This is good news for employees and bad news for employers who commit wage theft. For more information about overtime laws, see the Department of Labor's page on overtime pay.

Equal Pay Act (EPA)

What should you do about getting paid less for the same work?

It is old news that women are often paid less than men for similar work. Though this is not an issue that only caregivers face, it certainly affects caregivers, given that the ma-jority of them are women. So, when are pay disparities illegal?

It is unlawful for a company to pay a woman less than a man for similar work when the company does not have a legitimate reason for doing so. That's what happened to Linda Lovell. Ms. Lovell was an accomplished woman with an undergraduate degree in textile chemistry and a master's in business administration. After gaining significant work experience, Lovell joined a subsidiary of Verizon called BBNT, which provided con-tract research and development services to the Department of Defense. Although Ms. Lovell worked a reduced schedule of thirty hours per week, she often made herself available to clients on her day off. Ms. Lovell, the only woman in her workplace, was not rewarded for her extra effort. On the contrary, she was often taken advantage of by her male colleagues. For instance, though she would often let male counterparts perform billable work for her clients, which employees had to do to be eligible for bonuses, her male counterparts did not return the favor. Worse, some of her colleagues charged matters to her clients without informing her, resulting in budget overruns. And it goes on. Ms. Lovell was the only employee in her group who did not receive a laptop com-puter, though she made multiple requests for one. She was also not invited to some company training sessions. For all her trouble, Ms. Lovell learned that she was paid less than her male colleagues, at least one of whom did the exact same type of work she did. In addition, in 2003, Ms. Lovell received a lower raise than her male colleagues. So, she sued. The name of her case is *Lovell v. BBNT Solutions*, 295 F. Supp. 2d 611 (E.D. Va. 2003). The opinion in the case was issued by Judge Thomas S. Ellis of the US District Court for the Eastern District of Virginia.

She sued under two statutes: the EPA and Title VII of the Civil Rights Act. I won't go into all the details here. The intersection of these two laws is highly technical. If, after reading this, you believe that your employer may be paying you less than your male colleagues, go talk to a lawyer. (The law would apply equally to men: that is, it would be illegal to pay a man less than a woman for the same work just because he's a man, but that is a rarity.) Here are some basics so that you have a sense of what to look for.

The EPA makes it unlawful for an employer to pay an employee at a rate less than that paid to employees of the opposite sex for equal work. This law is part of the FLSA, which is, in many respects, very favorable to employees because it does not require a showing that the employer intended to discriminate. You can find the text of the law at 29 U.S.C. § 206(d)(1). To bring a case for a violation of the EPA, a plaintiff must be able to show the following three factors:

1. The employer paid different wages to employees of the opposite sex. This can include someone hired to replace the terminated employee.
2. The employee holds a job that requires equal skill, effort, and responsibility.
3. The jobs are performed under similar working conditions.

When comparing jobs, the title of the job is not the deciding factor. An employee must show that a specific male—called a "comparator"—was paid at a higher rate even though they shared a common core of tasks. When comparing pay, it is generally the rate of pay, rather than a difference in the total amount of pay, that is relevant. So, a woman on a part-time basis could win an EPA claim against a full-time male employee if she is paid at a lower hourly rate. When looking at the "equal skill" factor, a court should look at the skill required for the job, not just skills possessed by the employees.

For instance, an employer could not take a male employee in a marketing department and point to his PhD in physics as justification for a higher pay rate when that degree was not required for the job.

The powerful aspect of the EPA is that, once an employee has met these factors, it is the employer's burden to disprove that a violation has occurred, and this burden never shifts back to the employee. This is different from claims brought under antidiscrimination statutes like Title VII. Also, unlike Title VII, to win an EPA claim, the employee does not have to show *why* the employer established the pay rate the way it did. Title VII requires an employee to show evidence of what was going on in the employer's head, which can be difficult. This tilted playing field makes these cases easier to litigate and settle. All that is required is a review of the relevant records and perhaps a deposition or two to establish the pertinent factors. That's not to say they are easy to win—no case is. But it does make the EPA, and other claims under the FLSA, powerful ones for employees treated wrongly.

Even if an employee shows the three factors above, an employer can win an EPA lawsuit if it can demonstrate that the difference in pay rate was based on one of the following four factors:

1.   A seniority system,
2.   A merit system,
3.   A system that measures earnings by quantity or quality of production, or
4.   A difference based on any other factor other than sex.

As you can imagine, the last one, "any other factor other than sex," is a wide-open door. Two of the big factors that employers try to use are education/background and offering a higher starting salary to induce someone to accept an offer. The first thing to remember is that it is not enough for the employer to throw up one of these reasons and win. It must prove to the fact finder (i.e., the judge or jury) that one of these reasons justifies the disparity in rate of pay.

Education/background is particularly fertile ground for employers, given that there is almost always at least some difference in background in employees. The key to remember is that to rebut an EPA claim on this basis, an employer must prove the male employee has a combination of education and experience that is more valuable—not merely different—than the woman bringing the case. For instance, in the *Lovell* case discussed above, the employer argued at trial that it was justified in offering the male employee, Mr. McNamara, a higher rate of pay because he held an undergraduate degree in mechanical engineering and a master's degree in structural engineering. Moreover, he had played a significant role in preparing multimillion-dollar bid proposals for a competitor before joining BBNT. But in declining to overturn the jury award, the court-noted evidence at trial showed that Ms. Lovell had a similar level of education, she had significant work experience prior to joining BBNT, and she had an exceptional history at BBNT, which included a proven track record of winning new business. The judge noted that the jury reasonably could have concluded that Ms. Lovell's background was equally valuable to the company.

BBNT also argued that Mr. McNamara enjoyed a higher rate of pay because the company offered him a higher starting salary to lure him from a competitor. However—and this is an example of why deposition testimony is so important—the court noted that BBNT's department manager had testified in his deposition that if the market was such that the company had to offer a salary premium to attract talent, it likely would have raised the salary of current employees to retain them. So, the court noted, the jury could have concluded that the hiring starting salary for Mr. McNamara did not explain the continued difference in the rate of pay. Without that admission from the company's own witness, Ms. Lovell might well have lost this case.

Keep your eye on the defense that the employer had to offer a higher rate of pay to attract the male employee who now maintains that higher rate of pay. This defense, which is often rolled out by employers, could have the effect of making legal an unfortunate fact in the workplace. A number of studies have suggested that men sometimes receive a higher rate of pay for one primary reason: they ask for it. Women (again, as a general rule) are historically more reluctant to aggressively negotiate for a higher salary. At least one federal court has explicitly ruled that aggressive salary negotiations alone *cannot* be a defense to an equal protection claim: *Dreves v. Hudson Group*, No. 2:11-cv-4, 2013 U.S. Dist. LEXIS 82636 (D. Vt. June 12, 2013). In addressing the issue of salary negotiations, the court reasoned as follows:

Second, there is simply no basis for the proposition that a male comparator's ability to negotiate a higher salary is a legitimate business-related justification to pay a woman less. To hold otherwise would eviscerate the federal and Vermont equal pay provisions. It would also require the Court to accept a theory that is essentially indistinguishable from the repudiated argument that employers are justified in paying men more than women because men command higher salaries in the marketplace. *See Corning Glass Works v. Brennan*, 417 U.S. 188, 205, 94 S. Ct. 2223, 41 L.Ed.2d 1 (1974) ("That the company took advantage of [a job market in which it could pay women less] may be understandable as a matter of economics, but its differential nevertheless became illegal once Congress enacted into law the principle of equal pay for equal work."). Reliance on the difference in value that the market places on women and men "became illegal once Congress enacted into law the principle of equal work for equal pay." *Id.* In this Court's view, a pay disparity is no more justified when it is the result of a single negotiation than when it is the result of a market-wide phenomenon, for what is a marketplace other than an amalgamation of many negotiations? Permitting an employer to defend itself simply by showing that a disparity was the product of one negotiation with a male employee would lead to the same result: a marketplace that values the work of men and women differently.

In support, in a footnote, the court cited recent studies about gender disparity in salary negotiations:

The Court notes that there are a number of studies that suggest that gender plays a significant role in negotiation outcomes. *See, e.g.*, Hannah Riley Bowles, Linda C. Babcock, and Kathleen McGinn, "Constraints and Triggers: Situational Mechanics of Gender in Negotiation." 89 *J. Personality & Soc. Psychol.* 951 (2005). Other studies show that women and men face different social incentives when deciding whether to negotiate compensation, particularly when they must negotiate with a male supervisor or evaluator. See Bowles,

Hannah Riley; Babcock, Linda; Lai, Lei, "Social Incentives for Gender Differences in the Propensity to Initiate Negotiations: Sometimes It Does Hurt to Ask," 103 *Org. Behav. & Hum. Decision Processes*, 84 (2007).

Damages Under the EPA

If you win your EPA case, you can win back pay. If you were fired for raising an EPA issue while employed, you could also win front pay. If you can show that the employer "wilfully" set up a pay scale that differed based on sex, you could win liquidated damages, which generally results in a doubling of the underlying award. For instance, if you won $50,000 in back pay, liquidated damages would be another $50,000, bringing the total to $100,000. You cannot win emotional distress or punitive damages under this law.

Title VII

As is evidenced by Ms. Lovell's case, an employer that pays a woman less than a man doing the same work may violate Title VII of the Civil Rights Act of 1964 in addition to the EPA. (These claims can be brought in the same lawsuit.) There are advantages and disadvantages to bringing a claim under Title VII. The two advantages are relaxed standards for the proper comparator and available damages.

Under the EPA, you must prove that the comparator has a job, performed under similar working conditions, that requires equal skill, effort, and responsibility. There is a fair amount of wiggle room in that definition for an employer to put up a fight. In contrast, with Title VII, you have to prove only that your job is "similar" to higher-paying jobs occupied by males.

As for damages, under the EPA, you cannot win a claim for emotional distress or punitive damages, though this may be a wash, given that you can win liquidated damages under the EPA and not Title VII.

Here is another, less universally applicable, benefit to a Title VII claim. Unlike the EPA, in some jurisdictions, you could win a Title VII case based on the fact that a male comparator consistently received a higher raise that you did. This universe of cases would be small, limited to those cases where the pay raises differentials were consistent and stark in the differential. You could never successfully bring an EPA claim based on a differential in raises alone.

There are also significant disadvantages to a claim under Title VII versus one under the EPA. To win in a Title VII lawsuit, you must prove that your employer intended to pay you differently because of your sex. Moreover, as discussed above, you have to prove discrimination, whereas under the EPA your *employer* would have to prove that the difference in pay rate was based on a permissible factor.

There is also a procedural difference between Title VII and the EPA. To bring a lawsuit under Title VII, you must file a charge with the EEOC within either three hundred or 180 days, depending on where you live (crazy, I know). Only if and when (usually when) the EEOC issues a right-to-sue letter can you file in federal court. In contrast, with an EPA claim, you have 180 days to file a claim, but you don't need to go to the EEOC first.

What Happened to Ms. Lovell?

Ms. Lovell teaches us a lesson about thinking through the pros and cons before beginning a lawsuit. Before proceeding, you should make a clear-eyed assessment about what verdict and damages you may receive. The good news about Ms. Lovell is that she won her case before the jury on all counts. The jury found that BBNT had violated the EPA and Title VII. It awarded Ms. Lovell $400,000—$325,000 in compensatory damages and $75,000 in back pay—and $100,000 for the EPA claim. (If this verdict had stuck, Ms. Lovell could not have received a double payment for back wages, so she would not have been eligible to receive both $75,000 in back pay under Title VII and $100,000 under the EPA.) Remember that under both Title VII and the EPA, Ms. Lovell was entitled to seek all her attorney's fees from the defendants, an amount well over $100,000. Of course, BBNT's attorneys didn't work on this case for free. The company likely had already paid over $250,000 just to get the case to trial. So, BBNT was initially looking at writing some very big checks.

But that never happened—at least, not all of it. After the trial, BBNT doubled down on its position and paid its attorneys another chunk of change to file a motion with the trial court asking for it to essentially disregard the jury's verdict and enter judgment in favor of the company. (Yes, that is possible. So much for trusting juries!) If the judge was not willing to do that, the company asked for a new trial.

The good news for Ms. Lovell was that the judge ruled that there was enough evidence produced at trial for the jury to find that it paid her less than Mr. McNamara for no other reason except that she was a woman. However, the court found that there was not sufficient evidence as a matter of law to conclude that the company discriminated against her in awarding her a lower raise than Mr. McNamara. Losing on this basis was not such a big deal because the court found that she won, at least in some respect, under Title VII, so the amount of money she put in her pocket would not have been affected. But here comes the kicker. The court found that Ms. Lovell was not entitled to *any* of the $300,000 in compensatory damages because she did not testify concerning how she felt about being paid less than a man for the same work. As a matter of common sense, I think we can all agree that it probably felt pretty bad. But Ms. Lovell had to say that under oath at some point for a jury to award compensatory damages like pain and suffering. Because she did not do so, the court slashed the $325,000 award in compensatory damages to zero. While that certainly was tough medicine for Ms. Lovell, she likely would not have gotten all that money anyway, even if she had testified through tears about her emotional distress. In many jurisdictions, like the Eastern District of Virginia, where this case was tried, it is difficult to win big damages based on emotional distress alone, particularly when it is only the plaintiff—as opposed to a doctor or psychologist—who testifies about the distress. Called "garden variety" emotional distress claims, courts will usually allow awards of only between $15,000 and $30,000 (which is certainly still better than zero). Finally, the court looked at the back wages damages—as it was required to by law—and found that Ms. Lovell was entitled only to the difference between what she made and what Mr. McNamara was paid. The difference turned out to be $3,125. So, at the end of the day, that's what Ms. Lovell got. Even with this win, she would have (and likely did) submit a request to the court that BBNT pay her attorney's fees and costs. (If she had a contingency fee arrangement, she likely had not paid any attorney's fees out of pocket.) I'm sure the court required that BBNT pay some of that amount. The problem is that there is a bunch of case law saying that an employee's attorney can recover only for time he or she spent on those claims on which the employee won. That is clearly in question here now.

I don't know Ms. Lovell, but I would be curious how she feels about her case now. Knowing what she does about how it turned out, would she have done it again? Surely, the financial gain of less than $4,000 was not worth the time—more than a year—that it took for the case to work its way through the system. While Ms. Lovell would not have been involved during that entire time, she had to meet with her attorney a bunch (fun!), sit through a deposition, and endure at least a couple days of trial. But, as with most things in life, the money tells only part of the story. Maybe it was worth it for her to bring her company to heel. At the end of the day, no matter the money, BBNT lost and paid its attorneys a bunch of money to do so. We also don't know whether Ms. Lovell got any satisfaction from watching the superiors who wronged her have to sit for a deposition, under oath, in some windowless room for a number of hours (I'm just imagining the scenario). She couldn't have gotten any of that without filing a lawsuit. Or maybe she got no benefits out of this, found the whole process disheartening, and still sends her former attorney hate mail. (Let's hope not!)

Breast-Feeding

Marie is a woman who is breast-feeding her child and working full time. This means that Marie frequently needs to pump at work. However, her employer makes her pump in a bathroom and often limits the amount of breaks that Marie may take to pump. Is this legal?

Usually, this behavior is illegal. The Fair Labor Standards Act (FLSA) requires that an employer provide reasonable, unpaid breaks and a private place other than a bathroom for a mother to express breast milk for up to one year following the birth of a child. However, if the employer has fewer than fifty employees, and the employer can show that allowing a mother to pump would cause an undue hardship, significant difficulty, or substantial expense (in relation to the employer's size and financial resources), then the employer is not required to permit pumping breaks. Additionally, if your employer is required to give you breaks for pumping, then it is prohibited from retaliating against you for taking advantage of those breaks. . You can learn more that the website for the U.S. Department of Labor (http://www.dol.gov/whd/nursingmothers/).

Some states require additional protections for breast-feeding mothers. For example, California requires that breast-feeding mothers be allowed "reasonable accommodations" similar to those with disabilities, including accommodations such as a modified work schedule and job restructuring. New York expands on the FLSA regulations and requires that a mother be provided pumping breaks for up to three years following the birth of her child instead of just one year. Moreover, the Affordable Care Act, also known as "Obamacare," requires that employers provide a place for mothers to pump and follows the requirements under the FLSA closely.

Additionally, while it is an emerging area of the law, many courts are recognizing breast-feeding as being related to gender discrimination under Title VII and include breast-feeding discrimination as a form of gender and pregnancy discrimination. Recently, a woman in Texas was fired after requesting time to pump at work twice. In *EEOC v. Houston Funding II, Ltd.*, the Fifth Circuit ruled that breast-feeding discrimination violates Title VII because breast-feeding is "a medical condition related to pregnancy and childbirth." This seems logical enough, and the court made its decision based on the dictionary definition of *lactation*, which is "the physiological process of secreting milk from mammary glands and is directly caused by hormonal changes associated with pregnancy and childbirth."

Chapter 11
Fair Housing Act Claims

Another statute providing some protection for caregivers is the Fair Housing Act. Section 3604(a) of this law says that it shall be illegal to "refuse to sell or rent after the making of a bona fide offer, or to refuse to negotiate for the sale or rental of, or otherwise make unavailable or deny, a dwelling to any person because of race, color, religion, sex, **familial status**, or national origin" (emphasis added).

Courts have interpreted this provision to mean that a landlord cannot refuse to rent to a person solely because he or she has children. For instance, in *Potter v. Morgan*, the court awarded damages to the Potters based on these facts:

> Complainants had been living in LaGrange, WY, but needed to relocate to Cody, WY, approximately 400 miles away, because Mr. Potter's new job started in July 2011. During the course of searching for housing, Complainants contacted Respondent on June 10, 2011, but were wrongly denied Respondent's property on Draw Street (Draw Street Property). Complainants failed to find other available housing in Cody before Mr. Potter's job began and were forced to move to Clark, which is 37 miles north of Cody. After six months of commuting from Clark to Cody for both work and amenities, Mr. Potter received a conditional job offer from the Cody Police Department and Complainants broke their lease and moved to a house in Cody, at Gabbi Lane, in December 2011.

The opinion by the administrative law judge (ALJ) noted:

> At the heart of this matter is a one and a half to three minute tele-
> phone conversation, some of the content of which is in dispute. The
> parties agree that Respondent spoke with Mrs. Potter on June 10,
> 2011.... Based on its observation of the witnesses and their demean-
> ors while testifying, the facts enumerated at paragraphs 21–31, *su-
> pra*, constitute the Court's findings with regard to the interactions
> between Mrs. Potter and Respondent.... The salient statements
> are as follows: 1. Respondent told Complainants that the ages of
> Complainants' children were Respondent's "business" because
> Respondent was concerned with the children's safety, as the steps in
> the Draw Street Property could pose a safety problem. 2. In response
> to Mrs. Potter's statement that Respondent could not discriminate
> against Complainants because of her children, Respondent replied,
> "Yes, I can, and I will" [then hung up the telephone].

The ALJ found that an "ordinary listener could easily conclude that the statement was
in violation of § 3604(c)."

The court (technically, the US Department of Housing and Urban Development) awarded the Potters monetary damages, including $15,000 for "intangible damages," which
covered the emotional distress from being denied housing and the fact that Mr. Potter
was unable to participate in his son's school activities because the family was forced to
live away from where he worked.

A second example is the Ninth Circuit's decision in *Gilligan v. Jamco Development Corp.* In
this case, the federal appeals court found that it could be a violation of the Fair Housing
Act for the managers of an apartment complex to refuse to rent to a couple because
they received Aid to Families with Dependent Children (AFDC). The facts of the case
were as follows:

> In January 1994, Catherine Gilligan contacted Ruth Fischer about
> renting an apartment at Verdugo Gardens in Burbank, California.

According to the Gilligans' complaint, she informed Fischer that her family's source of income was AFDC, and Fischer replied that the Gilligans could not inspect or apply to rent an apartment because they were receiving AFDC benefits. The Gilligans maintain that Fischer never inquired about the amount of their monthly income or informed Catherine Gilligan of the monthly rent at Verdugo Gardens. They further allege that Fischer was aware of a vacant apartment unit in the building when she refused to discuss a rental with Catherine Gilligan.

On February 16, 1994, a fair housing tester posing as a prospective tenant contacted Fischer to inquire about the rental of an apartment unit for her family. The tester told Fischer that she received welfare payments, and Fischer responded that Verdugo Gardens was not a "welfare building." Fischer also stated that she had no apartments available to show until the following week. Fifteen minutes later, a second fair housing tester contacted Fischer and inquired about the possibility of renting a unit for her family. In response to Fischer's questions, the second tester stated that she was working and did not receive welfare payments. Fischer promptly showed her an apartment that was being vacated.

Because *Gilligan* was a decision about the standard necessary to move forward on a claim, the decision did not indicate how the Gilligans fared in their lawsuit. However, by allowing the case to move forward, the court recognized that it would be illegal for an apartment manager to discriminate against an applicant simply because he or she has children.

In short, The Fair Housing Act provides a powerful tool to protect families from housing discrimination.

Chapter 12
Caregiver Discrimination in Education

Consider these two scenarios:

Stephanie Stewart, pregnant with her first child, is an honors student in community college. She asks the professor of her *women's studies* class whether she can make up assignments that she will miss due to labor, delivery, and doctors' appointments. The professor, a *woman*, denies her request. (Check out "New Lawsuits Shine the Light on Pregnancy Discrimination," by Jessica Grose of *Slate Magazine* (http://www.slate.com/ blogs/xx_factor/2013/05/02/stephanie_stewart_amy_clark_and_others_battle_pregnancy_discrimination_in.html).

Or how about this one:

Gina is a student in a college course. She is pregnant and due to give birth toward the end of the semester. She talks to her professor, explaining that she will need time off for the baby. The female professor says no problem. Before the baby shows up, Gina misses some class time for reasons related to her pregnancy. When midterm marks come out, Gina gets a five out of twenty-five for class participation. Gina raises this with the professor, who says, "You can only get credit for class participation if you are in class." When Gina protests that she wasn't skipping classes for the fun of it—she missed class because of her pregnancy—the professor says, "Too bad, the university says I can set any attendance policy I want." Gina calls the department head, who helpfully explains, "Well, university policy does say she can set up any attendance policy she wants, so..." (For the full version of Gina Crosley-Corcoran's blog, visit

http://resources.thefeministbreeder.com/education/pregnancy-parenting-at-school/
did-you-know-pregnant-students-have-rights-neither-did-i/.)

Is what happened to Gina and Stephanie legal? Not under the federal law Title IX. In fact, both women got their respective universities to back down, but only after they threatened to take the legal action under Title IX for pregnancy discrimination.

Title IX

All educational institutions that receive federal aid, including private universities that accept it, are covered by Title IX, 20 U.S.C. § 1681(a). Title IX has justifiably received significant attention in the press for its use in combating inequalities in female athletics and sexual harassment on college campuses. As noted in an article, "Title IX and Pregnancy Discrimination in Higher Education: The New Frontier," by Mary Ann Mason and Jaclyn Younge: (http://www.law.berkeley.edu/files/bccj/Title_IX_Law_Review_Article_Final_5.29-3-5.pdf), Title IX is a powerful tool available to teachers and students subject to pregnancy and caregiver discrimination. This is a critically important issue for women in education, especially for students in lengthy courses of study such as PhD and professional programs. These programs often span a time in their lives when they may start and raise families. Similarly, students in community colleges are often older and more likely to be balancing school with family responsibilities. Those who work in education as teaching assistants and in postdoctoral programs, because of their part-time status, may not be covered by other laws like Title VII or the FMLA, but they are covered by Title IX. (Title IX is similar to Title VI, which makes it illegal to, among other things, exclude anyone on the basis of race from an educational program that received federal funding.)

The language of Title IX is very broad. It reads:

> No person in the United States shall, on the basis of sex, be excluded from participation in, be denied the benefits of, or be subjected to discrimination under any education program or activity receiving Federal financial assistance.

It also explicitly makes discrimination on the basis of family status and pregnancy illegal:

A recipient shall not apply any policy or take any employment action:

(1) Concerning the potential marital, parental, or family status of an employee or applicant for employment which treats persons differently on the basis of sex;...

(b) Pregnancy. A recipient shall not discriminate against or exclude from employment any employee or applicant for employment on the basis of pregnancy, childbirth, false pregnancy, termination of pregnancy, or recovery therefrom.

(c) Pregnancy as a temporary disability. A recipient shall treat pregnancy, childbirth, false pregnancy, termination of pregnancy, and recovery therefrom and any temporary disability resulting therefrom as any other temporary disability for all job related purposes, including commencement, duration and extensions of leave, payment of disability income, accrual of seniority and any other benefit or service, and reinstatement, and under any fringe benefit offered to employees by virtue of employment.

(d) Pregnancy leave. In the case of a recipient which does not maintain a leave policy for its employees, or in the case of an employee with insufficient leave or accrued employment time to qualify for leave under such a policy, a recipient shall treat pregnancy, childbirth, false pregnancy, termination of pregnancy and recovery therefrom as a justification for a leave of absence without pay for a reasonable period of time, at the conclusion of which the employee shall be reinstated to the status which she held when the leave began or to a comparable position, without decrease in rate of compensation or loss of promotional opportunities, or any other right or privilege of employment.

Title IX actually has significant advantages over actions brought under the PDA. Unlike the PDA, Title IX states that pregnancy must be treated as a temporary disability. This means that a woman bringing an action under Title IX must be given light duty or other accommodations recommended by her health-care provider. Not so under the PDA. Also, Title IX has no caps on compensatory damages (e.g., pain and suffering). In contrast, the PDA tops out at $300,000 for the biggest employers. But as a practical matter, this makes very little difference. It is a rare case where a court will allow a compensatory damages award that exceeds $300,000.

Taking Action Under Title IX

If you want to take action under Title IX, you have two options. You can file an administrative claim with the US Department of Education (DOE), Civil Rights Division. No attorney is required, and there is no cost to file. The downside of filing this way is that the DOE has a short statute of limitations of 180 days after the discriminatory event. Also, like most administrative agencies, the DOE is understaffed and overworked. So, for many cases, it conducts a cursory investigation and denies most claims. Still, DOE does take action in some cases. Simply filing is often enough to get a university to wake up and comply with the law. However, the DOE will not award monetary damages.

The second option is to file in federal court. You need not file with DOE first—you can go straight to court. The downside to this is that you will probably need an attorney, and there is an expense involved. The filing fee alone is $400. The upside is the availability of money damages and speed. In court, you can ask for a temporary restraining order to quickly force the university to take action. For instance, let's suppose that you are a postdoctoral student, and your supervisor has just told you that you can take time off to recover after a difficult delivery, but that he is going to have to give your lab to someone else because, "You know, I just can't afford to have the thing sit empty." This is bad. It took you two years to pull that lab together, and you are working on some research that literally could make your career. All of that goes down the tubes if you lose lab privileges.

What can you do? Going to the DOE isn't going to help. The department moves too slowly. You're going to need to file in court immediately and ask the court to enter a temporary restraining order (TRO) against the university to stop your director from taking away your lab. Most courts will hear a TRO in a matter of days. (Note that this does not mean that your lawsuit gets resolved in matter of days. A TRO basically means the court—if it finds that you have a likelihood of winning and that, if the court doesn't take action immediately, you will suffer irreparable harm—will basically stop things in place while the case goes forward.)

Part III: Leave Issues

Chapter 13
Laws That Protect Employees While on Leave

Family and Medical Leave Act (FMLA)

The FMLA—for you intrepid souls who want to read it—can be found at 29 U.S.C. § 2601. This is the only federal law that explicitly provides a right for employees to take time off from work to provide self-care (e.g., you just had surgery and need time to recover) or time to care for immediate family members.

Unfortunately, the law has a limited scope. To begin with, it applies only to employers with fifty or more employees within a seventy-five-mile radius. This excludes a wide swath of American employers, including almost all mom-and-pop operations. It also excludes companies that have dispersed places of business. For instance, if an employer had forty-nine employees in Virginia and another forty-nine based in Connecticut, it would not be covered by the FMLA. The second major limitation of the act is that it provides only for unpaid leave. For this reason, its use is not a reality for those families living paycheck to paycheck.

> **Additional Resource:**
> The American Bar Association recently released a 330-page report, *2013 Midwinter Meeting Report of 2012 Cases*. You can find it at the FMLA Insights Blog (http://www.fmlainsights.com/2013%20FMLA%20report%20(ABA).pdf), a very useful site for FMLA law.

This doesn't mean that you are automatically out of luck if your employer has fewer than fifty employees. Some states, like California and Massachusetts, as well as the District of Columbia, have their own laws that govern medical leave. (As is sadly often the case, we have no such luck in Virginia.)

Nevertheless, the FMLA provides important protections to eligible employees. Covered employees are entitled to at least twelve weeks of unpaid leave, and employers are liable for any attempts to interfere with an employee's efforts to take leave or to retaliate against those who seek its protections.

On the plus side for the FMLA, there is no requirement that you go to the EEOC or another state administrative agency before going to court. You can file a lawsuit any time within two years after the violation occurred. You have up to three years if the violation was willful, which means your employer knew its conduct was prohibited by law or that it acted with reckless regard for the law. The interpretation of what will satisfy the "willful" standard will vary by jurisdiction, so it's best not to wait three years to file. Moreover, the longer you wait to file the claim, the less likely you are to win, as memories fade and documents disappear.

Sample Scenario
Gabriela has worked as a receptionist at a large company for the past five years. She has two sons, ages fifteen and thirteen. She never had any problems at the company until she got a new manager, Marcy. Marcy believed that she had been hired to "whip this place into shape." She made it known that she planned to "crack down" on "excessive leave." Marcy made good on her promise, giving everyone a hard time about taking

days off. She even commented when she believed an employee was taking "excessive trips to the ladies' room."

At the beginning of the school year, Gabriela's oldest son was injured in a sporting accident. He was taken to the emergency room and told that he had torn a ligament and would need surgery in the coming weeks. In the meantime, he could wear a knee brace. Gabriela returned to work the next day with medical documentation of her son's injury. She told Marcy that she would like to take that Thursday and Friday off to help care for her son after his surgery. Marcy said that it would be difficult to find someone to cover the shift and asked whether the surgery could be rescheduled. Shocked, but afraid to lose her job, Gabriela rescheduled the surgery for the following week.

The following week came, and Gabriela came back to work with her sons in the car. She went in to talk to Marcy about who would cover her shift while she was out on FMLA leave. Marcy rolled her eyes and asked, "Do you really need to take this time off? It seems like you've been out a lot." Gabriela had not been out a lot—hardly at all. She explained to Marcy that, following her son's surgery, he would not even be able to get out of the bed to use the bathroom without help. Marcy laughed and said, "Just teach him to pee in a bottle!" Gabriela started to cry. Co-workers began to notice, so Marcy ushered her out of the building. While Gabriela stood crying in front of her car, Marcy tried to calm her down. She asked to be introduced to her sons. Gabriela complied. The oldest son asked why his mom was crying and Marcy, as if it were a joke, said, "I told her that you could just pee in a bottle."

Gabriela took two days off as scheduled. When it became clear that her son would take more time than expected to heal, she wanted to ask for more time off, as she still had plenty of FMLA leave. But given her last attempt to get time off, she decided not to. Plus, the leave was unpaid and, as a single mother, she could not afford it. She went back to work, leaving her son to be cared for by his grandmother in the morning and her thirteen-year-old son when he got home from school.

When she returned to work, her relationship with Marcy was strained. Marcy barely spoke to Gabriela and openly excluded her from lunch invitations with co-workers.

Three weeks after returning to work, Marcy wrote her up for an incident that occurred two months before Gabriela took FMLA leave. It involved an upset customer who had complained about something. When the incident occurred, Marcy confronted Gabriela about it. Gabriela tried to explain, but Marcy cut her short and said, "I don't want to hear it." Now, months later, the regional manager came through the office and asked to meet with Gabriela. The only private place to meet was the lunchroom. There, the regional manager asked Gabriela for her version of events. He told her to wait while he went to "check out her story." An hour later, he came back and told Gabriela to turn in her key card and collect her things. She was being fired. Incredulous, Gabriela asked why. The regional manager said, "Because you lied to Marcy about what happened."

Gabriela found herself without a job in the worst economic downturn in a generation. She found part-time work in a restaurant, but it was not nearly enough to pay her mortgage. She made it as long as she could on credit cards, but ultimately fell behind on her mortgage and lost her house.

Can Gabriela do anything about this? If so, what? What would be the potential value of any lawsuit?

First, Gabriela has two claims: (1) interference with attempts to take FMLA leave and (2) FMLA retaliation. A claim of FMLA interference is just what it sounds like. An employer cannot interfere with an employee's efforts to take FMLA leave. In this instance, Marcy was clearly hostile to Gabriela's efforts to take leave and discouraged her from doing so. She intentionally interfered with her efforts to take FMLA leave even though she ultimately granted her some.

Gabriela also has a strong claim of FMLA retaliation. Specifically, it certainly seems like Marcy set out to fire Gabriela because she took FMLA leave to care for her son. The company likely will argue that it legally fired Gabriela based on an incident with a customer. But the facts of this case suggest that this is what courts call "pretext." That is, the company is using the incident with the customer as a cover for firing Gabriela, when the real reason for her termination was the fact that she took FMLA leave. Evidence the company's cited reason for her termination was false, in that the incident with the customer took place months before she was fired. The company acted only after Gabriela took leave. Moreover, based on the regional manager's comments, it sounds like Marcy made up the story that Gabriela lied about the incident. But the truth was that Marcy would not even allow Gabriela to explain what happened. She could not have lied even if she wanted to.

One other matter that the company may try to hide behind is the fact that it was the regional manager, not Marcy, who made the decision to fire Gabriela. In essence, the company will argue: "Well, even if Marcy arguably wanted to discriminate against Gabriela, she didn't make the termination decision." This is called the "cat's paw theory." This derives from a fable in which a monkey tricks a cat into scooping some chestnuts from the burning embers of a fire. The cat does so, burning its paw. The monkey then takes off, chestnuts in hand. In this context, the idea is that the regional manager fired Gabriela even though he had no discriminatory motive. Rather, he was duped by Marcy into firing Gabriela. Some courts have thankfully stopped these maneuvers by disallowing cat's paw tactics. Thus, here, the company will be liable because it is apparent that the regional manager relied solely on Marcy's account in deciding to fire Gabriela. (The company might win on this point if it could show that the regional manager made the decision after conducting his own independent investigation, even if Marcy had initially raised the issue. But it is clear here that the manager simply relied on Marcy's untruthful account in making his decision. And now the company is going to get burned!)

What does Gabriela get if she sues and wins? She would be entitled to get lost wages and reinstatement or front pay. Lost wages are the amount of money she would have earned had she stayed employed. For the sake of easy math, let's say Gabriela made $5,000 per month and, by the time her case went to trial, she was out of work for a year. So, $5,000 times twelve is $60,000. She would also be entitled to interest on this amount.

Gabriela might also be eligible for front pay. Front pay is wages she would have earned after the judgment. Let's assume in this case that Gabriela got another job after a year, but it paid only $4,000 per month. As front pay, Gabriela would be entitled to the difference between what she would have made and what she currently makes for some time out into the future. Here, Gabriela is out $1,000 per month, or $12,000 per year. If a court awards her two years' front pay, she gets two times $12,000, or an additional

$24,000. (The amount of front pay is generally up to the court to determine. Front pay awards are usually in the range of two to five years, though courts can award more or less than these amounts.) So, Gabriela here would be eligible for $60,000 plus $24,000, or $84,000.

One great aspect of FMLA is that it allows for something called "liquidated damages." These damages are added to punish a company for bad behavior. A court can award liquidated damages by doubling the underlying award. In this case, that bumps Gabriela's award up to $168,000. A company can avoid liquidated damages by arguing that, even if it violated the law, it had a good faith belief that it was not acting illegally. That would be tough for the company to get by with here, given Marcy's blatant behavior.

Another plus to the FMLA is that employees who sue and win are entitled to an award of attorney's fees. Sweet justice. This means that the company will have to pay its attorneys and Gabriela's! Unless Gabriela's fee agreement provides otherwise, she will get to keep her $168,000 (minus what the IRS will take).

Unfortunately, Gabriela cannot recover damages for pain and suffering under the FMLA, although she would have been able to under other discrimination statutes. If this were a sex-discrimination lawsuit, she could. She also cannot recover for other losses. For instance, she won't be able to get the company to pay for the loss of her home and other associated costs.

Case Study
"Crappy" is a technical legal term that I will not define here. But this is essentially what a federal court in Connecticut found in *Wanamaker v. Westport Board of Education*, 899 F. Supp. 2d 193 (D. Conn. 2012). This is a well-reasoned case that is a must-read for attorneys who represent clients subject to pregnancy-related or caregiver discrimination.

Here's what happened:

Since 2004, Sally Wanamaker worked as a computer teacher in the Connecticut public school system. She was a star employee. In 2009, she gave birth to a daughter and was injured during the delivery. Her doctor informed the school system that she would need an additional thirty to sixty days to recover. At first, the school system told Ms. Wanamaker that the temporary teacher covering her position would continue to do so until she could return. However, the school later told Ms. Wanamaker that the substitute teacher would take her job permanently, but she could return as a substitute teacher. Ms. Wanamaker followed up with the school, saying that she could return if the school allowed her to teach while sitting down and allowed her to take some brief medical leave. The school said thanks, but no thanks. When Ms. Wanamaker appealed through the school system's internal procedures, the system backed down, but still refused to put her back into the computer teacher position. Throughout this time, the school superintendent was alleged to have said some unfavorable things about employees taking medical leave.

Ms. Wanamaker sued, claiming, among other things, that the system had interfered with her FMLA leave and had retaliated against her for attempting to take leave. The defendants filed a motion to dismiss. A key issue for this case was the school system's position that it could not have interfered with Ms. Wanamaker's FMLA leave because it offered her a full-time teaching position, even if it wasn't the one she had held for the past eight years.

Under the FMLA, an employer has to return an employee to her original job or its equivalent upon her return from leave.

Here, the school system said that returning Ms. Wanamaker to a full-time teaching position was the equivalent of, if not the same as, the position that she left. The court noted:

> In order to constitute an adverse employment action, it is not enough that defendants gave plaintiff a subjectively less preferred teaching assignment; the assignment must be "materially less prestigious, materially less suited to h[er] skills and expertise, or materially less conducive to career advancement."

Sotomayor v. City of New York, 862 F. Supp. 2d 226, 255 (E.D.N.Y. 2012) (quoting *Galabaya v. New York City Bd. of Educ.*, 202 F.3d 636, 641 (2d Cir. 2000)). The court disagreed with the defendants, finding that the complaint (which it had to accept as true at this stage) alleged that the school first tried to put her in a substitute position. It then tried to put her in a regular teaching position, despite the fact that her doctor requested that she be placed back in her computer teaching position. Thus, the court reasoned, the replacement assignment was "materially less suited to her skills and expertise."

The court also included a meaty review of the legal basis for interference and retaliation claims, individual liability and governmental immunity under the FMLA, as well as ADA coverage for temporary disabilities. As an added bonus, the court discussed Ms. Wanamaker's claims under the Connecticut Fair Employment Practices Act (CFEPA), a unique state statute providing additional protections to employees in that state.

I don't want to overstate this win; this is a decision on a motion to dismiss at the inception of the lawsuit. At this point, Ms. Wanamaker still has to prove her case. Moreover, this case is a trial court opinion from a federal court in Connecticut. Other courts need not follow the court's reasoning here. Still, the thought and care that the judge obviously put into these issues means that other courts likely will cite this opinion as persuasive authority. And employees everywhere can use it to argue that an employer cannot move an employee to a crappy job and then successfully hide behind the equivalent position provision of the FMLA. Best of luck, Ms. Wanamaker!

Leave as an Accommodation Under the ADA

The ADA specifically provides that time out of work can be a reasonable accommodation. Note that this is particularly useful when you have a combined right to FMLA and ADA leave. If you have a medical issue that counts as both a serious medical condition under the FMLA and a disability under the ADA and run out of twelve weeks of FMLA leave, you may be protected by the ADA if you need to extend that leave. But, for this to stick, the leave must be of a reasonable duration. At the very least, this means that the leave must be for a definite period. For instance, assuming that your job is not a crucial one for your workplace, you are probably safe if you have a disability and a doctor's recommendation that you should stay out of work for a month. The further you push out that time frame, the more likely you are to risk that your employer will claim that continued leave is unreasonable and have a court agree.

You can read more about this issue in chapter 9. For detailed discussion on the law in this area, check out an article by attorney Ramit Mizrahi, "Leave As A Reasonable Accommodation Under The Americans With Disabilities Act," 3 LABOR & EMPLOYMENT LAW FORUM 29 (2013). You can find it online at http://digitalcommons.wcl.american.edu/cgi/viewcontent.cgi?article=1055&context=lelb.

If you find yourself facing a possible need for extended leave due to a disability, see a lawyer to find out how courts in your area deal with this issue.

Employee Retirement Income Security Act (ERISA)

What happens when employers take away or deny your benefits?

A significant perk of employment for many—besides the obvious paycheck—is the benefits package. This is often particularly true for pregnant women and caregivers who are, or will be, facing significant health-related expenses.

What protections do you have when an employer starts to screw around with your benefits? ERISA is the primary federal statute that regulates employer benefit plans. Some state laws apply that often have more favorable damages—for instance, punitive damages and in some cases treble damages, which are not available under ERISA. For that reason, most employers want to litigate cases under ERISA rather than state law claims. If you think your employer may have discriminated against you in denying benefits coverage, or if you think your company is just plain wrong about how it made a decision with regard to benefits, arrange a consultation with an attorney who handles these claims.

When you do, look for an attorney who represents employees, ideally one with experience handling cases involving benefits. Many attorneys who do this work will specifically clarify that they handle ERISA cases. Note that ERISA is an extraordinarily complicated law. The pool of attorneys who handle these cases is small, and even smaller for those who represent employees. This means you might have to do a bit of digging and may need to look outside your immediate area, especially if you do not live in or near a big city. A good place to start is the attorney-finder function of the NELA, which you can find at http://www.nela.org.

But it is important that you at least be able to spot the issues, particularly because ERISA cases are easy to miss. It's is also important that you spot them because you may be able to use ERISA to your advantage even if you find the initial reason you sought a lawyer—e.g., wrongful termination or some type of discrimination—is, because of some loophole in the law, not a viable claim.

Here is a short list of the categories of issues you should look for:

- Denial of benefits because you or someone your plan covers is about to incur significant medical expenses.
- Any kind of differential treatment (e.g., higher plan costs) charged to you or someone on your plan as compared to other members of the plan. This is not always illegal, but it should be a red flag.
- Differential coverage of any benefits related to pregnancy, including refusal to cover contraceptives.
- Improper management of investment accounts. Do you think there is something strange about the way the company, or its administrator, is handling your retirement account? Are a lot of your funds invested in a company owned by the brother-in-law of the company president? This could be an ERISA violation. However, just because investment accounts are performing poorly does not mean that your plan is violating ERISA. But if there is a question, it is worth having an attorney take a look.
- Failure to provide notice of your rights by providing you with plan documents (e.g., not providing you information about your right to continued health-care coverage [under COBRA] if you lose your job).
- Retaliation against you for raising issues about your benefits.

As with most issues involving ERISA, there are no bright-line rules. For instance, it may be legal in some jurisdictions and under some plans to deny expenses for childbirth under preexisting condition exclusions. In some instances, it is not legal. This legal landscape is continuing to change with the passage of the Affordable Care Act. Still, if you find yourself affected by one of these issues, recognize that it may be an illegal act and consult an attorney.

Here's a quick tip that you should use if you are facing trouble with your employer and have a benefits package: ask for your "plan documents." You can do this while you still work for the company or after you have been fired. The plan documents are the paperwork that explains your benefits. Your employer is required by ERISA to provide them to you upon request. You can win some damages, including attorney's fees, if your company fails to provide them within sixty days after your request.

How do you request them? Put the request in writing; e-mail is fine. You will need to send the request to the plan administrator. This may or may not be an employee of your company. Companies sometimes hire a third-party administrator to handle benefits. I know of one pregnancy discrimination case that was financed, in part, when the company had to settle an ERISA claim involving the failure to provide plan documents.

ERISA Case Study
In this case, an employer fired a woman because she had a baby who required expensive medical care.

Thelma Fleming worked as a nurse practitioner for a nursing home, Covington Manor, three years before she gave birth to her first child. Her child was premature and required hospitalization for three months. Ms. Fleming's medical expenses for her delivery were $4,000. The baby's hospitalization resulted in an $80,000 bill. (And these were 1983 dollars.)

Ms. Fleming planned to return to Covington, but she decided to seek a position with a nursing home owned by the same company, Brownsville Manor, which was located closer to her home. To do so, she had to resign her position with Covington. Afterward, she applied to Brownsville and was offered a part-time position with the intent that she move to a full-time spot when one became available. Before she could start, however, the company called Ms. Fleming and told her not to report to work. The company admitted that it decided not to let Ms. Fleming start her new position because it did not want to pay the high cost of health insurance through its self-insured plan for

Ms. Fleming's child, who would require ongoing medical treatment. So, she sued, claiming that the company discriminated against her on the basis of her pregnancy in violation of Title VII of the Civil Rights Act.

After a bench trial, the court found that the company did not violate Title VII because there was no evidence that it discriminated against Ms. Fleming on the basis of her sex. Interestingly, the court, of its own accord, asked the parties to address whether the company had violated ERISA because it admittedly declined to have Ms. Fleming report to work after offering a job because the company did not want to pay the high cost of her benefits. The court pointed to language in ERISA, stating that:

> It shall be unlawful for any person to discharge, fine, suspend, expel, discipline, or discriminate against a participant or beneficiary for exercising any right to which he is entitled under the provisions of an employee benefit plan…, or for the purpose of interfering with the attainment of any right to which such participant may become entitled under the plan.

The employer—now locked into the position it took at trial—tried to wiggle out of this one by arguing that Ms. Fleming was not an employee because she had not been officially hired at the time the company told her not to bother showing up for work. It also argued that she was not a plan "participant" because she was not a full-time employee. The court rejected both of these arguments. First, it observed that the company had offered her a position and afterward had Ms. Fleming start the onboarding process, reviewing employee manuals and the like. Thus, she was an employee when the company essentially reneged on the deal. Second, the court found that ERISA explicitly includes in the definition of plan those who *may* become eligible to receive benefits. The company conceded that it initially anticipated that she would become full time.

So, Ms. Fleming won, sort of. She had asked in her lawsuit only that she be given her job back at Brownsville. But the trial court found that although reinstatement is often a favored remedy, it was not appropriate here because she later quit the job she found after being fired at Brownsville, found herself a man, and had a another child. Thus, the court reasoned, the woman didn't really want a job. On that basis, it awarded her only back pay from the time she was fired up to the point when she quit the job she subsequently found. This amount came to $5,000.

Are you thinking what I'm thinking? Some version of: Huh? Did the court really just say that? You and I are not the only ones. One of the judges on the panel (Judge Nathaniel Jones, who worked as an attorney for the NAACP before becoming a judge) wrote a separate opinion in which he said pretty much the same thing. Here's what he wrote:

> In the instant case, the district court denied reinstatement because it found that Fleming voluntarily quit her position at Maplewood Nursing Home in May 1985 and that she would have quit her position even if she had been working at Brownsville.... The court found her reason for quitting to be "her mental and physical condition resulting from the stress and tension of the new baby".... Fleming contends that she quit because the thirty-one mile commute from Brownsville (where she lived) to Jackson (the location of the Maplewood Nursing Home) forced her to be too far away from her sick baby. She contends that had she received the job at Brownsville, she would not have had to quit because the job would have been located in her home town.

> This dispute seems to be one of fact, and I ordinarily would not suggest disturbing the district court's finding. In this case, however, the district court's rationale for denying full back pay and reinstatement seems to me problematic. After concluding that Fleming would have quit even if she had been employed at Brownsville, the court goes on to state that "[p]laintiff had someone else who helped to support her in 1986, and she had another child in 1987. Clearly, plaintiff was not interested in working full-time from May 1985 until May 1988, at which time she obtained other full-time employment."

> That conclusion seems to me problematic because it is based upon two stereotypical presuppositions that the PDA was designed to alleviate. First, the court assumes that women would not work if they

could find other means of support. Second, the court assumes that Fleming's decision to have another baby is somehow fundamentally inconsistent with a desire to work full-time. The facts that Fleming sought to work full-time at Brownsville after the birth of her first child and that she later obtained full-time work at Maplewood suggest that Fleming would have worked full-time despite her having another baby. Further, the court's attribution of a desire not to work to the decision to have a child is precisely the sort of presumption that employers are prohibited from making with respect to women's decisions regarding pregnancy and childbirth. Therefore, it seems to me that the district court's rationale is at best a highly questionable if not wholly impermissible ground on which to refuse Fleming the legitimate remedies of reinstatement and full back pay. Thus, I would reverse on this issue, reaching the conclusion that the district court's finding here was clearly erroneous.

Fleming v. Ayers & Associates, 948 F.2d 993, 1001-02 (6th Cir. 1991) (internal citations omitted).

I tend to agree with Judge Jones. There could have been any number of reasons that Ms. Fleming would have stayed at Brownsville even though she subsequently left another job to stay home. Maybe it was closer to where she lived, had better management, paid more—you get the picture. Perhaps the best indication that she would not have quit was that she asked only to be reinstated, instead of asking only for back pay.

What if your employer pulls a similar stunt and fires you because it doesn't want to pay your benefits, but it isn't honest enough to admit it? That is often the case. (This was a strange case because apparently no one had thought about ERISA as an issue before the trial was over. The case started as one about sex discrimination. The company's defense was straightforward. Oh, no, Judge, we didn't care about the fact that she was a woman. We just didn't want to pay high insurance costs for her sick kid. Had we known about that little bugger, we wouldn't have hired her in the first place. Sorry, Judge? What about ERISA? Um, dang. Can we get a do-over?)

In the event that your employer knows better than to admit an ERISA violation, it will come up with another reason. These are the usual cast of characters: she was a poor employee, she falsified her time cards, or this was just a reduction in force. If your employer offers up one of these reasons, the case becomes just like any discrimination case in which you will have the ability to put on evidence that the reason offered by your employer is a "pretext," or a made-up reason to cover up its real motive, which was to wiggle out of its obligations to pay benefits. In that case, you could show things like you received excellent performance reviews; your time cards were accurate and, in fact, you worked overtime for which the company did not pay you; or you were the only one let go, so this was not an actual across-the-board reduction in force.

Short- and Long-Term Disability

Some companies offer short-term disability (STD) and long-term disability (LTD) as part of the benefits package. The terms of these plans vary. They can be a good option to use in tandem with FMLA and ADA leave. Sometimes, a health problem that qualifies you under one of these laws will also qualify you for STD. The benefit of using STD along with FMLA or other leave is that you can continue to receive at least a portion of your salary while you are out. A company is not required to pay you while you're on FMLA or ADA leave. As is the case when requesting any medical leave, it is important that you communicate clearly to your doctor about your health condition and the requirements of the insurance policy. If the insurance company denies your application, there will be an appeal process provided by it. Appeals are primarily conducted by submitting documents and are not costly proceedings. If the insurance company wrongly denies your appeal, you can bring a lawsuit under ERISA.

LTD policies operate under the same principles, but, in my experience, companies will fight these harder, likely because the payout can be extensive. You will need all your medical providers working with you, and you probably will have to be examined by a company doctor for an "independent" review. I put this term in quotes because these doctors are often friendly to the company.

Note that, in many cases, to qualify for long-term insurance benefits, you must have a medical professional state that you cannot return to work, even without an accommodation. Keep in mind that in doing so you are removing yourself from the protections of the ADA, which requires that you be able to perform the essential functions of your job. Of course, if you require LTD benefits, you likely do not want continued protection under the ADA, which requires that you, at some point, be able to return to work.

Supplemental Social Security Income

People who earn below a certain income threshold may qualify to receive SSI benefits. These benefits are governed by a completely different set of laws that are outside the scope of this book. Many attorneys specialize in this area of law. Most do not require any up-front payment. SSI differs from many LTD policies in that you can apply for and receive SSI and still be protected by the ADA. The US Supreme Court has held that this is so because qualifying for SSI benefits means only that you are unable to work, not that you are unable to work with an accommodation. But it does require you to thread a difficult needle. You have to be impaired sufficiently not to be able to work at your current job, but if your workplace made some reasonable accommodation, it would be possible for you to return.

Chapter 14

Overlapping Protections of the ADA and the FMLA

The FMLA and the ADA are the two primary laws that protect those requiring leave from work. These laws overlap in some respects, yet they have significant differences.

Which employers are covered by the FMLA?

The ADA applies to any employer with fifteen or more employees. The FMLA applies to employers with fifty or more employees within a seventy-five-mile radius. So, if your company has thirty employees in Fairfax, Virginia, and another thirty in Albany, New York, it is not covered by the FMLA, but it is covered by the ADA.

Which employees are covered?

The ADA covers any employee with a disability who can perform the essential functions of their job with or without accommodations. In most respects, the ADA does not protect those who need to provide care to family members.

The FMLA covers any employee who has worked for the company for at least one year and for at least 1,250 hours during that year. The employee must suffer from a serious medical condition—one that requires hospitalization or a continued course of treatment. The FMLA also covers the birth of and bonding with a child, including an adopted child. An employee can also take FMLA leave to care for a parent, spouse, or child suffering from a serious health condition. For those in military families, the spouse, child, parent, or next of kin of service members can take up to twenty-six weeks in a one-year period to care for the service member. There are additional FMLA benefits for service members and their families.

Does the FMLA require an employer to make changes to my work space?
No. The FMLA requires only that your employer provide you with leave from work. The ADA, however, does require your employer to make reasonable accommodations that allow you to perform your job.

Does the ADA require my employer to provide me with leave from work?
Maybe. Leave from work can constitute a reasonable accommodation, though the law does not specify any time period. So, a week could be the longest reasonable accommodation required under the ADA. Under the FMLA, however, a covered employee is entitled to a full twelve weeks per year.

Significantly, for those with health problems, it can be possible to stack FMLA and ADA leave. For instance, you could exhaust your FMLA leave and qualify for additional leave under the ADA, though the duration of leave will vary depending on circumstances.

Can I take ADA leave when I give birth to my child?
No, unless you become disabled, as defined by the ADA, while giving birth. A normal pregnancy will often not result in ADA coverage. If you are protected by the FMLA, however, you are entitled to twelve weeks of unpaid leave, regardless of whether you are disabled.

Must my employer give me leave from work to take care of a sick family member?
Not under the ADA. The ADA requires an employer to accommodate only you. In contrast, FMLA requires covered employers to give employees protected under the law up to twelve weeks of unpaid leave to care for a child, spouse, or parent suffering from a serious health condition.

My son has to travel overseas for work, but he is not in the military. Do I qualify for FMLA leave to care for my grandchild while he is away?

No. FMLA offers leave to provide for only spouses, children, or parents with a serious medical condition.

Can I sue under both the FMLA and the ADA if my employer fires me while I'm on leave?

Possibly. Unless your employer can show that it would have eliminated your position even if you were not on FMLA leave, you can sue for interference with your FMLA rights. It is possible that your employer also violated the ADA, if you were out as the result of an accommodation request under the ADA. (Though, as a tactical matter, it makes little sense to request leave under both statutes simultaneously. Take FMLA leave first, then follow up with a request for leave under the ADA if you suffer from a disability.) You might also have a claim for both under a set of facts like these: You requested an accommodation at work, a quiet office to work in while you recovered from post-concussion migraines that have plagued you for almost a year now. Your employer eventually gave in, but only after you hired an attorney. Even after that, someone overheard your boss complaining about the "disruption" you caused and saying that he believed you were faking it. A day later, you were in a car accident and took FMLA leave while you were in the hospital. The day before you were to be discharged, your boss called and fired you, saying, "Things just aren't working out."

Here, you have a claim for both. You have a retaliation claim under the ADA because it appears that your boss fired you because he did not like that you asked for the protection under the ADA. You also have a claim for interference and retaliation under the FMLA because, by firing you, your boss unlawfully interfered with your FMLA right to leave. It also looks like he may have fired you because you sought protection under the FMLA.

Is my company required to give me FMLA leave if I qualify for it even if I didn't mention the FMLA law in my request?

Yes, your company is required under the FMLA to tell you about your right to leave if you do something that reasonably put your company on notice that you are entitled to the leave. For instance, if you are in a car accident and require a week of hospitalization, your employer must give you FMLA leave even if you don't know to ask for it.

Case Studies

Scenario 1

I suffer from ADHD and depression. Both worsened for a period of months and, as a result, I missed some important deadlines. Given my previous high performance, it should have been clear to everyone that I was experiencing health problems. One of my co-workers even asked me whether I had ever thought about taking Ritalin. I recently was denied a promotion. My boss told me it was because I missed the deadlines. Do I have a claim under the ADA?

Probably not. Unlike the FMLA, which requires an employer to affirmatively apply the law to you where you qualify for protection (except in limited circumstances), an employer is actually prohibited from assuming that you suffer from a disability. Here, there is no indication that your employer knew of your disability, and both ADHD and depression qualify as a disability under the ADA. Even if your employer were on notice, you did not request an accommodation, and under the ADA, your employer is under no obligation to offer you one absent a request. So, even though you could have been entitled to an accommodation that might have allowed you to meet the deadlines—for instance, time off to see a doctor or a quiet office space—your employer is not liable because you chose not to make the request.

Note that it would be different if there were evidence that your employer denied you the promotion because of your disability. Let's say that your performance had never suffered and your boss had said, "We just can't promote you because of your depression." This would be a violation of the ADA, even though you never requested an accommodation.

Scenario 2

I suffered a seizure last year as the result of my epilepsy. At my doctor's request, I asked my company to put different lighting in my office. I gave my boss a letter from my doctor explaining the reason why. My company refused outright. I later suffered another seizure at work, injured myself, and had to be hospitalized. I was out for a week under FMLA leave. When I came back, my boss told me that the company had reassigned me to a different position with lower pay. Someone else took my job. Did my employer violate the ADA and the FMLA?

Yes, and yes. Epilepsy is covered under the ADA, and a change in lighting is almost certainly a reasonable accommodation. Your employer violated the law by refusing to even entertain your request. Your employer also violated the FMLA because that law requires that your employer reinstate you to the same or equivalent position, if one is available. Your job was still open, and you were entitled to it.

But here's the thing. You can bring an action against your employer for the FMLA violation but not the ADA violation. You have at least two years to sue for a violation of the FMLA. You can file a complaint with the US Department of Labor, but this is not required. You can go straight to court. In contrast, you have anywhere from 180 to three hundred days to file a charge with the EEOC for an ADA violation. The ADA requires that you file a charge with the EEOC and let it attempt to investigate your allegations before you sue in court. Because you didn't file with the EEOC, you cannot now protect your rights under the ADA, even though your company clearly violated the ADA.

Okay, so I can sue for only the FMLA violation. Does this really matter?

It might, at least in terms of what you can recover. Under the ADA, you can recover for emotional distress and for punitive damages. How much those damages would be is hard to say. I'm guessing that the denial of the lighting request was something of a figurative slap in the face. You could win emotional distress damages for that, though likely not a significant amount, unless the denial resulted in severe depression and you have a doctor to testify about that. But it doesn't sound like it. Punitive damages to punish the company could also be available to you if you were to win at trial. It sounds like this was a blatant violation. Depending on how the courts are where you live, you could receive punitive damages. But, again, these would not be large amounts. First, no jury is likely to slap a company with six-figure damages for this kind of violation. Yes, it's bad, but it's not terrible in the grand scheme of things. Second, courts have held that punitive damages must be proportional to underlying damages. Here, damages for the emotional distress would be low, so that would limit the amount of punitive damages available to you. Under the ADA, you could have also gotten back pay: here, it's the difference between what you would make if you had kept your old job minus what you actually made. That's not such a big deal, because you can get those damages under the FMLA.

Under the FMLA, you can still receive the salary that you lost as the result of your employer's actions, and that likely is the biggest source of damages for you. The FMLA does not allow you to recover emotional distress or punitive damages. However, you can recover liquidated damages, which is not available under the ADA. Liquidated damages are usually double the underlying damages. So, if you had $30,000 in lost back wages, you could recover $60,000 total if the court awarded liquidated damages. You can receive these if you can show that your employer acted willfully. It certainly sounds like it from these facts.

Chapter 15
Privacy

Sample Scenario[1]

You work in accounting for a government agency. You've been there five years. After trying to get pregnant for more than a year, you are thrilled to find out you're carrying a baby. Although you want to share the news with an assistant accountant who is also a close friend, you wait until you start to show to do so. You are less thrilled about telling your boss, Nancy, who is a vice president. Nancy is universally disliked. She has been known to yell and throw things when she gets upset. Childless and single, she lives for her job and seems not to understand that not everyone chooses to live like that. Your relationship with her is poor, though you have tried everything and gone out of your way to get along with her. Fed up after her most recent outburst, you called your agency's EEO office to report that this vice president was creating a hostile work environment.

Six months into the pregnancy, tragedy strikes. While at home one day, you start to bleed profusely. Your husband rushes home to take you to the hospital. You have a big agency report due tomorrow. Despite being in a panic about the bleeding, you tell him to make sure to call Kathy, your friend and co-worker, so that she will know why you are not at work.

---

1   This hypothetical is based on a modification of the facts in the case *Walker v. Gambrell*, 647 F. Supp. 2d 529 (D. Md. 2009).

When you arrive at the hospital, the doctor gives you some horrible news. The baby is in cardiac arrest. You are rushed into the OR. Though distraught, your husband remembers to call Kathy. He knows her because she has been to your house for dinner with her husband. Through tears, he tells her that you are in the hospital "losing the baby."

This hits Kathy like a punch in the gut. Looking at the photos of her five-year-old daughter sitting on her desk, she starts to sob. She quickly gets up to leave. As fate would have it, she runs into Nancy at the elevator bank. Noticing how distraught Kathy is, Nancy asks, "What's wrong?" Kathy replies that it's personal. Nancy presses on, saying, "Listen, I'm sorry for whatever is going on, but we have this report to get out tomorrow. Do you know where Mary is? I just can't have her out today." Kathy blurts out, "For the love of God, Nancy, Mary is at the hospital right now losing her baby. Is that a good enough reason for you?" Nancy pauses briefly and says, "Does anyone else know about this?" As the elevator door closes, Kathy says, "I don't know. I haven't told anyone."

In less than a minute, Nancy sends out an e-mail to the entire staff asking them to meet in the conference room. At the meeting, Nancy tells everyone about your miscarriage. She expresses sympathy and says she "understands that everyone is upset about this tragic news." She goes on to say, "We will be sending her flowers as an office today. But you all know that we have a big report to get out today. I know that she would want us to get that done, because she's put a lot of hard work into it."

For some reason, Nancy then goes rogue. She drafts a letter to you, expressing "deep sympathy for your situation," then noting "I assume you will need time off to deal with this difficult situation. Just for our HR purposes here to arrange FMLA leave, can you let me know if you have any history of depression, including in your immediate family? Again, this isn't to pry. I'm just trying to help out."

Is what Nancy did legal?

The answer is complicated and likely depends on your jurisdiction and court. There are two potential violations: Nancy's disclosure of your private medical information and Nancy's inquiry about your medical history.

Some courts, including district courts in the Fourth Circuit, have ruled that an employer is not required to keep confidential any medical information that it discovers through any means outside of an employer-initiated exam or inquiry. Therefore, because your co-worker voluntarily blurted out the information about the miscarriage to Nancy, you likely do not have a claim.

However, Nancy has no reason to ask you about your history of depression, which is completely unrelated to your miscarriage; moreover, you have not yet asked for FMLA leave due to your medical condition. In addition, under the ADA, employers can only ask disability-related questions that are job-related and consistent with business necessity. Here, the question about your family history of mental illness has no bearing on any job-related decision. Therefore, it is unlawful.

Read on to learn about several laws that can protect your confidential medical information. At the end of this chapter, I'll share some strategies to protect you in the event that you face a scenario like the one above.

Medical Privacy Laws

Medical privacy in the workplace is protected by four federal laws:

1. The Health Insurance Portability and Accountability Act (HIPAA)
2. The Genetic Information Nondiscrimination Act (GINA)
3. The Americans with Disabilities Act (ADA)
4. The Family and Medical Leave Act (FMLA)

Depending on what state you live in, you may also be protected by state laws.

Health Insurance Portability and Accountability Act (HIPAA)

HIPAA primarily applies to health-care providers and, in limited circumstances, to employers. The HIPAA privacy rule protects personal health information from unauthorized disclosure. Health information is considered personally identifiable if it relates to a specifically identifiable individual. Under 45 C.F.R. § 160.103, it generally includes the following information, whether in electronic, paper, or oral format:

1. Health-care claims or health-care encounter information, such as documentation of visits to the doctor and notes made by physicians and other provider staff;

2. Health-care payment and remittance advice;

3. Coordination of health-care benefits;

4. Health-care claim status;

5. Enrollment and disenrollment in a health plan;

6. Eligibility for a health plan;

7. Health plan premium payments;

8. Referral certifications and authorization;

9. First report of injury;

10. Health claims attachments;

11. Health-care electronic funds transfers (EFT) and remittance advice; and

12. Other transactions that the US Department of Health and Human Services (HHS) may prescribe in future regulations.

Normally, an employer will only deal with covered entities and not actually be one. However, if an employer has any kind of health clinic operations available to employees, provides a self-insured health plan for employees, or acts as the intermediary between its employees and health-care providers, it will find itself handling personal health information that is protected by the HIPAA privacy rule. So, if your employer is not a health-care provider, generally HIPAA will not apply to disclosures of your personal health information by your employer. However, as mentioned above, if your employer needs information from your doctor to verify a claim under the ADA, FMLA, or Rehabilitation Act, you will probably need to provide your doctor with a HIPAA form authorizing a release of medical information.

HIPAA is enforced by the HHS; this is the only agency that will accept your report of a HIPAA violation.`

Genetic Information Nondiscrimination Act (GINA)

GINA protects against the use of genetic information in health insurance and employment determinations. GINA's confidentiality regulations are contained in 29 C.F.R. § 1635.9. The regulations define "genetic information" as including information about genetic tests of an individual and her family members, her family's medical history, the request for or receipt of genetic services, or participation in related clinical research. It excludes information about sex, age, and race or ethnicity that is "not derived from a genetic test."

If an employee asks for medical leave to care for herself or for a family member with a serious health condition, an employer may receive this information as part of the certification provisions of federal, state, or local laws that require employees to provide information about a family member's illness to support the need for leave. An employer cannot use this information to make hiring, firing, job placement, or promotion decisions, or to make any change in the terms or conditions of employment.

Note that GINA applies only to employers with fifteen or more employees.

ADA
The ADA requires your employer to keep confidential any medical information you share during the hiring process, the results of a work-related medical exam, information about a disability that you share to get an accommodation, information shared as part of an employer's wellness program, and the results of drug tests. Note that the ADA does not protect information relating to your use of illegal drugs.

FMLA
The FMLA allows employers to obtain medical records from your health-care provider to verify your claims. For example, if you are taking leave under the FMLA to care for a sick loved one, your employer can ask for medical verification that you or your family member has a serious health condition. The Department of Labor's website has a verification form that you may use to provide this information to your employer, but it is not required. Your doctor may require a HIPAA form to provide information to your employer.

Laws That Apply to Federal Employees
The records of those who work in the federal government may be protected by the Privacy Act of 1974. You can find the statute at 5 U.S.C. § 552a. The Rehabilitation Act of 1973 prohibits discrimination by federal employers and contractors as well as in programs administered by federal agencies and programs that receive federal financial assistance. This law is interpreted according to the standards applicable to ADA claims.

Record Keeping

So, you are making a request under the ADA or FMLA, but you're worried about the claim being in your employment file for all to see, right? Well, don't fear. The results of medical exams and any medical records obtained must be kept confidential and kept in a separate medical file apart from your employment personnel file.

Your employer is not bound by the regulations under HIPAA, because it is not a health-care provider. It must keep your medical file confidential, but under the ADA, it can release the information to your supervisor or managers who need to know about your restrictions or accommodations. It may also share this information with first aid or safety personnel, if your disability requires treatment in the event of an emergency. Additionally, your employer may share the information with government officials investigating compliance with these acts. Finally, your personal health information may be disclosed for worker's compensation and insurance purposes.

If you are applying for a job, the employer *cannot* ask whether you are disabled or whether you are associated with (meaning that you take care of) anyone who is disabled. Nor can it ask about the nature or severity of a disability. However, it can ask whether and how you can perform the job with or without a reasonable accommodation.

Medical Exams Under the ADA, FMLA, and Rehabilitation Act

If your employer requires you to undergo a medical exam, do you have to submit to one? It depends.

An employer cannot require you to take a medical examination before offering you a job. Following a job offer, an employer can condition the offer of employment on your passing a required medical examination, but only if it requires all employees in that job to take the same examination. Furthermore, an employer cannot reject you because of information about your disability revealed by the medical examination, unless the reasons for rejection are job-related and necessary for the conduct of its business. Finally, the employer cannot refuse to hire you because of your disability if you can perform the essential functions of the job with an accommodation.

Once you have been hired and started work, your employer cannot require you to take a medical examination or ask questions about your disability unless they are related to your job and necessary for conducting business. Your employer may conduct voluntary medical examinations that are part of an employee health program, and it may provide medical information required by state workers' compensation laws to the agencies that administer such laws.

Tips to Protect Your Privacy

Keeping your medical records private in the workplace is difficult, and it's even more challenging because the right thing to do is often the opposite of what your instincts might tell you to do: namely, to share your information freely with your supervisor. Here are three things you can do to help protect your information.

1. Don't tell your boss about your medical condition unless she asks you to.
Even then, be careful. Most people like to do their jobs well and don't like to make a supervisor unhappy. For that reason, it is not uncommon to see an employee volunteer confidential medical information in response to a general question.

Let's suppose that you have to be out of work for a terrible migraine. Your supervisor e-mails you and asks, "Hey, just checking in. What's going on?" You then send a lengthy e-mail to your boss telling her about this migraine, your course of treatment, and the medication you are on. Assume that your employer has one hundred employees. Is this information covered?

According to a federal appeals court, no. In *EEOC v. Thrivent Financial for Lutherans*, the court held that this information was not covered by the ADA because the question from the supervisor did not require the employee to share medical information. Thus, the information **volunteered** by the employee was not confidential.

Here is a brief summary of the facts in *Thrivent*. The employee lost his job for excessive absences. The employee later applied for other jobs. When prospective employers called his former boss for a reference, he described the reasons the employee was fired, which included sharing that he suffered from debilitating migraine headaches.

The employee sued, claiming a violation of ADA confidentiality. The court dismissed his case for the reasons noted above.

What should you do if you get this call?

You should do one thing <u>before</u> you even get this call. If your employer has a policy that requires you to call in due to illness, follow it. In some instances, courts have dismissed lawsuits by employees who were protected by law but failed to follow the company's policy on sick leave.

As for this specific instance, *don't answer what isn't asked.* Here, your boss has just asked a general question: "What's going on?" If you are out for a medical reason, say something vague. For instance, "Sorry, boss. I'm under the weather. I should be back next week. I called and left a message for HR this morning." If your supervisor presses you, you have little protection if the company has fewer than fifteen employees. You have to tell her something. But avoid sharing specific information. Instead, offer to bring in a doctor's note when you return or to fax it that day if you can. Can your employer fire you for refusing to answer questions that implicate your medical information? Unless you are protected under some state law, if your employer has fewer than fifteen employees, the answer is probably, and sadly, yes.

If your employer has more than fifteen employees—and is thus covered by the ADA— tell your supervisor that you have a medical condition and will be happy to talk further to HR. Chances are, your supervisor wants to know as little as possible about your medical condition and will welcome a chance to have HR step in. If your supervisor is dissatisfied with that response and presses you for information, confirm that she is asking for your medical information. That way, your answer is protected by the ADA.

Here's what you need to say to protect your rights under the ADA.

> Boss. What's going on? Why are you out?

> You. Sorry, I left a message on the HR hotline. I'm a bit under the weather today. I will be back in tomorrow.

Boss. What do you mean "under the weather?"

You. I'm just sick; it's personal. Look, if you need to know more, I'm happy to give more detail. But this involves confidential medical stuff. If you want, I can call HR again as soon as we hang up.

Boss. No, look, I've got to know what's going on. Do I need to cover one shift? Two? More?

You. Sure, I get it. So, you're asking me for my medical information?

Boss. Yes.

You. Okay. This is confidential, right?

Boss. Ah, sure. Yeah. Need-to-know basis only.

You. I have severe migraines that make it difficult for me to function. I woke up with one this morning and went to see my doctor. I am on medication for them. They usually pass in a day or two. I called this morning and left a message on HR's voice-mail just like the policy manual says.

By clarifying that your boss is asking for confidential medical information, you make sure that your discussion is covered by the ADA.

As soon as that conversation is over, hang up and call HR. Tell your HR representative that you are seeking protection under the ADA. You actually do not need to use the initialism ADA. HR should know.

2. Tell HR.
Due to amendments to the ADA, many more conditions now qualify as a disability, even if they are sporadic: acute instances of asthma, for instance. So, even if you don't

consider yourself or your family member "disabled," you may very well qualify for protection under the ADA. But you can't get that protection if your employer does not know that you have a medical condition that might qualify as a disability.

So tell HR. Tell HR even if you don't need time off or a change in your work conditions. This provides you the two protections offered under the ADA:

1. The right not to be discriminated against simply because you have a disability, and
2. The right to receive reasonable accommodations if you need them to perform your job.

An accommodation might involve a move to an office in a quiet location for someone with an anxiety disorder or time off to get medical attention for occasional migraines, for instance. But you can't get any of these protections—or sue to vindicate your rights—if you cannot demonstrate that your company was aware of the disability.

When can the company ask you for your medical information?

The ADA allows for three instances when an employer can make medical inquiries or request that an employee receive a medical exam:

1. When an employer has objective evidence to question whether an employee can perform essential job functions;
2. When necessary to evaluate an employee's request for an accommodation; or
3. When necessary to determine whether an employee poses a direct threat to others.

This doesn't mean that an employer can ask just any question about your medical condition. The questions must be "job-related and consistent with business necessity."

Here are some examples offered by the EEOC in its *Enforcement Guidance on Disability-Related Inquiries and Medical Examinations of Employees Under the Americans with Disabilities Act (ADA)*:

Example A:

For the past two months, Sally, a tax auditor for a federal government agency, has done one-third fewer audits than the average employee in her unit. She also has made numerous mistakes in assessing whether taxpayers provided appropriate documentation for claimed deductions. When questioned about her poor performance, Sally tells her supervisor that the medication she takes for her lupus makes her lethargic and unable to concentrate.

Based on Sally's explanation for her performance problems, the agency has a reasonable belief that her ability to perform the essential functions of her job will be impaired because of a medical condition. Sally's supervisor, therefore, may make disability-related inquiries (e.g., ask her whether she is taking a new medication and how long the medication's side effects are expected to last), or the supervisor may ask Sally to provide documentation from her healthcare provider explaining the effects of the medication on Sally's ability to perform her job.

Example B:

A crane operator works at construction sites hoisting concrete panels weighing several tons. A rigger on the ground helps him load the panels, and several other workers help him position them. During a break, the crane operator appears to become light-headed, has to sit down abruptly, and seems to have some difficulty catching his breath. In response to a question from his supervisor about whether he is feeling all right, the crane operator says this has happened to him a few times during the past several months, but he does not know why.

The employer has a reasonable belief, based on objective evidence, that the employee will pose a direct threat and, therefore, may require the crane operator to have a medical examination to ascertain wheth-er the symptoms he is experiencing make him unfit to perform his job. To ensure that it receives sufficient information to make this determi-nation, the employer may want to provide the doctor who does the examination with a description of the employee's duties, including any physical qualification standards, and require the employee to pro-vide documentation of his ability to work following the examination

Example C:

Six months ago, a supervisor heard a secretary tell her co-worker that she had discovered a lump in her breast and is afraid that she may have breast cancer. Since that conversation, the secretary still comes to work every day and performs her duties in her normal efficient manner.

In this case, the employer does not have a reasonable belief, based on objective evidence, either that the secretary's ability to perform her essential job functions will be impaired by a medical condition or that she will pose a direct threat due to a medical condition. The employer, therefore, may not make any disability-related inquiries or require the employee to submit to a medical examination.

3. Tell your doctor what's going on at work.
Your doctor is a key player in any claim for leave under the ADA or the FMLA. Some doctors are familiar with the legal requirements of these laws, but many are not. To the extent that you can anticipate that your employer will contact your doctor, give him or her a heads-up.

Step 1: Get a HIPAA release. You will need to sign a HIPAA release before your doctor can speak to your employer. Most doctors' offices can help you with this.

Step 2: Get the proper diagnosis. It helps to let your doctor know what the law requires so that he or she can give your employer an accurate picture of your health condition.

For instance, generalized anxiety disorder (GAD) may or may not be covered under the ADA. If your health-care provider merely indicates a diagnosis of GAD, your employer may fight you on whether you are disabled under the act. If, however, your health-care provider gives you a diagnosis of GAD and describes how it affects "a major life activity" or your brain function, then your employer will be less likely to win an argument that you are not disabled.

Step 3: Have your doctor read and sign any forms. Finally, sometimes your employer will give you forms for your physician to fill out related to your disability. Or you might request those forms or a letter from your doctor in support of your request for accommodation. Make sure that your doctor reads the forms and signs them.

I know this sounds like a no-brainer, so how can this go wrong? This is how. The nurse tells the doctor that you have been by four times that day asking for this form. The staff wants to get you out of the lobby. The nurse sticks the form in the doctor's face, and she signs it while simultaneously wolfing down a sandwich. This will become important if your doctor has to testify about the form.

I had such a case go to trial. At issue was whether the defendant company knew about the nature of my client's disability and whether she was, in fact, disabled. My client had given her employer several letters signed by her physician indicating the nature of her disability. These letters were drafted by the client and signed by the physician. There is nothing wrong with this practice, if the physician agrees with the content of the letter. In this case, though, the doctor testified that he didn't remember reading the letter. When asked why, he said something like, "I sign a lot of papers in the course of my practice. As I recall, [the client] needed for me to sign this, so I did." Suddenly, our expert doctor looked a lot less like an expert.

Tip:
The EEOC has published a great resource regarding the ADA that you may want to share with your health-care provider. It is titled *The Mental Health Provider's Role in a Client's Request for a Reasonable Accommodation at Work* (http://www.eeoc.gov/eeoc/publications/ada_mental_health_provider.cfm).

Taping Your Employer

Privacy requirements go both ways—you also must pay attention to your state's laws on privacy before recording any conversation, depending on your jurisdiction.

It is very easy to record conversations at work. Indeed, chances are that you could do it with your cell phone. Recordings of conversations can be extraordinarily valuable for employees suffering from mistreatment by a boss or co-worker, helping to avoid a "he said, she said" situation. But is it legal?

The answer is that it depends on what state you're in and the nature of the conversation. Both Virginia and the District of Columbia are "one-party" states; that is, you can record any conversation as long as one party consents to the recording. Thus, if you are one of the people in the conversation, it may be legal to record the conversation, even if the other person does not know about it. But recording the conversation could still be illegal if the other person had a "reasonable expectation of privacy" in the conversation (Virginia) or if the recording is made with "injurious intent" (District of Columbia). In Maryland, both parties to the conversation must consent to the recording. Keep in mind that if you work in a heavily regulated industry, like health care or defense, other privacy laws may apply. Visit the Reporters Committee website (http://www.rcfp.org/can-we-tape) for a state-by-state listing of laws on recording. Clearly, the legality of recordings can be a tricky issue, but I have seen them used to great effect in two cases in Virginia.

Here is an example of one case involving pregnancy discrimination and FMLA retaliation where a recording played a significant role. A marketing manager was told by her HR department that she would no longer have a job if she took time off to have a baby. HR told her that she was not covered by the FMLA, which may have been true, as the FMLA applies only to companies that have at least fifty employees in a seventy-five-mile radius. It is possible that the company would have violated the PDA, but only if it had fifteen or more employees and only if it applied the leave policy in a different manner to employees who were not pregnant: that is, say, if they held a job open for a man who broke his leg skiing and had to take time away from work to heal. In any event, the employer backed down and allowed her to take leave after the woman's lawyer contacted the company and indicated that the woman had taped the conversation with HR. (You can listen to the tape on *The Huffington Post*'s website.) Score one for the little guy (woman).

Part IV: Nuts and Bolts: How to Protect and Win Your Case

Chapter 16
Prelitigation

In many cases, you should—or must—take several steps before filing a claim of discrimination against your employer. In this chapter, we'll cover the preliminary steps that normally precede pursuing a claim with an agency or a court.

Step 1: Beat the Filing Deadline

The first step is to retain your attorney and determine the time limits to file your complaint. A dizzying array of statutes limits the time you have to bring a complaint—these are appropriately called statutes of limitation.

For instance, if your boss punches you, in most jurisdictions you have at least two years to bring a lawsuit. But if you work in the private sector and your boss denies you a promotion because you are pregnant, you have at most three hundred days to file a charge with the EEOC. If you fail to meet this deadline, you lose your right to sue forever, no matter how good your claim is. And, if you are a federal government employee, you have only forty-five days to file a complaint with the EEO office.

The first thing your attorney will try to find out is how much time you have to file a complaint. If you have a lot of time, the attorney will likely spend at least a couple of weeks getting the facts of your case straight before taking action. If you have only a couple of days to get something filed, then filing clearly becomes the priority. Your attorney is likely to focus on the bare bones necessary to get the filing done and then, after you have filed, will circle back to learn all the details of what happened. You sometimes will hear attorneys talk about "stopping the clock" on the statute of limitations. This means preventing the clock from running out on your claim. An attorney need not know all the facts to file a claim with the EEOC—just enough to know that you have a case. Once your claim is filed, the attorney has time to work with you to get a complete understanding of the details of your case.

Step 2: Develop the Facts

Next, you'll meet with your attorney to develop the facts of your case. Attorneys differ on how they handle this process. Some like to do extensive investigation before filing a charge with the EEOC or other administrative agency; others like to wait and develop the case as it proceeds through the agency. Attorneys sometimes fail to be explicit with their clients about how they investigate cases. It is understandably frustrating when you meet with an attorney and experience the excitement of preparing your filing, only to have your attorney go radio silent for weeks or even months after you file a charge or complaint. While it may not be the best customer service, being ignored for a time by your attorney does not necessarily mean that your case is going down the tubes. It may just mean that not much is happening at the agency, so there is not much to do. These peaks and valleys are par for the course in litigation.

Step 3: Send a Demand Letter

The next stage in employment litigation is sending a "demand letter" to your employer. As the name implies, this letter demands something from the company. It lets your employer know that it violated the law and you plan to take action unless it wants to settle. The demand can take the form of money, more severance, extended benefits, and the like, or it can also ask for nonmonetary relief such as an agreed-upon employment reference, a requirement that your supervisor not speak badly of you, or an agreement not to oppose your application for unemployment.

Whether to send a demand letter is a matter of strategy. Most attorneys send them (I commonly do), but others consider it a waste of time because many employers won't do anything until forced to do so by the EEOC or other state agency, which rarely happens, or by the court during active litigation. I usually send them because I have had success settling cases without filing in court. But it is true that some employers will simply sit on such a letter or drag out negotiations without any real intent to settle. This becomes an issue because the longer you wait to file with the EEOC or a court, the longer it takes to resolve your case.

It is important to remember that the demand letter is not the same as suing your employer; it is technically not considered litigation (though it certainly is adversarial). Sending a demand letter is not something that is public, and it does not involve the courts.

Chapter 17
EEOC Charges

Most federal discrimination laws require that you file a charge with the EEOC or its local equivalent before you can file a complaint in court. The theory is that your employer should have notice of your complaint and the EEOC should be able to investigate your claims before you file an expensive and time-consuming lawsuit.

Important Deadlines

In many states, you have only 180 days to file a charge with the EEOC <u>or you will lose your right to sue forever</u>, no matter how blatant the discrimination. If you work for a government organization, you may have <u>as few as forty-five days</u>.

So, if you are pregnant and your boss fires you, saying, "Oh, I know you are doing a great job, but we know you're going to quit as soon as your maternity leave is over, and here's a letter saying just that," you lose if you wait 181 days to tell the EEOC.

If you have time before the 180 days, take the time to call a lawyer. If you don't, call the EEOC yourself (be prepared to wait for an hour or more). The toll-free number is (800) 669-4000. A lawyer can always fix things later. But no lawyer can fix the problem if you don't file. It's over—done. If you don't have to protect your case by filing within the 180 days—for instance, if you have a wage and hour claim, which is not covered by the EEOC—the intake officer will let you know.

In some instances, you may be able to file with a state or county agency and have a longer deadline of up to three hundred days. Filing with some of these agencies is the same as filing with the EEOC and may offer some other advantages. For instance, these agencies may conduct more intensive investigations and offer additional protections under applicable state laws. For a list of some state agencies that can help, visit this website (http://www.thelaw.com/guide/employment/list-of-state-fair-employment-practices-agencies/).

Filing a Charge of Discrimination

Filing with the EEOC is an easy process and primarily involves filling out a two-page form and checking some boxes. Though it helps to have an attorney, the system is designed to be used by nonattorneys, so it is not terribly complicated. You can find the complaint forms online. You can also just walk into your local EEOC office and sit down with someone to file a claim.

The sad truth is that the EEOC is an underfunded agency, so your complaint is unlikely to receive a thorough investigation before the EEOC declines to pursue it. So, don't get your hopes up. But you must complete this process before you can go to court, so stick with it.

After you fill out the form, the EEOC will notify your employer by mail that you have filed. Within a few weeks, your case will be assigned to an investigator, who will help you fill out a "charge." The charge, which is a summary of your complaint, is the official start of the EEOC process. The charge need not contain every detail of what happened to you at work—just the facts necessary to establish that discrimination occurred.

At some point after the charge is filed, your employer will submit its own position statement to the EEOC. This document is not provided to you, unfortunately. You can submit a Freedom of Information Act (FOIA) request and get a summary of the statement from the EEOC.

Once you've filed a charge, be prepared to wait. Your case is likely to languish for some time. This doesn't mean that you (or, ideally, your attorney) are prevented from continuing to work on your case. Indeed, you can settle with your company at any point in the process. So, just because the EEOC isn't moving quickly doesn't mean that you can't make progress on your case. Indeed, I have settled many cases while they are pending at the EEOC.

The Intake Process

Once the EEOC finally reviews your charge, it will put it in one of three informal categories: (1) charges that lack any merit, (2) charges that might have merit that the EEOC will investigate, and (3) charges that the EEOC has a strong interest in and may take to litigation.

Those in the first category are not offered mediation through the EEOC; instead, they are sent what is called a "right-to-sue" letter. This short form letter says that the EEOC has determined that there is insufficient cause to continue with your case, but that you can proceed to federal court if you choose. You have ninety days to file in federal court once you have received that letter. Indeed, you have to have this letter before you are even allowed to proceed with a case in court. Rest assured that nothing about the EEOC process can be used in court. So, the fact that the EEOC has refused to take your case means little. The EEOC rejects the vast majority of the charges filed with it.

However, if the EEOC rejects your charge quickly, while it may not mean that you will lose your case, it does mean that the EEOC found it weak enough not to proceed with an investigation. This is not a sign that you should give up, but you should use it as an opportunity to consider whether your case is worth pursuing. This is a discussion you should have with your attorney if you have one.

The second, and largest, category of EEOC charges includes the charges that the EEOC deems worthy of investigation. Before assigning it to an investigator, the EEOC will offer mediation through the EEOC. This is not mandatory, so either side can decline.

My view, which I believe is shared by most employment attorneys, is that mediation is worth doing, even if it is unlikely that you will reach a settlement. The reason is that it gives you a chance to sit down with the other side to talk about the case. At the very least, you may learn exactly what defense the company believes it has. (Your employer is likely to agree to mediation for the same reason; it may be the first time its attorney has a chance to see you—and your attorney—to size him or her up.) Mediation is an informal process conducted at the EEOC office. Everything said in mediation is confidential and cannot be used in the litigation. The EEOC will require both sides to sign a form indicating that these rules are understood. (By the way, almost all mediators use this same format, even outside the EEOC.) We will talk more about mediation in chapter 18.

Next Steps

As a result of underfunding, the EEOC's case managers rarely conduct a thorough investigation. For instance, they don't even conduct an in-person interview; it's all handled over the phone. The agency also litigates a fraction of the cases it takes in. If you want to really depress yourself, review the agency's litigation statistics, especially when compared to the number of charges it receives.

So, even though you may be required to file with the EEOC, expect that you may still need to go to court. At the end of the vast majority of cases, the EEOC finds no cause to take the case and issues a right-to-sue letter. Often, the agency takes a long time before it puts you out of your misery by giving you the right-to-sue letter. Sometimes it can take years.

Let me ask you this: Do you think your case is stronger or weaker after it sits around for a year or more? Time is not your friend. You should know that you are only required to give the agency 180 days to finish its investigation. It never finishes in 180 days. After that point, you can request a right-to-sue letter and the agency must give you one. Of course, you'd better be prepared to sue if you ask for that letter.

Regardless of what happens with the EEOC, you must receive a right-to-sue letter before you can file in court. And again, once you have this letter, you have only **ninety days** to file a complaint in court or you lose your right to sue forever.

Here's the moral: file with the EEOC soon. If you are offered the opportunity to mediate your case, take it. And hire a lawyer at least for that part. It's your best and probably only chance to get anything out of the case. If that fails, don't expect that the EEOC is going to help. Figure out how to move forward on your own.

Chapter 18
Mediation

In this chapter, we'll review the two options you have for mediating your dispute with your employer. For claims under Title VII, you can elect to have the EEOC mediate your dispute. Alternatively, you can hire a private mediator to hear your case.

EEOC Mediation

Mediation before the EEOC will begin with the mediator setting forth the rules of the mediation—for example, confidentiality and the like—and talking about the mediation process. Next, each side (usually you and your attorney—if you have one—and one representative from your company and the company's attorney) gets to give a short statement about how it views the case. This statement is not a conversation; it's just a presentation. Most of these statements are brief. The other side is not permitted to ask questions of you or your attorney during this presentation; likewise, you cannot ask them questions.

After the statements are complete, the mediator will separate each side into different rooms. The mediator will then begin a process of shuttle diplomacy. That is, he or she will start in one room and say, "I've heard your opening statement. What do you really want to get this resolved?" If the mediator starts with you, you might say, "I'm willing to dismiss my charge if I get my job back and thirty thousand dollars (or whatever) in lost wages." Ideally, you will have had a chance to talk with your attorney beforehand to develop a strategy that includes your bottom line for getting this resolved. It doesn't take a law degree to know that you don't start out with your bottom line. So, if you offer to settle for $30,000 and reinstatement, you should be prepared to take $15,000 with no reinstatement.

What happens next will depend on the mediator. A good mediator will likely give you some feedback on your case. For instance, "Ms. Employee, I've looked at your position statement and I've seen a bunch of these cases. I think if you want to get this done, you should be prepared to come down some on that request for lost wages. I'm not telling you to give me a number now; just think about it." The mediator will then leave the room and go talk to the employer, relaying your offer. A lazy or poor mediator will not attempt to give you guidance on your case or will give you ill-considered advice. Unfortunately, my experience with many EEOC mediators is that they will not be overly familiar with your case and will not move parties to a settlement. But on occasion, cases do get resolved.

After the mediator relays your offer seeking reinstatement and back wages, the employer might respond, "Look, we'd prefer not to spend our time fending off a lawsuit, but we didn't do anything wrong and feel like we can prove it in court. We won't offer her the job back, but we'd be willing to characterize the termination as a voluntary resignation and offer five thousand dollars in severance." Mediator: "Okay, I'll take this back to them. But I have looked at some of their documents and, at least as far as I can see, their claim is not baseless. So, is this your last offer?" Employer attorney: "No, it's not our final offer. We can come up, but not exponentially."

And the back-and-forth continues until the parties settle the matter or reach an impasse.

In my scenario, the mediator is pretty good, and by that I mean he is leaning on both sides to push them to an agreement. Many are not so good: they might push each side a bit, but will stop when they receive some real resistance. A good mediator will push through that, really spending time with both parties in an effort to help them see the case clearly. He or she also will display some creativity in helping everyone reach an agreement. For instance, the fired employee might be willing to come down on the settlement number if the employer is willing to write a glowing recommendation that she can use to find other employment. Neither side would have considered that option without the mediator spending a lot of time exploring the strengths of the claim with each side: explaining to the employee the risk of losing and explaining to the employer the risk that the employee might win.

At this point, let me take a detour and discuss the emotional aspect of mediation. As an employee, you will do better if you understand that this is a process and one that will not necessarily satisfy a thirst for justice. It is commonly said that a mediation is successful if an agreement is reached and both sides walk away a bit unhappy. As an employee, you will have to be prepared for this process to open old wounds. If you have come this far, you have invested a lot emotionally and financially in your case. And now you have to sit at a table across from your employer who wronged you and its lawyer, both of whom likely think you are just looking for a handout. After you or your attorney lays out the strengths of your case, you have to sit there and listen to the other side's smug attorney hold forth on why she believes your claim is weak and will lose in court. In preparing yourself, know that this is part of the game. I know, this is not a game for you. But this process is in many ways like a high-stakes poker game. If you are prepared for that emotionally going in, the process will be less distasteful.

You also need to be prepared for the process to take a while. A productive mediation can sometimes go on for hours, with the mediator going back and forth multiple times trying to work out a deal. So, bring with you any supplies you might need. A good book, a crossword puzzle, your favorite cigarettes, whatever. While the mediator is talking to the other side, you'll be sitting in a room waiting and waiting and waiting. Yes, you and your attorney will discuss the mediation for some of that time, but not the whole time. Also, be prepared for the highs and lows. I was once in a mediation that literally went all day and into the night. It actually exhausted the mediator, who essentially just decamped to his office and let the attorneys hash everything out. Around ten o'clock in the evening, we had something close to a final agreement, but at the last minute, the employer changed its position on whether the employee should be bound by a confidentiality clause. It initially agreed to a much lower settlement value in exchange for allowing the employee to talk freely about the lawsuit. But just before everyone signed, it decided it wanted a confidentiality provision. This essentially ended the mediation with no agreement reached. This means it was almost like it never happened. Ten hours spent going through all the highs and lows (and boredom) of mediation, all for nothing. This can be especially demoralizing if you are paying your attorney an hourly rate.

Not only did you not settle, but you now also have a $3,000 bill. This example is on the extreme side, but it is not uncommon. What to do?

Sit down with your attorney before mediation and come up with a realistic appraisal of your case and what you might accept in settlement. The most pressing issue is the money. What are you willing to accept to get this all over with? Really consider it. I understand that it is distasteful to put a price tag, one likely much lower than you want, on what may have been one of the most painful experiences of your life. But remember that mediation is about the art of the possible and will always—if it is to be successful—involve taking less than you want. Also, really think about the money. Of course, you want the most you can get. You'd rather get $100,000 than $30,000. But think about that $30,000 figure. (Let's assume for the sake of this exercise that this amount is after taxes.) I know few people for whom this is not a lot of money. It can pay off a car, a year of college, credit card debt—you get the point. I want you to think about what it would feel like to have a check like that. I want you to do it now because I have been in more mediations that I can count where my client went in wanting six figures or more, only to realize after hours of mediation that a lesser, more realistic amount was acceptable.

Now, some of this reassessment occurred because the mediation process worked. The client went in with a high figure, but once she heard the mediator talk about the weaknesses in her case (they all have weaknesses) and felt the unpleasant experience of having to face her dirtbag boss and his lawyer, she decided to take a lower amount to end the claim. That's fine. Like I said, that's how the process is supposed to work. But save yourself some of the highs and lows. Heck, just save yourself an hour or two of haggling. Be prepared for the emotional stress and have a realistic assessment of what you are willing to take in settlement.

I don't say this to push you to settle. Sometimes it is worth it to stick to your guns. There is certainly a lot of dignity to be gained by winning a lawsuit, regardless of the financial outcome. Also, know that settlement values change. Your employer may lowball you in an EEOC mediation, only to change its tune completely after being kicked around in a few depositions. The closer you get to trial, the higher that number goes up. Of course, you need to be prepared for the converse: that your case value might go down. Maybe you think you've got a great case until one of your key witnesses suddenly changes his story during depositions, virtually gutting your legal case. All of a sudden, you realize you just left the best money you were going to see in this case on the table at the last mediation.

Both sides face risks by going forward. You need to make a coolheaded evaluation of what kind of risk tolerance you have. Also, have a frank discussion with your attorney. Many retainer agreements have language that will allow an attorney to withdraw representation if you turn down what <u>the attorney</u> believes is a reasonable settlement offer. So, if the employer offers you $100,000 in mediation and your attorney says he's litigated a dozen cases just like this and the offer is the best you will see, you have the right to turn it down, but your attorney may withdraw, leaving you without representation and perhaps with a substantial bill for legal fees and costs. It's better to be clear on this before you walk into mediation rather than after a long day of mediation when everyone is tired and wants to go home.

Keep in mind that failure at mediation does not mean that all is for naught. It is not uncommon for parties to settle days after the mediation once everyone has had a good night's sleep and taken some time to reflect.

Private Mediation

You can also pursue your claim by hiring a private mediator. Private mediators are professional mediators. Private mediation firms can help you select a mediator with experience in your case. The costs vary, but generally range anywhere from $250 to $500 per hour. Each side will usually pay half of the cost.

Why a private mediator? Time and experience. Mediators with the EEOC usually work a nine-to-five gig. They may not be the sharpest tools in the drawer (though I've worked with some very good ones). These mediators may not have even read your file before the mediation, and they may never have worked as an attorney litigating a case like yours. All things being equal, they probably would like to settle your case, but if it means staying past five o'clock, forget it.

In contrast, a private mediator will generally be a retired judge or an experienced attorney who will spend a considerable amount of time preparing for the mediation before it begins. He or she will review all the relevant court documents, in addition to whatever else you want to share with him or her in confidence. During the mediation, the private mediator is almost guaranteed to be active, educating and pushing each side to settlement.

These mediators will go the distance to get a settlement done. Need to press on into the night to get a deal inked? A private mediator will more than likely sign on for that. Moreover, a private mediator will often stay involved even if face-to-face mediation fails. Good ones will stay in touch with each side, searching for creative solutions to find common ground for settlement.

Who would you be more willing to listen to, a tired EEOC mediator in a wrinkled suit or a retired judge who has seen a dozen or more cases like yours tried in his courtroom? Not even close, right?

Chapter 19
Settlement

Your ability to reach a favorable settlement is related to two primary factors: (1) the objective strength of your case and (2) the "burn rate" associated with the litigation process.

The objective strength of your case depends on the existence of objective "hard" evidence that is difficult for the employer to deny. Note that this has nothing to do with what actually happened in your case. If I offer to represent a client, I do so only when there is no doubt in my mind that the person has been wronged and I can help.

But proving what happened is a different matter. Often in employment cases, the issue is state of mind. For instance, there may be no dispute that you were fired. The question is whether you were fired because the company needed to downsize or because your boss doesn't like pregnant women. If you have "hard" evidence of what your boss had in his head when he fired you, then a defendant is more likely to settle.

Let's suppose that you secretly recorded your boss and on that tape he says, "Look, missy. Our department operates on a shoestring budget. If we have to pay for maternity leave, there won't be a job waiting for you when you get back." That's hard, unequivocal evidence. Presented with such a recording, most employers will want to settle. But rare is the case in which a defendant is honest about his motives. Usually, it comes down to circumstantial evidence: for example, you had great performance reviews, but your boss hired and promoted only men. When it came time to cut staff, he fired only one person—a pregnant woman—you. He says it is because you had the least experience.

Technically, that is true. You were at the job for months less than the most junior male employee. But he had been placed on a performance improvement plan. So, what was in your boss's head when he fired you? You know without a doubt, because you lived it. Your employer, though, knows it might be able to convince a jury otherwise. As a result, the company is in no hurry to settle.

However, the company must also consider the burn rate, which is the amount of money it will cost to defend the lawsuit. This money amount is closely tied to how much work the company's attorneys will have to do to mount a defense. The lower the burn rate, the longer your employer is likely to drag things out to see what happens. Maybe you'll go away. Maybe your attorney will drop the case. Why not wait to find out?

This calculus changes when things get busy in the case. For instance, when your company starts getting invoices from its law firm in the amount of $10,000 to $20,000 per month, it might rethink settlement. Not only is the company having to pay its lawyers, but it's also probably having to take staff time to help find evidence to support the company. Once depositions start, the company may be looking at losing days of time from senior staff. When the company starts to experience pain, it will revisit settlement. It will do this because now it is looking at increased costs to defend the lawsuit, and on top of that, there is the possibility that the company might lose if it proceeds to court.

What about the risk of publicity? It is generally a mistake to think that companies care. Many clients mistakenly believe that a company will settle rather than risk a lawsuit that includes allegations of discrimination. Had I not done this for a while, I probably would have thought the same thing. But it's just not the case. Companies are used to getting sued. It's just not news for an employee to claim discrimination. In the years that I have been doing this, only once did the press report on a case after we filed it.

The reason companies often blow off a demand letter and participate only tepidly in an EEOC proceeding is because the burn rate is low. To respond to a demand letter takes only a day or two of an attorney's time. This usually includes a minimal "investigation": that is, the attorney will call the manager and ask, "What happened?" Most employers don't want to settle and so will play hardball at this prelitigation phase. Similarly, while employers would prefer not to defend an EEOC action, it doesn't take a tremendous amount of time. They have to produce a statement defending the company's actions and take a few calls from an EEOC investigator, but that's about it.

Also, consider that the employer's attorney knows only what the company is telling her. As far as she knows, you're a straight-up liar because that's what your former boss said about you. She'll think differently when she sees your attorney take the deposition of your boss while he sweats buckets because he's having difficulty keeping his different stories straight. But often that has to happen before the company will offer significant money to settle.

The burn rate starts to go up when we get into later stages of litigation.

Here's another thing to think about. Up to this point, none of this has been public, and the courts have not been involved. I often get the question about when the lawsuit starts. Up to this point, it hasn't. Technically, someone could file an FOIA request to find out that you filed with the EEOC. I have never seen this happen. Up until this point, everything has been under the radar.

What are your chances at settling before things go public? It depends on how much you want. If you're looking for three to six months' worth of salary, then good. Better than half. If you want more, be prepared to go into the next stage.

Chapter 20
The Life Cycle of a Lawsuit

Let's talk about the stages of your case. I will discuss them further below, but first I want to address two common questions: (1) What is litigation? and (2) When does the lawsuit start?

Litigation is a broad term and could mean any time you start an adversarial process: for instance, when you or your lawyer sends a letter to your employer threatening a lawsuit. But when most lawyers talk about litigation, they are talking about a lawsuit.

That brings me to the second question: When does a lawsuit start? A lawsuit starts when you (or your lawyer) has filed a complaint in court and "served" the complaint on the company. I often have clients concerned about starting a lawsuit. They know they want to, say, get a better severance, which may involve raising the possibility of a lawsuit in a letter to the company. When I discuss this with my clients, sometimes they express concern that they will somehow slide into a lawsuit without knowing it. If this is you, let me assure you that this will not happen. Filing a lawsuit requires several steps and your input. In some ways, the commitment is like signing a lease for an apartment. Before you sign a lease, you may have significant discussions with a landlord. These discussions are a prerequisite to entering a lease, but they will not result in you accidentally signing a lease. You'll know when it comes time to do that.

Now we're getting into the real lawsuit part. The procedures for a lawsuit all are laid out in the Federal Rules of Civil Procedure. This uniform set of rules governs federal courts. Each state system will have a different set of rules, but they will likely mirror the federal rules in most respects. You're not required to read these rules, but they are a useful guide if you want to go to the source of much of what I'll talk about in this chapter.

Complaint

The filing of the complaint is the opening salvo in a lawsuit. The three most important parts of the complaint are the heading, the facts section, and the claims section.

The heading will contain your name as the plaintiff and then list the defendant(s). Sometimes there will be only one defendant, the company. Sometimes there will be more than one defendant: for instance, when you sue your company and boss..

The second important section is the one setting forth the facts of your lawsuit, generally set out in individually numbered paragraphs. The facts section can go on for pages. It need not (and probably should not) contain everything that happened to you at the company.

This brings us to the third section: claims. The claims are the specific violations of the law that the company committed. You can have more than one claim under the same law. For instance, you might sue your company after being fired following a request for leave to take care of your newborn. Let's assume your boss at first told you that you could not file for FMLA leave to care for your child. This is an illegal attempt to interfere with your right to take FMLA leave. This is claim number one. When he tells you this, he says, "Child rearing is incompatible with this workplace." This is illegal gender stereotyping based on sex. This is claim number two. Let's further assume that, after some effort, you get HR to sign off on your FMLA leave. But six weeks into your twelve-week leave, you are fired. The company alleges that you left several invoices unpaid when you went on leave. This is untrue, and you can prove it. Everything suggests that the company fired you simply because you took FMLA leave. This is unlawful retaliation: claim number three. So, this complaint will have three separate claims under two laws.

Each claim is further made up of "elements." These are the basic building blocks of the claim. The building blocks are the law required for a plaintiff to "state" a claim. Take, for instance, an FMLA retaliation claim. The elements of this claim are that (1) you were entitled to take FMLA leave, (2) you requested leave, (3) the company took an "adverse employment action" against you as a result of your request for leave, and (4) you suffered damages as a result of that action. So, to "state a claim" for FMLA retaliation, you would have to say in the facts section something like this:

1. Mary Smith worked for AMC Welding as an accountant. She had held this position for two years, working full time both years. (This statement is required because you must work for at least a year and more than 1,250 hours to be eligible for FMLA leave.)

2. AMC Welding has one hundred employees who all work in Arlington, Virginia. (An employer must have at least fifty employees within a seventy-five-mile radius for FMLA to apply.)

3. On March 3 of this year, Ms. Smith applied for FMLA leave to care for a newborn. (An employee can take leave under the FMLA to bond with a newborn child.)

4. Six weeks into the leave, AMC fired Ms. Smith, who had a strong record of performance prior to her leave.

5. On information and belief, AMC fired Ms. Smith in retaliation for taking FMLA leave. (This is the illegal act. Note that Ms. Smith need not have all the facts necessary to *prove* retaliation at this stage and may use the phrase "on information and belief.")

6.   Since her termination, Ms. Smith has been unable to find work, and remains unemployed as of the date of this complaint.

In this case, Ms. Smith had a strong record of performance at the company, never receiving less than an "excellent" rating in her three reviews. In her last review, she received "excellent" ratings across the board and was granted a 5 percent raise, the highest available. These facts are not included in the complaint in this example. An attorney could include them, and might in this case to rebut the employer's claim that Ms. Smith was fired for misconduct. But understand that this is not required. The complaint is only to set forth what we call the "*prima facie* elements" of each claim. It is not meant to include everything about your case.

Don't "Hang It Out Like a Christmas Tree"
I have had numerous clients who want to include everything they can in the complaint. I had one client who said he wanted to "hang it out like a Christmas tree." While you want your complaint to be thorough—in part because you want to force your employer to answer your allegations—you don't want to make your complaint too extensive.

First, this can weaken your credibility with the court. You may have some claims that you could bring, although they are weak. It doesn't help you (or your lawyer) to be up before the judge defending a bad claim. You run the risk of running into the boy-who-cried-wolf syndrome. Bringing weak claims can make your other claims suspect.

Second, and related, litigation is expensive. The defendant will take every opportunity to get a weak case dismissed. Defending weak claims requires a lot of time to research and write briefs to file with the court. This will slow down your case and cost you money.

Where Should I File My Complaint?
There are several courts that you may file your discrimination or retaliation claim in once you have exhausted your administrative remedies by filing with the EEOC

or a state agency. There are state and federal trial courts. Most federal laws permit discrimination claims to be brought in federal or state court. However, many times you will have state law claims as well, such as intentional infliction of emotional distress, negligent infliction of emotional distress, or an independent state law discrimination or tort claim. If you have federal law and state law claims together, you can also file these in either federal or state court under the doctrine of "permissive joinder."

Generally, a federal judge is not required to allow state law claims in federal court, but may allow the state law claims to be brought alongside federal claims if both the federal and state law claims arise out of the same facts. This is a strategic decision, but often, if you have federal law claims (such as under Title VII) and file in state court, then the defendant has the option to remove the action from state court to federal court.

Filing Is Only Half the Battle

Once you have written the complaint, you must file it with the court. This means someone must take the complaint to the clerk and have it entered into the court system. There is a fee associated with this. In federal court, the fee is currently $400. You will also need a summons for each defendant. This is an order from the court that requires the defendant to file a response. You (or your attorney) will also need a cover page, which the court uses for administrative purposes.

Once you have paid the fee, the court will take your complaint and file stamp it with an official time/date stamp. You'll see this on the first page of any complaint in any court. Congratulations, you have filed a lawsuit!

But guess what? If that's all you did, your case would go nowhere. The next step is to serve the complaint on the defendant. This must be done according to specific rules of civil procedure that allow the court to certify that the defendant has been served. Why? Because if a defendant fails to respond to your complaint with a legal document called an "answer," the court can enter what's called a "default judgment." This, in essence, means that you win. There would have to be a hearing to determine how much money you are entitled to, but you'd be awarded something. And if the defendant failed to pay, you could get an order from the court directing law enforcement to take anything owned by the defendant and sell it. Clearly, this is a big deal.

Given those stakes, the court has to have proof that the defendant received your complaint and the summons, which essentially orders the defendant to answer the complaint and warns about the consequences I discussed above. This proof is called "service of process." In federal court, anyone who is over eighteen can serve the complaint through a number of methods, the most direct, of course, being to hand deliver it to the defendant. You've likely seen something like this in movies. The process server throws papers at an unsuspecting person and says, "You've been served!" And it really can happen like that!

The person serving the complaint then fills out an affidavit describing who was served and how that person was served, and he or she files the affidavit with the court under penalty of perjury. In most cases, it's not quite so dramatic. For instance, businesses are required to have a designated agent whose job it is to accept service. Many corporations hire companies that specialize in this sort of work. So, to serve, say, McDonald's in Virginia, you can look up the company's registered agent with the State Corporation Commission and just send a process server to the agent to serve the corporation. No drama there.

Sometimes it can be difficult to serve an individual. You have to find that person or a family member and get the complaint in that person's hands. That's why the courts usually will give you some time to serve the complaint. In federal court in Virginia, you have 120 days. In state court, it's one year. Sometimes it makes sense to wait to serve the complaint. For instance, you may need to file a complaint to stop the statute of limitations, but you want to negotiate with the defendant before you kick litigation into high gear.

Tip:

A few times a month I get a call from someone who has received a right-to-sue letter. Now they need a lawyer, but don't have enough time to find one before the ninety-day period expires. Here's a trick if you can't find a lawyer in time and your back is against the wall: file the complaint yourself.

The complaint need not be perfect. Though I don't recommend it, you could even handwrite it. Consider making a trip down to the courthouse to the civil clerk's office and ask how to file a complaint. You'll need a certain number of copies, a summons for each party, and likely a cover sheet. (Many courts have a website with this information.)

After you file the complaint, you have some time to find a lawyer before you have to serve the defendant. What happens if you don't ever serve the complaint? Nothing. Your complaint will eventually be dismissed, and you'll lose your right to sue. But, if you do find a lawyer to take your case, she can always file what's called an amended complaint to fix any problems.

Motion to Dismiss

Once you have served the defendant and the affidavit of service has been filed, then the litigation gears are truly in motion. In most cases, the defendant has twenty days to file a legal document called an "answer" to the complaint. The defendant must answer, even if it is just to deny the numbered paragraphs in your complaint. Or, instead of filing an answer, the defendant can file a motion to dismiss.

A defendant can try to get your case thrown out of court at several stages during the litigation. The first is at what is called the motion to dismiss stage. The second involves a motion for summary judgment. Before I get into those, let me briefly describe what lawyers call "questions of fact" and "questions of law."

A question of fact is what it sounds like—an issue of whether something did or did not occur. A straightforward example is a car accident. Let's suppose an orange truck hits a blue car in an intersection. The person driving the blue car that is struck suffers a broken arm. This person sues the driver of the orange truck. The issue in the lawsuit is whether the driver of the orange truck ran through a red light before hitting the blue car.

There is no issue of law in this case; it doesn't take a law degree to know that it is negligent to run a red light. The issue here is one of fact: did the orange truck in fact run the light? The driver of the truck says that the light was green when he passed through it.

You can imagine the evidence you might want to see if you had to decide that issue. You'd probably want to hear from both drivers and any witnesses in the area. It would probably also be helpful to have records about the time of day the accident occurred and records from the computer that controls the light. For instance, does the light change from red to green at certain times, and can you match this up with when the accident occurred? These facts could help you decide whether you believe the truck ran a red light.

In a lawsuit, questions of fact are supposed to be decided by the trier of fact. This is often a jury. Jurors listen to testimony and other evidence, and then come up with a verdict. In some cases, the trier of fact is the judge. In these cases, the judge does the same thing a jury does: he or she listens to testimony, reviews evidence, and then makes a decision. (In some cases, the law determines whether the person suing is entitled to a jury trial. In all cases, the plaintiff—or the defendant in a criminal trial—can opt for a judge or "bench" trial rather than a jury trial.)

Judges are not supposed to decide questions of fact before the fact finder—again, often a jury—has a chance to hear the evidence. In particular, our legal system emphasizes having the jury eyeball a witness. Sure, you can say on paper whatever you want, but if someone watches you tell your story, he or she might or might not find you believable. So, a judge is not supposed to decide questions of fact by just looking at what people say on paper.

However, a judge can decide questions of law without any fact-finding hearing. (Some situations involve mixed questions of fact and law, but those are not as common.) That is because questions of law generally do not depend on deciding what facts are true.

Let's say that your neighbor sues you for emotional distress because you stuck your tongue out at her. We all know that it is not illegal to stick your tongue out at someone. It's bad manners, but it's not illegal. In this case, you would file a motion to dismiss after your neighbor filed the complaint. Note that you can file a complaint about anything under the sun. The clerk will not screen cases to see whether they state a claim. In a motion to dismiss, your argument would go like this: "Your Honor, I'm not saying that I did or did not stick my tongue out at my neighbor. If I did, she had it coming. But it doesn't matter whether I did or I didn't. It's not illegal for me to do that. So, you should dismiss this case." And the judge would.

Increasingly, defendants are filing motions to dismiss in employment cases. As a tactical matter, it is a way to delay the case and force you and your attorney to spend time and money defending it. (This is one reason why it doesn't make sense to bring weak claims.) When the defendant files a motion, the court must treat all the facts in the complaint as true. Assuming those facts are true, the issue is whether your complaint states something that is against the law.

The court will decide the issues you raised on a claim-by-claim basis. Indeed, a defendant may file a motion to dismiss only as to certain claims in your complaint. If the court grants a motion to dismiss only some of your claims, your lawsuit will proceed. If the court grants a motion as to every claim (some lawsuits have only one), then your case is over.

The good news is that, even if the court grants a motion to dismiss, it will usually do so "without prejudice," which means that you can refile an amended complaint. Of course, you will need a factual basis to do so. That is, you must have something different to say in the new complaint that would justify filing it again. If the court grants the motion but some claims survive, your lawsuit goes forward. You can later file an amended complaint to include the dismissed claims, again, if you have a factual basis to do so.

Remember we discussed the burn rate above. The burn rate for an employer at this point is not substantial, but it is starting to grow. Paying an attorney to draft, file, and argue a motion to dismiss can be expensive. But the case still hasn't required a tremendous amount of time from company officials.

Note that filing an opposition to a motion to dismiss will not take a tremendous amount of your time, and you are not required to attend the hearing, though you can if you wish. At the hearing, only the attorneys will make arguments to the judge. The judge is very unlikely to ask you anything.

Answer

If your employer does not file a motion to dismiss, it must file an answer, as discussed above. This filing does not require a hearing, and the case will proceed to discovery after the answer is filed.

Sometimes a court will require both sides to attend a hearing to discuss how the case will proceed, setting deadlines for discovery and for motions to dismiss. If both sides can agree on these issues, they can sometimes file a joint discovery plan and avoid a hearing.

Discovery

Discovery is the stage when parties begin to formally investigate the case by asking questions and taking testimony. It is roughly divided into two parts: "paper" discovery and depositions.

Paper discovery consists of interrogatories, requests for production of documents, and requests for admissions. Interrogatories are written questions that each side can send to the other. The party answering interrogatories is required to sign the answers as being true. Each party is usually limited to thirty questions. So, if there are two defendants, you can send a separate set of thirty questions to each. Each defendant can also send you thirty questions to answer. The questions and answers are not filed with the court, and thus they do not become public unless they are attached to a motion or used at trial.

A request for the production of documents (RFP) is just what it sounds like. You can request that any party turn over documents that are relevant to the case. There are usually no limits on how many RFPs you can serve on an opposing party.

Requests for admissions are written requests that the other side admit something as true. You can use these for basic facts, such as "Admit that Ms. Smith worked for your company from January 1, 2013 to December 4, 2013." The purpose of obtaining admissions is to get these facts "in the record."

Let's detour for a minute and discuss what "in the record" means. When facts are in the record, it means that they are properly before the court. For instance, the complaint, answer, answers to interrogatories, documents produced during discovery, and deposition testimony are all part of the record. If a fact is in your head but not in one of these documents, it is not in the record and cannot be considered by the court as part of the record. Of course, trial testimony can put facts in the record. It is often the simple facts that attorneys sometimes forget to put in the record.

Let's suppose I want to write in a motion, "Ms. Smith, at fifty-five years old on October 4, 2013, was the oldest employee at AMC Welding." If your birthday or that fact is not stated somewhere in the record, the court cannot consider it, even if your attorney says it is true. This fact would likely be in the complaint. But if it weren't, I might use a request for admission to the employer to obtain the information: that is, "Admit that on October 4, 2013, Ms. Smith, at fifty-five years old, was the oldest person working for AMC Welding." If the employer knows this fact to be true, it must admit it.

Back to the all-important burn rate. The burn rate is increasing at this point because the attorney will have to go to the company to help learn the answers to these questions and dig up relevant documents. It takes time for the attorney and company officials to gather all this information. It can get particularly expensive if the company must search computer records, which most discovery requests require these days.

> **Tip:**
> Most people know that work e-mail and social media can get you in trouble. You should also know that there is a federal statute called the Computer Fraud and Abuse Act, 18 U.S.C. § 1030, that allows employers to sue you if you "access" a work computer "without authorization." This broad language gives employers wide latitude to go after you if use a work computer for personal gain or to help you in a lawsuit. If you removed material from a work computer before your employment ended, let your attorney know right away. There are ways to handle this situation to help limit any potential liability to you.

As a general rule, the burden of the paper production falls more heavily on defendants. Companies have more people to talk to, more databases to search, and so on. But it will be work for you, too. The defendant will ask for every piece of information you have that could be relevant to the case. The most difficult part of this is that some of this information may be very personal. For instance, if you are claiming emotional distress, a defendant may have the right to request certain medical records. You cannot refuse to turn these documents over if they are relevant.

I once had a case in which my client noted in her lawsuit that she suffered from emotional distress as a result of the events that had happened to her at work. Prior to the lawsuit, she had worked with a therapist regarding these issues. As part of her therapy, she kept a diary. Although it was embarrassing to her, she turned the diary over to the defendant. Initially, she resisted, noting the personal nature of the records, until I explained that she had no choice. Why? The rules of civil procedure are designed to prevent either side from hiding evidence.

Courts don't like "gotcha" tactics. They want both sides to share the evidence relevant to the case. This promotes earlier settlement. If one side refuses to turn over evidence, the other can file what's called a "motion to compel production," where the party asks the court to force the other side to turn over the requested information. Not only can a court require the production, it can also sanction the other side for failing to comply with the discovery rules. The discovery rules are far from perfect, and defendants often obfuscate and refuse to turn over documents, requiring motions to compel. Depending on how heated this part of discovery becomes, it can raise the burn rate dramatically.

Costs—those expenses not associated with attorney's fees—can begin to creep up here. Again, this is more likely on the defense side, but there can be expenses for you as well. These might include large copying jobs and perhaps even a computer forensics firm to retrieve electronically stored information from your phone or computer.

> **Tip:**
> Litigation involves two types of expenses: attorney time and costs. Costs include court filing fees and deposition expenses. Depositions require hiring a court reporter to take down testimony, and then you have to pay for the written transcript. As a general rule, a deposition costs approximately $1,000 per day. It is not uncommon for even a simple case to involve five or more days of depositions. Other expenses include hiring process servers, retaining investigators, and copying documents. Most single plaintiff cases involve between $5,000 and $15,000 in costs. Even attorneys who take cases on full contingency often require clients to cover costs.

Depositions

This is where the burn rate kicks up substantially. During a deposition, one party gets to ask questions of someone from an opposing party under oath. It's not exactly the same as courtroom testimony, but it is close. A deposition can last for less than an hour to more than seven. A court reporter takes down testimony, which can be used in motions filed with the court or in the courtroom during the trial.

Depositions themselves are stressful enough, but they are made worse by the time it takes to prepare for them. It can take hours to review information relevant to the case and prepare for the proper way to answer questions. The other side has to do the same. Preparation is even more critical when the depositions are videotaped, as the recorded testimony can be shown at trial.

But depositions have many benefits as well. This is the part of the case where you can force people from your company to sit down across the table from your lawyer and answer questions. Now, the burn rate increases substantially because of the attorney time involved and, for the defense, time that key personnel have to take away from the company.

Depositions can be useful because they get everyone in the room for an extended period. That allows time for the attorneys to communicate in person, which is often effective in moving the ball forward in settlement. Depositions also give attorneys a more realistic review of the case. For instance, defense counsel may lose some faith in the strength of the company's case when the senior executive, who appeared so reasonable when talking from the secure confines of his office, suddenly comes across as both ill-informed and dismissive in a lengthy videotaped deposition.

Of course, the stakes will be high for you, too. The value of your case will drop like a stone if you can't offer evidence in support of your claims or come across in *your* taped deposition as whiny and evasive.

Motion for Summary Judgment

Summary judgment is the main event short of trial. It is what defendants pin great hopes on. The result of this stage often ends the case, one way or another. Unlike the motion to dismiss stage, a court here is supposed to evaluate the facts. The legal question is whether there is a genuine dispute of material fact relevant to the claims at issue. (You can look at the exact language in Federal Rule of Civil Procedure 56.)

Let's take, for example, a classic discrimination case, one in which the employee claims that the employer fired her because it did not believe a woman with a new baby could perform at a high level. The employer claims that the termination had nothing to do with the employee's sex. Rather, it occurred because the employee had not been performing well at her job.

After completing discovery, the defendant files a motion for summary judgment attaching your answers to interrogatories, some pages from various depositions, and some e-mails produced during discovery. In the motion, the defendant's main argument is this: "Your Honor, at the motion to dismiss stage, you could not look at facts or the evidence. Now you can. Looking at all these facts produced by the plaintiff, there is no way a reasonable juror could find in favor of the plaintiff."

Here, the judge is supposed to look at the evidence in a light favorable to the non-moving party, which is usually the employee. That means that a tie at this stage goes to the employee. What the judge is looking for—and it is the judge at this stage, not the jury—is a "factual dispute" about an issue relevant to the legal claims. The idea is that the judge is not supposed to act like a juror or fact finder. She is supposed to put herself in the shoes of a hypothetical reasonable juror and decide whether, given the facts that have been developed through discovery, this juror could decide the issue in favor of the employee. The judge is not supposed to decide the case at this stage. She is not supposed to say, "Well, I don't think it happened this way. I don't find the employee's story credible, so I'm granting summary judgment." She should deny summary judgment if she says to herself, *Well, I don't think the employee's story holds water, but I can see, given these facts, that a reasonable person could think differently. That's what a jury is for, so I'm letting the case go forward.*

Motions for summary judgment and (if you are the employee) oppositions to them are a big deal. Unlike a motion to dismiss, which usually involves only legal arguments, this motion involves factual and legal arguments. The facts have to be supported by evidence. To do this, both sides must attach numerous documents, including deposition transcripts. For instance, a single sentence like "Ms. Smith's manager knew full well that she performed at a high level throughout her time at AMC Welding" might need support from an interrogatory answer from the defendant, a string of e-mails produced during discovery, and three pages of testimony from a deposition. You can imagine how much time it can take to comb through a deposition transcript several hundred pages long to find the exact statement you need. It is for these reasons that motions for summary judgment and oppositions to them take dozens of hours of attorney time and can result in a filing over a hundred pages long. Indeed, it is in some ways like writing a book.

There is a good reason to have a standard tilted in favor of letting the case move ahead. At the summary judgment stage, the judge will usually have yet to hear from a single witness. Motions for summary judgment are decided based on the written evidence put forth by each side. Our system likes for the jury (or the judge) to be able to hear from a witness on the stand before making a decision. At this stage, parties can submit testimony from depositions. But this usually happens by printing out pages from a cold deposition transcript and attaching them to the motion as an exhibit. For instance, the employer might attach a page from the deposition of the employee's manager that reads like this:

> Q: Why did you fire Ms. Smith?
>
> A: Because she routinely came in late and failed to follow my instructions.
>
> Q: Did the fact that she had just had a baby in any way affect your decision?
>
> A: No.

In a transcript, this seems pretty straightforward. But imagine the same testimony at trial.

> Q: Why did you fire Ms. Smith?
>
> A: [*Long pause; witness fidgets in his seat, appearing uncomfortable, eyes downcast.*] Because she routinely came in late and failed to follow my instructions.
>
> Q: Did the fact that she had just had a baby in any way affect your decision?
>
> A: [*Swallowing hard.*] No.

Different, right? His answer sounded solid on paper, but if you see him answer those questions, you might find him a liar based on the nonverbal signals.

However, the sad truth is that federal courts have increasingly used motions for summary judgment to dismiss cases. Judges do what they aren't supposed to do, though they don't come out and say so: they actually decide what they think happened and often throw the case out. Why? Federal courts are busy, busy places, with each judge having to decide all kinds of cases, including a crush of criminal cases and other civil matters. For this reason, there is an institutional bias to "clear out the docket" by getting rid of cases before trial. Trials take up a lot of court time and resources. Judges generally won't dismiss a strong case, but when there is a close call, they now tend to find in favor of the defendant and toss the case out.

But what about the court of appeals? Sure, you can appeal. But appeals are expensive and time-consuming. Many individuals who lose at this stage just decide to pack it in and go home. Even if you do appeal, courts of appeal in this area are not considered employee-friendly. So, you could very well spend more money, only to lose at the appellate level, too. And, even assuming you could pull together an appeal to the US Supreme Court, it is not required to hear every case appealed to it. In fact, the Court hears only a small percentage of cases presented to it.. Chances are, it wouldn't even look at yours.

All this is to say that the summary judgment stage often decides the case. If the employee loses, the case is often over. If the judge rules in favor of the employee and lets the case go forward, then the next stage is trial. At this point, the advantage in some sense shifts to the employee. Trial offers risk to both sides, but particular risk to a defendant:

- *A trial is public.* While defendants generally don't care so much about the public nature of complaints and motions, they care more about a trial. For instance, no employer wants to spend days in the spotlight trying to defend claims that it doesn't like women with kids.

- *The burn rate for trial is very, very high.* Now the company has to pay for the defense attorney—and sometimes a team of them—to take the case to trial.

Also, the company witnesses have to be prepared to testify. No business wants its employees—sometimes high-level employees—sitting around the courthouse waiting to testify rather than working.

- *The risk is higher.* If a defendant loses, it likely will have to pay its own attorneys as well as the attorney's fees for the employee. Even in a simple case, that could be a combined cost of more than $250,000. Of course, the company then has a very public loss on its record.

For this reason, settlement offers will sometimes increase dramatically—I've had them increase tenfold—after a company loses at summary judgment. With real money on the table and a risk that they could also lose at trial, employers frequently choose to settle.

Summary judgment, then, is often the high-water mark for cases moving through the litigation process. As a matter of numbers, employers win more often than employees.

Given this, employers look at settlement as a business matter. The first issue is cost. A good rule of thumb is that it will cost an employer anywhere from $50,000 to $100,000 just to get through discovery and file a motion for summary judgment. The best-case scenario at that stage for the employer is that it wins. But that's all it gets. It won't get most of that money back. It is true that the loser has to pay costs (not attorney's fees). For an average single plaintiff employment claim, these are usually between $5,000 and $10,000. That's right; if you lose at this stage, you have to pay your former employer. Now, in many instances, employers will agree to waive their ability to collect costs in exchange for an agreement by the employee not to appeal.

Since the employer is looking at paying around $100,000 just to win, anything less than that is a good business decision. It makes a lot more sense just to pay you $30,000 to go away. The employer saves $70,000 and will usually settle only if you sign a confidentiality agreement, which means it buys your silence, too. The employer doesn't get a confidentiality agreement if it fights and loses.

The closer your settlement number gets to six figures, though, the more likely an employer is to roll the dice. The employer will take a shot at summary judgment and come to the table with six-figure-type money only if it loses. In fact, big companies are notorious for taking a shot at summary judgment no matter what. Do you think a company like General Electric cares much about spending, say, $60,000 to take a shot at winning? No, it doesn't. In those cases, the employer will only make a "nuisance value" offer, likely under $10,000, until after the court decides the motion for summary judgment. Then, if the company loses, it will talk turkey.

There are reasons other than finances that companies do this. The second reason is setting a precedent for settling. The last thing a company wants is a reputation for early and generous settlements. I think the fear of this is overblown—that employees will line up around the block to sue if the company settles—but that fear is out there. The thinking here is, *Let's fight this tooth and nail. Even if we lose, our other employees will think twice about taking us on in court.*

The third reason is that employees sometimes will just go away rather than sue. Gearing up for summary judgment, not to mention trial, is a big deal for anyone. Relying on this, employers will call your bluff. You can send a demand letter, only to get no response or a very low offer. The employer is counting on the fact that you will read a book like this or talk to any attorney about the process and decide it is just not worth the time and money. The other problem is that, even if you are willing, you may have trouble finding an attorney willing to sign on if you need a contingency fee. You can imagine how strong a case must be before an attorney will agree to put her own payment at risk. The workload is high, and the chance of a big win is low. It often just does not make financial sense for an attorney to take a risk that she will do all that work, only to get nothing in the end. Even if you love the work and the clients, that can be a good way to go out of business.

Don't get me wrong. It's not all doom and gloom. If you're properly prepared for the litigation process, it can be empowering. Remember that senior vice president who would not even bother to take your call after you were fired? This is the same vice president who signed off on a letter to your attorney saying that you were fired for incompetence. Now, after receiving a subpoena from your attorney, he has no choice but to answer questions under oath. You can imagine a conversation with the company's attorney:

> VICE PRESIDENT. Look, I'm not going to meet with her attorney. It's just not going to happen. We had good reason to fire her. End of story. I'm scheduled to be in Washington State that day.

> ATTORNEY. I understand, but here's the deal. You have been subpoenaed to appear. I cleared this date with you last month. You have to come. I'm sorry. We have to show up.

> VICE PRESIDENT. I'm not going. Tell them they can forget it.

> ATTORNEY. If you don't show up, you will be in violation of a court order. Her attorney will file a motion to show cause. The court will set a hearing, and you and I will have to explain to an unhappy federal judge why you should not be held in contempt. There is nothing I can do about that. It's the law.

> VICE PRESIDENT. (*Long silence.*) Fine. But I can only stay for two hours.

> ATTORNEY. You need to be prepared to stay all day. I'll also need at least four hours the day before to prepare you for the deposition.

> VICE PRESIDENT. (*Clearly fuming, through clenched teeth.*) As you wish. (*Slams down phone.*)

This is good stuff. And the only way to force that kind of issue is to file a lawsuit. The question is how much it's worth to you. For some people, that revenge plus a $50,000 settlement is worth it. For others, it's not. You should consider what you hope to get out of the litigation, considering monetary and nonmonetary goals. Have a frank conversation with your attorney about accomplishing those goals.

Trial

Very few cases go to trial. For the reasons noted above, the economics favor settlement, particularly if the employee survives summary judgment. But it does happen. I won't address the topic here. If you make it this far, you will have an attorney, and he or she will spend a lot of time preparing you for it.

Chapter 21
The Judge and Jury

Which Court Should You Choose?

It depends on several factors, including whether you decide to sue under federal or state law (or both). States often have laws or statutes similar to the federal antidiscrimination laws. Many states also do not limit the damages on these actions, unlike the federal laws, which cap the damages depending on the number of employees your company employs. If you file your claims in federal court and the court takes jurisdiction over your state law claims as well, then it will apply the law of the state when deciding those claims.

In addition, recent studies have shown that because of a very demanding standard in federal court, many employment discrimination claims are being dismissed at summary judgment. On average, only 15 percent of federal court plaintiffs won their employment discrimination claims, compared to an average win rate of 51 percent for other types of claims. Therefore, depending on your state, it may be more beneficial for you to file your lawsuit in your state court.

Furthermore, while you probably do not have any control over which jurisdiction you will file your claim in (usually your claim is filed where the action arose, which is typically your place of employment), there are important differences between courts. For example, the Fourth Circuit—which covers Virginia, Maryland, North Carolina, South Carolina, and West Virginia—has a reputation for being very conservative and often overturning large discrimination verdicts. However, the Ninth Circuit—encompassing Alaska, Arizona, California, Guam, Hawaii, Idaho, Montana, Nevada, the Northern Mariana Islands, Oregon, and Washington—is very liberal and often upholds large jury verdicts, and has more case law that is favorable to plaintiffs.

Additionally, deciding what local court to bring your claim in is very important as well, especially if you have the option of bringing your claim in more than one court. For example, the US District Court for the Eastern District of Virginia in Alexandria is called the "rocket docket" because it likes to move cases in and out quickly and often disposes of cases on summary judgment. Therefore, if you need a longer time to build up evidence or prepare your case and you have the opportunity to go to another court, that may be a good option for you. Each court, and even each judge, is very unique in how it rules, and a good local attorney who has practiced in those courts will be able to advise you on the reputation of your local court system. If you are able to proceed only in one court, your lawyer will advise you on how to manage the difficulties or benefits that a specific court may offer.

A Word About Juries

Very few cases—particularly civil cases—actually make it to a jury. They often get dismissed or settle. If you Google the "vanishing jury trial," you'll find a number of articles.

I've learned some surprising things about juries over the years. Here are just a few.

Jurors sometimes decide cases by the time the opening is over. TV shows and movies love the closing argument. How many times have you seen a lawyer on the silver screen making an impassioned closing argument before an enthralled jury? Lawyers dream of it, too. But, according to most social scientists, the truth is that jurors come to any case with their own set of conscious and unconscious biases that predispose them to view a case in a certain way. Jurors, like all humans, rely on this set of values and viewpoints to make snap judgments. This means that, in a trial, a juror will often reach a conclusion about the verdict by the end of opening statements. It doesn't matter how tear-inducing your closing argument is: the case is over long before you get there.

I do not mean to say that jurors take their obligations lightly. When I first started trying cases—having read too many articles about runaway juries and ridiculous verdicts—I had low expectations of jurors. To my surprise, however, almost all the jurors I was able to speak to (judges often asked willing jurors to stay after trial to talk to lawyers) took their obligations very seriously. They pored over facts and struggled with jury instructions.

This doesn't mean that they considered important the same things I thought they would. That is one of the wild cards about juries. They might latch on to something that was not even on the lawyer's radar screen. In one of my first trials as a prosecutor, there was testimony that the officers cursed at the defendant as they chased him. This case involved a "jump out" in a public housing area plagued with open-air drug dealing. It did not occur to me that this would be important: it wasn't an what a lawyer would call a necessary "element" of the offense, and the defendant was caught with seventeen zips of crack in his pocket. This wouldn't matter, or so I thought, so I didn't address the foul language. I later learned, after a not-guilty verdict, that a number of elderly jurors found this language very troubling. They thought that an officer who used such language would—as the defense argued—be willing to plant drugs on the defendant. In another case, I found out that jurors struggled in deliberations with whether a police cruiser was the same thing as a patrol car. I got a conviction in that case.

Even if unpredictable, jurors try hard to do the right thing. People do their best to be fair. You can just never predict what logic the group will use to reach a decision.

Mock Trial

Recently, I had an experience that brought home the truth that people make up their minds quickly. Earlier this year, I participated in a mock trial that involved high school students as jurors. The mock trial involved a civil case. The plaintiff was the widow of a man who died in a car accident and was suing an insurance company. The insurance company claimed that the man killed himself. The insurance policy contained a provision that let the insurance company off the hook if the policyholder committed suicide. Some facts in the case seemed to indicate that the husband and father intended to kill himself so that his family could get the multimillion-dollar policy. But there were some tear-jerking facts, too. For instance, the man was a father of two, and his wife had just given birth to a third child a week before his death. So, the stage was set. Are you more likely to believe insurance companies are evil and looking for a way to save money? Or do you take a hard-nosed look at the facts and decide that a deal's a deal: if he killed himself, then there should be no payout?

As lawyers, we set about preparing our case by worrying over details of witness examination, introducing evidence, and, of course, giving closings. There were dozens of teams of lawyers, and we all tried at least one case over the course of two days before juries of high school students.

Now, you might think high school students aren't the best example (unless you are one). But recall that juries are made up of all kinds of people, some who may be just out of high school, and many who didn't even make it through. So, high school students, particularly diligent ones like these, are not a bad approximation of most juries.

We videotaped the jury deliberations and talked to the students afterward. One of the questions we asked the jurors was at what point in the proceeding they reached a decision. Now, an important thing to recall about this mock trial and question is that, unlike real life, the jurors had no incentive to tell us what they think they are "supposed" to say. No jurors want to admit—even to themselves—that they made up their mind in the first fifteen minutes of the case. Here, there was no such restraint. What did we learn? Most jurors readily admitted that they made up their mind very early in the case. Some jurors even said they had done so when the judge read a summary of the case before the first lawyer even opened his or her mouth. "Oh, the insurance company denied payment? Those guys are never up to any good," or a similar, but opposite reaction. None of the jurors were swayed by the closing arguments.

Jury Selection

While procedures vary from state to state, the basics of jury selection are the same. When a case is ready for trial, the judge calls for a panel of potential jurors. This group is called the "venire." The judge and the lawyers then ask this group a series of questions designed to pick twelve (or sometimes six) jurors who can fairly decide the case. Individuals in the venire are called up until the jury and alternates are selected. Some jurors can be "struck" for cause. These decisions are made by the judge. For instance, a juror who said she could never believe a police officer cannot be fair in a criminal trial. Each side also gets a number of peremptory challenges. That is, each side gets to strike jurors for any reason, as long as it is not discriminatory. For example, the defense team could not try to strike just black jurors. A litigant or the judge can stop jury selection to address a charge that one side is discriminating. This is called a Batson charge.

But outside of improper discrimination, a litigant can strike a juror for any reason. Got a bad feeling? Don't like his shoes? Fine. An example of a proper peremptory strike would, in a criminal case, look like this: The potential juror, in response to a question from the judge about whether he has ever been involved in the criminal system, says that his house has been broken into three times over the past five years. Asked whether this affected how he viewed the police, he says, "Well, they never caught anybody. That frustrated me. At least they tried, I guess." The judge asks whether he can, despite this experience, be fair to a case involving witnesses that are police officers. The potential juror says, "I think so. I'm sure I can." The judge will not strike this juror for cause. But a prosecutor might well think to herself: *He says he can be fair. Maybe he means it. But he's had a bad experience with the police. That might affect his view in a close case. I'm going to strike him.*

Jury "Deselection"

Some say that jury selection is actually the incorrect term, given that neither party actually gets to "select" the jury. The best each side can do is use its peremptory strikes strategically and judiciously. Peremptory strikes are limited. A lawyer can't strike with impunity. And there is a fair amount of chance involved. A venire panel is selected randomly. It is possible that you could have a bad run of luck and the first six panel members might appear hostile to your side (but not hostile enough for the judge to strike for cause). In that case, you might have to burn through your strikes early, only to find that the other half of the panel is even worse for your side. There is a fair amount of guesswork involved in this procedure.

In the District of Columbia Superior Court, where I tried most of my jury cases, potential jurors are called up and questioned by the judge, with lawyers on each side. After the judge asks a question or two, each side gets a very limited option to follow up. Judges, wanting to move proceedings along, don't let lawyers question jurors for long.

Once there are fourteen jurors in the jury box (twelve, plus two alternates), each side is allowed to exercise two strikes or to pass. After a round of strikes, the process starts over. This goes on until the strikes are exhausted. In almost all my cases, I had jurors I believed might or might not be good for my case. But I had to predict whether that person might be better than a panelist who would rotate into the box if I exercised a strike.

For instance, as a prosecutor, I might get someone on the jury who had a bad experience with the police. If given my druthers, I'd strike that person. But I might decide not to exercise that strike if I looked out into the panel and saw a male with a green Mohawk and a tattoo that reads: DOWN WITH THE MAN. I have to make a decision then about the best of what may be bad options. If I have one more strike, I can use it and get the Mohawk guy. Now, the truth is that I know nothing about either of these people. Maybe I'm prosecuting a drug case and Mohawk guy is really in the seminary with a passionate belief that drugs are tearing apart the fabric of our society. As a lawyer, the most I can do is "deselect" the jury in the best way to maximize my chances of success.

Part V: Other Considerations

Chapter 22
Workplace Investigations

In most nonworkplace situations, you know when you might have a criminal law problem. Rob a store or get pulled over while driving drunk, and you know you'll be in trouble with the law. However, in white-collar investigations—ones that often start in the workplace—it can be difficult to tell when you have violated some obscure regulation. This is particularly true in heavily regulated businesses like government/military contracting, pharmaceuticals, shipping, and import-export companies. It is also true for multinational corporations with significant dealings with second- or third-world countries. So, any time you are involved in a workplace investigation, you should be concerned about potential problems with law enforcement.

The difficulty with workplace investigations is that they are conducted without regard to an employee's constitutional rights. For instance, if you work for a pharmaceutical company and get interviewed by compliance, you may have no idea what the investigation involves, and you may not realize that what you say could be turned over later to federal law enforcement. The company could use that interview against you without regard to your right to speak to law enforcement or your right to contact a lawyer.

In short, workplace investigations are nothing but a tangled mess of trouble for employees. It can sometimes be difficult for a lawyer to decide what rights apply and when. So how are you, the employee, supposed to make sense of it? I know I am a bit of a broken record on this issue, but it is almost always worth your time to sit down and talk to an attorney any time you are involved in an investigation, even if you are not the one being investigated.

Even if you meet with an attorney, you should learn the basics so that you know the right questions to ask. To that end, in this chapter, I provide an overview of your rights in a workplace investigation.

The first issue for you to consider is whether your employer provides a process for an investigation and your rights in it. For instance, if you are a member of a union, your union contract may give you the right to have a representative at some meetings with management. Similarly, your company may have published guidelines that it is supposed to use when conducting an investigation. These guidelines may, for instance, indicate that you have the right to bring a representative. Understand that there are no absolute rights in many instances. Strangely, there is nothing necessarily illegal about a private company choosing not to follow its own guidelines. Still, if you find yourself involved in an investigation, you know what the company's internal rules are. You can often find these in the employee handbook and on the internal company website.

The next important issue depends on whether you are a government employee or a private employee. A government employee may have some due process rights provided by state law. For instance, public schoolteachers, particularly if they belong to a union with bargaining power, may have specific, enforceable rights to some process. By process, I mean a certain type of hearing and the right to bring representation.

Importantly, government officials have the right not to be fired for refusing to answer questions that could be self-incriminating. There are a couple of important points here. First, everyone has a right against self-incrimination when *questioned by law enforcement* when *in custody*. But, in the private sector, this right does not provide job protection. For instance, if a police officer stops you and says, "You can't go anywhere. Did you just take that Snickers bar without paying for it?" you have a Fifth Amendment right to refuse to answer. Let's assume that the officer asks you this question while standing in your conference room at work beside your boss. After the officer asks the question, you say, "I'm taking the Fifth." Then your boss says, "Hey, you answer the question, or you're fired." Is that legal? Yes. You have an absolute right to refuse to answer the officer's question, but that right does not include job protection.

Things are different if you work for the government, and sometimes even if you work for a government contractor. In the case *Garrity v. New Jersey*, 385 U.S. 493 (1967), the US Supreme Court held that it was unconstitutional to make police officers choose between answering law enforcement questions about the alleged fixing of traffic tickets and losing their job. The court reasoned that this choice resulted in coerced testimony, which violates the Constitution. The government used its power as an employer to force these officers to give potentially incriminating testimony. Of course, the same pressures apply to a private employee making the same choice. But in the private sector, the government is not on one side of the equation and thus, at least as far as the courts are concerned, cannot be said to coerce your testimony.

The rights are referred to as *Garrity* rights, and government employers are required to inform government employees subject to investigation of the right to both keep their job and refuse to answer incriminating questions.

A *Garrity* rights statement for a federal employee might sound like this:

> You have the right to remain silent if your answers may tend to incriminate you. Anything you say or do may be used as evidence in both an administrative proceeding and any future criminal proceedings involving you. If you refuse to answer the questions posed to you on the grounds that the answers may tend to incriminate you, you cannot be discharged solely for remaining silent. However, your silence can be considered in an administrative proceeding for its evidentiary value that is warranted by the facts surrounding your case. This interview is strictly voluntary, and you may leave at any time.

However, if you are not subject to criminal prosecution because the government is giving you immunity, it can make you choose between answering questions and keeping your job. The US Court of Claims resolved this issue in a case called *Kalkines v. United States*, 473 F.2d 1391. *Kalkines* held that an employee could be disciplined or fired for refusing to answer questions—even incriminating ones—if the government has agreed not to prosecute. This is true even if the answers could get your fired. The reasoning here is that there is no government coercion to subject yourself to criminal (as opposed to employment) penalties because the government has taken criminal prosecution off the table. You will know if this is the case because the government is required to give you a *Kalkines* warning, which is essentially that "you can be fired if you don't answer."

The warning that your employer should read to you—and will typically ask you to sign—will go something like this if you are a government employee:

> I want to advise you, [Employee], that you have all the rights and privileges guaranteed by the laws of the state of [your state] and the Constitution of this state and of the United States, including the right to be represented by counsel at this inquiry and the right to remain silent, although you may be subject to disciplinary action by the [name of government employer] for the failure to answer material and relevant questions relating to the performance of your duties as an employee of the [United States/state/locality].

> I further advise you that the answers you may give to the questions propounded to you at this proceeding, or any information or evidence that is gained by reason of your answers, may not be used against you in a criminal proceeding except that you may be subject to criminal prosecution for any false answer that you may give under any applicable law, including [any law applicable to false statements].

Let's go over two important points here. First, under *Kalkines*, you have the right to counsel, and you can still be prosecuted if you lie. This is why it is important to get an attorney immediately. He or she can be another pair of ears in the room working on your team. If you talk without representation, what happens when the investigator later says he or she believes that you were lying? All of a sudden, you are looking at possible criminal prosecution.

Garrity/Kalkines situations often come up with investigations by the Office of the Inspector General, a government body with various branches given the authority to investigate wrongdoing within the government. These officers do not have the authority to conduct criminal prosecutions, but they can refer cases to federal prosecutors. They can also "debar" individuals and companies from selling services to the federal government. This is very serious and can result essentially in an economic death sentence for a company, and potentially for an individual whose entire career has been in selling products to the government.

Here's a weird curveball for you: the police do not have to give you these warnings. If FBI agents show up at your workplace, they can bring you into a room and, assuming that you are not "in custody," can ask you anything they want, even if it is incriminating—and in a complicated workplace investigation or white-collar investigation, it may not be immediately clear whether you are in trouble.

What about an investigation that is not criminal—what rights do you have then? Not many. Let's say, for instance, that you work for a car company and report to human resources that your boss is a sexually harassing creep. (Your words, not mine.) Two days later, you get a call to come down to HR. When you walk into the room, you see Pete, the vice president of HR, sitting there with his assistant, pen in hand. Pete says they are conducting an "investigation" into your "complaints." This would be great, except that Pete and your creepy boss are buds, often golfing together on weekends. There is just no way this is going to be a real investigation. This is going to be a whitewash, no doubt.

What are your rights here? Can you refuse to participate? Can you demand that you be allowed to bring a lawyer? Unless you have a union contract (and how many people have one these days?), the answer to both questions is probably no. This is not a criminal investigation. Your employer is a private organization, so no constitutional rights are at issue. This means that you have no right to keep your job if you refuse to participate in the investigation. In fact, it would probably be legal to fire you for refusing to participate, even though you were the one harassed. A number of courts have held that refusing to participate in an investigation is not an activity protected under antidiscrimination law. Eventually, you've got to play ball, or you risk losing your job.

However, you do have some legal protections if you raise your allegations though a lawyer. (Of course, showing up with a hired gun may have some long-term implications for your job. That's a different conversation.) Let's try it out in the example above.

Instead of going straight to HR, you first hire a lawyer. She tells you that you likely are protected under federal law prohibiting sexual harassment because your company has more than fifteen employees. The lawyer recommends that she write a letter to HR raising the issue through the company's process for handling these complaints, and that she help you file a complaint with HR and file a charge with the EEOC. Sounds good. You hire yourself a lawyer. The lawyer sends the letter to HR, noting that she is representing you and that, the day before the date of the letter, you filed a charge of sex discrimination with the EEOC.

Now you've got a little (but, unfortunately, only a little) something to work with. Cue the music—you're now a "represented party." This does not mean that you can refuse to speak to your HR department. But it does complicate things if your company wants to bring in its lawyer to talk to you. Under the rules of professional responsibility, a lawyer cannot talk to someone represented by an attorney on the other side of a dispute. He or she can speak only to the other attorney.

So, let's say in the example above, you show up to the meeting, and HR Pete is sitting with the company's lawyer. In that instance, it very likely violates the lawyer's professional obligations to speak to you if he or she knows that you have an attorney. In that case, you could rightfully throw a wrench in the works and say, "I'm happy to help with the investigation, but not while your lawyer is here. If he's going to be here, I want, and am entitled to, my lawyer." Now watch Pete's smirk vanish.

In truth, if you were to bring your complaint in the first instance through a lawyer, this all would be worked out beforehand. Instead of getting called to a meeting with no advance notice, the company's lawyer would talk to your lawyer about setting up a meeting and who could—and could not—attend.

But lawyer or no lawyer, you cannot refuse to participate in the investigation if your employer is not the government. And that often is not a bad thing. You should be prepared for it. If you are prepared, it is an opportunity to give your side of the story.

A word here for those who are accused of wrongdoing in the office that is not of a criminal nature. Let's say that *you* are the one accused of sexual harassment. Brenda from marketing sent a letter to HR saying you grabbed her derriere at the office holiday party. This is categorically untrue. Yes, you were at the party, and you talked to Brenda for a bit. But you spent most of the time watching the game in the hotel lobby. You're fairly certain it was Ted from accounting with the wandering hands. How people often mistake the two of you, given your rugged good looks contrasted with his weak chin, you'll never know. But it happens often.

The company holds an investigation. It even hires an outside law firm to do the interviews. You have nothing to hide, so you freely go and tell the truth. Two weeks later—after fifteen years of solid service—the company fires you without warning. Though you are never able to get an official answer from the company, you hear though back channels that the powers that be believed Ted and not you.

This is outrageous. You're now unemployed with one kid in college and another on the way. Don't you have rights? This was demonstrably the wrong outcome. Sadly, there is very likely nothing to be done here. This is not a criminal investigation, and you are not a public employee, so you don't have the right to due process or to an appeal. The company got it wrong. That's sad, but it's not illegal.

That's not to say there is no circumstance under which this would be unlawful. Let's return to the example above. You are African American and Brenda is Caucasian, and so is Ted. The same events occurred. The company fires you. The next day, as you are trying to figure out what to do, the phone rings. It's the secretary for the vice president of HR. He's speaking in a hushed voice. "Look," he says, "I don't have much time. But I couldn't sleep unless I did something. Yesterday I overheard the attorney tell the CEO that he talked to three people, and all of them said you didn't do it. And then he said to the attorney, 'Look, it is common knowledge that a black man will take his shot at a white woman if given half an opportunity.' The attorney literally sprinted to the door to close it. I don't think they know that I heard. I still can't believe he said it. I mean, he's black, too. Anyway, I thought you should know."

Now, you've got something. This wasn't someone making the wrong call in an investigation, which is not illegal. This was flagrant discrimination based on race and sex. You'd better call your lawyer.

I don't mean to blow this out of proportion or to suggest that all HR investigations are a threat. Many are not. Sometimes HR (or the company's law firm) is really making a good faith effort to figure out what happened and to stop wrongdoing. You need not go in with guns blazing in every situation. But sometimes it's hard to know the difference. Regardless, at the end of the day, it is important to keep in mind that HR and the company's attorneys are there to protect the company, not you.

This is a lot, I know. So, here's my quick chart on how to handle workplace investigations.

What Happens	The Protections You Have	What to Do
FBI agents show up in your office and "just wants to talk."	• You have the right against self-incrimination. • You have no workplace protection.	Don't talk, no matter what, even if they tell you that it is in your best interest. This is almost always a lie. Get a lawyer or say that you want to talk to the company's lawyer. What if you could get fired? Better to get fired than risk criminal prosecution. In truth, your risk of getting fired is low. Most companies would probably prefer that you talk to a lawyer before deciding whether to cooperate.
OIG investigators show up and say they are conducting an investigation. They read a *Garrity* statement and ask you to sign it.	• You have the right against self-incrimination. • You have *Garrity* job protection even if you refuse to answer.	Don't talk, ever, unless they later offer immunity. Regardless, talk to a lawyer as soon as you can.
OIG investigators show up and say they are conducting an investigation. They read a *Kalkines* statement and ask you to sign it.	• You have the right to counsel. • You will not be criminally liable (unless you lie). • You have no workplace protection if you refuse to answer.	Tell them that you want to talk to a lawyer. Go talk to a lawyer. Explore whether you face any possible criminal liability. If you do, it's probably best not to talk: it's better to lose your job than go to jail. If, after consultation with your lawyer, you decide that you face no criminal liability, agree to talk, but only with your lawyer present.

What Happens	The Protections You Have	What to Do
HR representatives show up and tell you that they are investigating something and need to talk to you. You do not work for the government.	• You have virtually no protections. • This is not law enforcement, so you have no Fifth Amendment protection. • You don't work for the government, so you have no rights under *Garrity* or *Kalkines.* • If it's just HR with no lawyer, 99 percent of the time the company is well within its rights to talk to you; in fact, the company can lawfully fire you for refusing to talk.	Ask for some time. Most companies will not walk you out of the building immediately for refusing to talk. They'll give you at least a day. Go talk to a lawyer see what risks might exist in talking and whether you have any rights (e.g., under contract or state law) to have legal representation. In some rare instances, it may be worth it to risk getting fired instead of talking. For instance, if telling the truth means admitting to a crime, don't talk. It's better to get fired. If you admit criminal liability to a private citizen, nothing would prevent that person from telling law enforcement, and there would be nothing illegal if law enforcement used that information to arrest you. If it's not that dire—for instance, if the investigation is based on a complaint that you raised—agree to talk. If you have time, talk to a lawyer about any traps that may lie ahead. For instance, it is possible that an HR rep in such an "investigation" might be trying to establish— without telling you—that you were in danger of getting fired well before you raised a complaint. HR would do this to prepare a defense for the company—using your words—that any disciplinary action taken against you was unrelated to your complaint, which may be illegal retaliation. If you game this out with a lawyer beforehand, you might be able to avoid these traps. Ask whether you can bring your lawyer or a friend. Ideally, you will have someone in the room on your side who can back up your version of events if it turns into a he-said/she-said situation.

What Happens	The Protections You Have	What to Do
		If the company's lawyer is in the meeting and you have your own lawyer who is not with you, raise this fact and ask that you be allowed to bring your counsel.
		When you go to the meeting, whether with someone or alone, keep your wits about you. Make sure you understand everything being asked of you. Though you don't want to hide the ball, particularly if you want the company to know about wrongdoing, generally, the less you say, the better. You can always follow up in writing later if you miss something.
		Don't let HR put words in your mouth. For instance, if an HR person says, "Earlier you said that you did not think your boss meant to do any harm" and that's not exactly what you said, then say so. "No, I said he did not do any physical harm to me. I do think he meant to insult me," or whatever the real story is.
		When you get out of the meeting, write down everything you can remember, in question-and-answer style. While it is not the same as having someone in the room on your side, it can be evidence later of your version of events. Plus, you may forget important details as you get further away from the event. Your detailed notes that you took while events were fresh in your mind may prove helpful later.

Chapter 23
Don't Quit

Rebecca was with a large insurance company. After working for years with the company, during which time she received good reviews and several promotions, she realized her dream of becoming pregnant. While the pregnancy went well, things at work did not. Her supervisors, none of whom had children, said the right things, but shortly thereafter, they took her out of a management-training program. When she protested, they said it would be better to start her in a different training class when she returned from maternity leave. That sounded reasonable, but it didn't happen.

In fact, when she returned to work, not only was there no opportunity to start with a new training program, she didn't even have a desk. HR had to find her a temporary space. When she asked her supervisor about the situation, she was told they had to make some changes in her position due to her "condition." One of these changes was to put her in a position that involved answering customer calls. Not only was this a demotion, it was also difficult for Rebecca because being on the phone meant a less flexible schedule and no private work space. This arrangement also made it difficult for her to pump breast milk. Disgusted, she filed a pregnancy discrimination claim with the EEOC while she continued to work. A month later, she felt she couldn't take it anymore. She wanted to leave her job, so she called me and asked whether she should quit.

There is no "right" answer to this question. It is certain that quitting your job will weaken your case. First, in most cases, if you quit your job, you may not be eligible for what lawyers call back wages. These are wages that you are entitled to if you are fired for discriminatory reasons and are unable to find a job or find a job making less. In some cases, like the one above, your employer is moving toward firing you. If it does, you can get back wages. But if you quit before it can fire you, you likely cannot get those wages. So then, you are just left with emotional distress damages, which are generally much lower than lost wages.

If you quit, you may also deprive the employer of the opportunity to retaliate against you by firing you. I understand the common-sense desire to prevent your employer from doing bad things to you. But the worse your employer acts, the higher the value of your claim. Now, understand that I am not asking you to try to provoke bad behavior. Keeping your record clean is crucial to winning your case. I am simply talking about letting your employer do what it is planning to do anyway.

But here are two things to consider.

1. Sometimes you can still recover back wages even if you quit. Courts will allow this recovery when your employer made working conditions so intolerable that you have to leave. This is called "constructive discharge." The standard to meet this is very high. Being unhappy is not enough.
2. Most important, this is your life, and you only get so much of it. I never advise people to stay in a job just because it may raise the value of their case. At the end of the day, you have to do what makes sense for you. But it is important that you don't make that decision without understanding what you might be leaving on the table.

Chapter 24
Filing for Unemployment

So, let's suppose that you have had a great employment history with no disciplinary action, but then all of a sudden you get laid off. What should you do?

Well, one of your first steps should be to file for unemployment through your local unemployment office. You are eligible for unemployment if your hours have been reduced or if you have been separated from your employer. Many states accept online or telephone applications for unemployment claims. You should have all the relevant information, such as your employer's address and contact information, your contact information, your Social Security number (or your alien registration number), and the information to any union that you may be represented by or have an employment contract with.

You will generally be ineligible for unemployment benefits if you quit your job without good cause (relocation with a spouse is not covered under unemployment benefits) or if you were fired for misconduct in connection with your work. Qualifying for benefits depends on the state in which you are applying. In Virginia, you must have earned at least $2,700 in the two quarters before filing. You must also be able to perform work and be available for interviews and job searching. Therefore, usually if you are on disability leave or FMLA, you will not qualify for unemployment benefits. You must actively seek work and accept any suitable offers you are given. Different states have different requirements, but generally, you will be required to report to the employment commission weekly or biweekly and give it information on whether you have applied for jobs, had any interviews, made any job contacts, or found employment.

What if I quit work or am fired because of discrimination?

Generally, once you file for unemployment, if your employer disputes your eligibility, then the employment commission will schedule a telephone fact-finding interview. Generally, both you and your employer will have the opportunity to present your side of the story and explain why you were fired or why you quit. You have the right to an attorney who can represent your interests during this hearing. The hearing is very informal, and in most cases, there will be very little investigation done or witnesses consulted. Generally, if your employer seems to have a valid reason for denying the unemployment, then the commission will side with the employer.

After the hearing, the hearing officer will make a decision in writing within ten days (in Virginia), and you will be notified via mail. You then have the right to appeal. You may appeal, or your attorney may appeal on your behalf. Your employer may also file an appeal if the employment commission finds in your favor. The days allowed for the appeal depend on the state, so look for the deadline in the written notification you received from the agency. Make sure that your appeal is filed or postmarked before the deadline for an appeal.

At an appeal hearing, you and the employer will have the right to testify under oath and present witnesses and documents to support your claims. You, or your attorney, may also ask questions of any person testifying against you. An appeals examiner will then review the testimony and make a determination. If you disagree with this determination, then you may file a commission appeal. Generally, this level of appeal is just a review of the evidence, and you cannot present new information or evidence unless you can show a good reason for not including it in the prior stages of the claim.

Finally, if you disagree with this opinion, you may then file a claim in your local court for review of the decision. You may file on your own or have an attorney represent you.

Epilogue: My Story

It was shortly before Christmas in 2005 when the call came. The US Attorney for the District of Columbia called to offer me a position as an Assistant US Attorney (AUSA). I was thirty-three and married with a ten-month-old son, and this was a long time in coming.

After graduating from Georgetown University Law Center in 2001, I returned to my home state of North Carolina to join a midsize firm in Raleigh. As a new associate, I worked in a section of the firm that represented school boards all across the state. My interest was in litigation, and that is what I did, handling everything from contested student suspensions to defending school systems when sued. I loved the job, but soon realized that I would see little courtroom time in a civil litigation practice.

After two years, I got engaged to a woman I had met in law school. She was in Washington, DC, and announced that she had no desire to move to North Carolina. (I knew it was a lost cause when, upon visiting the state with me for the first time, she said that she thought the trees in the state grew too close together. Not much I could do about that!)

So, I gave up that tug-of-war and got a job clerking for a judge in the Superior Court of the District of Columbia. Before taking the bench, the judge was a superstar in the US Attorney's Office, where he prosecuted many high-profile murder cases. Like me, he had started in private practice, only to realize that he would rarely see the inside of a courtroom. He told me that if I wanted trial experience, there was no better place to get it than the US Attorney's Office, particularly in the District of Columbia.

With his support, I applied right out of the clerkship. A spot in any US Attorney's office is highly competitive. These offices have their pick of bright, competitive lawyers who want to work on challenging cases that involve a lot of trial work. While many are motivated by the desire to serve the public, it doesn't hurt that many who serve as AUSAs go on to high-profile appointed positions or to lucrative jobs in private firms.

Just getting an interview is an achievement: getting the office to consider your application often requires a call from a VIP. The interview process itself is rigorous, with multiple rounds of interviews followed by the harrowing experience of delivering an opening statement in front of senior staff in the office. The final interview is with the US Attorney.

With the support of my judge, I got an interview and made it to the final interview, only to be turned down. It is not uncommon that applicants must apply more than once to get in. I was advised to get some criminal law experience (up to that point I had none) and reapply. So, I did. I got a job with a boutique law firm that specialized in white-collar criminal defense. It was a dream job in many ways: great work with some of the top criminal defense lawyers in the city.

I spent two years with the firm. While there, my wife gave birth to our first child, a boy. I had always wanted to be a father, but like most, I had no real idea what this meant. No one prepared me for how much I would completely fall in love with that little boy. I was also unprepared for how much work being a father would take. Harrison was not the best sleeper, and my wife and I spent many nights with little sleep. She worked as an attorney at a large law firm, so we shared child-care duties as evenly as we could. Fortunately, my work life was flexible and, for the most part, low stress.

It was a good thing, too, because we also had a high-maintenance dog, a cocker spaniel named Sawyer. I found Sawyer running around, lost, in front of the law school while I was studying for the bar. When no one claimed him from the shelter, I adopted him. A sweetheart of a dog, Sawyer soon developed multiple health problems, including diabetes. After many expensive trips to the vet, we found a combination of medications and twice-daily insulin shots could keep him healthy. However, Sawyer, being a dog, did not always cooperate with his treatment. If he found a sugar-laden treat—like an entire loaf of bread, for instance—that he could reach, he would eat it. This would make his blood sugar go haywire. As a result, he would often pee and poop all over the house, which, of course, had to be cleaned up. And Sawyer would occasionally have seizures, sometimes necessitating an emergency trip to the vet. We joked that Sawyer's care was so expensive that owning him was the equivalent of having another car payment.

Still, life was good. I had a good job and was able to get home to see and spend time with my son. I knew many attorneys who by choice or necessity were weekend parents. Due to heavy billing requirements and travel, their kids were asleep when they left in the morning and on the way to bed when they got home. After Harrison was born, it was clear to me that I would never make that choice. It wasn't so much of a conscious declaration; it just was. There was no way I would not be around him during waking hours every day. I quickly surmised that it would be difficult to cram parenting into a few hours on the weekend. (I know that many parents don't have a choice. I was, and am, lucky to have the ability to structure my life as I want, within certain parameters.)

But that choice was about to be much more difficult. I joined the US Attorney's Office in the fall of 2006. The District of Columbia US Attorney's Office is unique in that it handles both state-level criminal matters—primarily "street crime" like assault, drug crimes, etc.—as well as prosecutions involving violations of federal law. This is a real benefit for attorneys seeking trial experience because state-level prosecutions tend to take less time and go to trial more often. While an attorney in private practice might have a case go to trial once every five to ten years, and a federal prosecutor might have a trial twice a year, a prosecutor in District of Columbia Superior Court might have a jury trial every month—not to mention dozens of contested witness hearings before a judge. Indeed, a prosecutor in District of Columbia Superior Court literally lives in the courthouse.

All new prosecutors start in the misdemeanor section. This is a trial lawyer's version of trial by fire. District of Columbia Superior Court is high volume, with dozens of misdemeanor cases going on every day. Prosecutors handling these cases sometimes receive a file literally hours before a case goes to trial. As you might imagine, this is both exhilarating and terrifying. It is particularly difficult for type-A personalities who make it into the office. Like me, many of them got where they are by mastering every little detail of cases they worked on. If you had a matter go to court, you prepared the case and knew everything you could about it. This was impossible in the US Attorney's Office. The case volume was too high, and prosecutors in the misdemeanor section often were assigned cases they didn't prepare. Sometimes— many times—there would be mistakes: witnesses were not subpoenaed, evidence was not procured, etc. But the prosecutor in the courtroom could not soothe an angry judge by noting that someone else prepared the case. You just had to do the best you could.

This was a harrowing time for all new prosecutors. It was not uncommon for attorneys to lose weight, given the long hours and stress. I did. Slight to begin with, I dropped from approximately 160 pounds on a six-foot frame to somewhere under 150. My suits hung off me, my pants held up by a belt cinched as tight as I could get it. Many of my colleagues were younger than me. Some were unmarried. Most did not have children. As I soon figured out, this made a big, big difference. Like me in my childless years, these attorneys worked until they could work no more, then went home to relax and get a few hours of sleep before starting the process all over again.

I could not do that if I wanted to see my son during the week (not to mention my wife, or take on the many child-care duties). And as anyone who has had children will tell you, it is a wonderful thing to see your toddler after work—it is also a lot of work. You can't come home, kick off your shoes, have a beer, and unwind. Your child is on you from the moment you walk in the door. Some of this time is delightful. Your child is cute and full of energy, happy to see you. But you still must be "on." Sometimes it's not so delightful. Your child is tired and strung out, crying, throwing food, and so on. With him is the now strung-out person who has cared for him all day—just waiting for the opportunity to hand off the little darling. At this point, Harrison was walking but unaware of danger. Turn your back for a second, and he'd try to stick a finger in a light socket or come perilously close to tumbling headfirst down the steps. Just being with a child that age is nonstop, sometimes grinding, work. And this is when the child is in a good mood. Often toddlers at the end of a long day are not. Looking back on it and comparing him to his siblings, Harrison was high maintenance—on the move all the time. And when he was in a bad mood, he was in a bad mood. Coming home to a toddler in a good mood is work; coming home to one in a bad mood is like walking into a buzz saw. So, while my childless colleagues headed off to a bar with friends or went home to lie on the couch, I went home to chase after a toddler and tend to a high-maintenance dog. I know that many endure worse. We had it good in that my wife and I had jobs and everyone was healthy. But compared to life without kids, this was a lot of work—and stress.

I did well at the US Attorney's Office. I was good on my feet and excelled in court. As a result, I was put on a special "kid caseload," which involved misdemeanor prosecutions of child sex abuse cases. Unlike most misdemeanor cases, these were legally complicated and often involved expert testimony from nurses and doctors—not to mention the heartbreaking subject matter. I was thrilled with the assignment, but it took a toll. The long, stressful hours at work followed by stress at home caused health problems. The first and most difficult was insomnia. I began to wake up in the middle of the night, heart pounding, unable to sleep. And when I could sleep, I was many times awakened by a crying Harrison. I left the house early every day so that I could meet my witnesses before court. I left my suits downstairs because I couldn't see to dress in my room. Even if I could, I didn't dare make noise that would wake my wife and child. I sometimes came downstairs to find that Sawyer had peed and pooped on the floor. I couldn't just leave it. So, I'd clean it up, wolf down some breakfast, and sprint to catch the bus.

Eventually, my class rotated out of misdemeanors to the trial sections. "Guns and drugs" was the next rotation. If anything, it was more stressful than misdemeanors. Now we were trying jury trials. The case volume was crushing. It was particularly difficult starting a new rotation because you were taking another lawyer's caseload, as that lawyer rotated to other sections in the office. This meant that I had to learn an entirely new caseload and relevant law, as the cases kept on churning. All my colleagues were under immense stress. Many, including me, were thrown into situations where mastery was simply impossible. Survival was the name of the game. Of course, there were benefits. We wanted trial experience, and we got it. Within a year or two, a prosecutor in the District of Columbia office takes more cases to trial than many attorneys do in their entire career. It is, as the expression goes, like drinking from a fire hose. While I learned that the hard way, learn I did—and a lot. I don't think a lawyer ever gets over trial nerves, but I soon developed my own style and rhythm. I learned the coveted skill of trying jury trials.

My own routine became even more extreme. I stopped trying to eat breakfast at home. Instead, I'd drink a cup of coffee and eat oatmeal every morning in the office while meeting with officers or reviewing the cases scheduled for that day. I continued to sleep poorly. I often felt like I was in a fog. Unwilling to miss time with my family, I left every day at 6:00 p.m., no matter what. Some of my colleagues at this point were beginning to start families, too, though the majority still did not have children.

After surviving "guns and drugs," I rotated to another trial section in domestic violence. Though less brutal, this was a busy rotation. The cases were more serious, involving violent crimes that required putting witnesses before the grand jury. The domestic violence section was great. The supervisors were supportive and understanding.

During this time, my wife gave birth to our second son, Jonah. He was born healthy and (relatively) happy. We were thrilled. However, I was unprepared for how difficult having a second child would be. Sure, I knew it would be more work, but having raised one son to two years of age, I figured that I had seen the worst of the learning curve. Not true. Adding a second for us was exponentially more difficult. With one child, there was always at least the possibility of getting a break. If the spouse could take the child for an hour or so, one of us could take a shower, read a book, or go for a run. With two, neither of us got a break—ever. To make matters worse, we had a small house, and the boys shared a room. This made coordinating naps difficult, and pretty much no one slept all the way through the night.

If coming home to one had been work, coming home to two was a test of patience and strength. I remember times walking up to the house and being able to hear our newborn crying, Harrison screaming (he was discovering tantrums by now), and the dog howling. I wish I could say that I were being funny.

I continued to make family my priority. I did my half of the child care and shared the household duties: I did most of the shopping and cooking in my family. This meant that I pretty much did nothing but work and raise children, as did my wife.

By then I was chronically sleep deprived and, as I now know, depressed. I would cry for no reason, had little appetite, and could not sleep, even though I was exhausted.

I finally confided in my doctor, who sent me to a psychologist. She put me on antidepressants and prescription sleep aids. She said I suffered from generalized anxiety disorder.

Despite this, I continued to perform well at work, receiving high marks and even winning an award for my performance in the domestic violence unit. No one at work had any idea what I was going through, and with good reason. It was a high-stress environment—everyone was operating in the red zone.

One might reasonably ask why I didn't look for another job or ask for a different assignment within the office. As my doctor said, "You know, in many other parts of the country, working like this would be considered insanity. Someone might say, 'Why are you doing this? Just find another job.' But this is a different sort of town. My husband is an attorney. I know that your job is considered by many to be the Holy Grail."

I didn't consider scaling back or quitting an option. It's just not something that people in the office commonly did. Moreover, it was not in keeping with how I wanted to view myself. I didn't need help. I just needed to tough it out.

Certainly, women have challenges balancing child care and work. In some ways, women face more complicated issues. Certainly, only women can be pregnant. Still, men face their own headwinds. Unlike women, men are rewarded for having a family. Research has shown that a résumé indicating that a man has children (e.g., "Other activities: coaching son's Little League team") is more likely to get selected for interviews than the same résumé with a woman's name on it. Employers, consciously or not, like the picture of a male worker with a family. So, men have it easier in that regard. The same studies suggest that men with families are penalized more harshly than women if they ask to take time off to care for a child. It seems we like men to demonstrate virility and stability by having a family, primarily because we assume they will perform better at work. If a man betrays that notion by indicating that he occasionally prioritizes family over work, then he is summarily kicked off that perch.

I, no doubt, internalized that idea. Sure, I could want to participate in the life of my children, but that had to be on my own time, and only after I had done well at work.

I want to note here that no one at the US Attorney's Office ever suggested that I sacrifice family for work. Indeed, the office, particularly the domestic violence section, was rightly known for being family-friendly. I shudder to think of working with family stress in a job that is openly hostile to caregiver responsibilities. And yet I hear about it daily in my practice. This is shameful behavior on the part of employers. I marvel at what some of my clients have had to endure.

Eventually, I realized I could not sustain the way I was working. Indeed, trying to balance work and family was backfiring at home. Because I was in a constant state of exhaustion, I had little patience and was short with my wife and children. It was taking a toll. I went to my supervisor and requested an early rotation to the appellate section, known for being not nearly as hectic. To the office's credit, it quickly complied with this request. I moved to appellate, but not before I came down with a terrible respiratory tract infection. I hobbled to that section, broken in many respects.

After completing that rotation, I left the office to open my own firm. For years, I dealt with guilt over my departure. Many of my colleagues expressed admiration that I would leave the safety of a government job—in the midst of an economic meltdown, no less—to hang out a shingle. But for me, it felt different. It's true that I had always wanted to start my own firm. I'd had that dream since before I graduated from law school. But the way it happened felt far from heroic. I felt like a failure.

I have since made my peace with that time in my life and recognize that my choice did not reflect a weakness on my part. It was just a very difficult time that I dealt with the best I could.

As I look back on it, I realize that what made that balancing act nearly impossible for me was having children. You will not find it surprising—particularly if you have kids—that becoming a parent is a profound stage of life. There are many wonderful things about it, but also some not so wonderful. In part, I faced the difficulties I did because I simply was not willing to forgo playing a significant daily role in my children's lives. This is not heroic. This decision was as much for me as it was and is for them. I would like to think that in the long run my family will benefit from having me around, though, to be honest, I'm not sure this is a given. Still, that is the choice I made. Some of it was structural. Perhaps it would have been different if my wife had stayed at home, but she didn't. We relied on her salary, so it wasn't an option. Perhaps I wouldn't have felt the rush to get home if we, as a family, had structured our lives so that Anne took responsibility for most of the child-care and household duties. I don't know that that would have been ideal—and it would have involved a lot more unrelenting work for Anne. In any event, that was not how our family structure worked.

Other attorneys make different choices. I recall hearing a story about a prosecutor who cross-examined Kenneth Lay in the federal prosecution following the collapse of Enron. This was a career-making case. This AUSA will carry that badge for the rest of his life. When he went back into private practice, he could add "cross-examined Mr. Kenneth Lay in the Enron prosecution, leading to a guilty verdict against Mr. Lay" to his bio, which would literally make him millions of dollars over the course of his career. A story I heard mentioned that after the trial, he went straight home to see his wife and children. His youngest daughter, I believe, was around two. It said that he had not seen her for six months. **That was a quarter of her short life.**

I recall thinking at the time that I would never make that choice, even if you could guarantee that I would have a successful, front-page prosecution like that. I just would not be away from my children for that length of time.

I am not claiming hero-parent status. I don't mean to criticize this prosecutor or many other workers like him for making that choice. He likely is a great father. There is no question that the time he spent on that case and away from his family will—through the income it will ultimately generate—give his children options that mine will not have.

However, what this AUSA and I do share in common is that we both had the luxury of making those choices. Many parents, perhaps most, don't. Working is not so much a quality of life issue; it's a matter of survival. A mother works two jobs and rarely sees her kids, not because it allows her a higher standard of living, but because it's what she has to do to afford rent and food.

All this is a very long-winded way of sharing with you why I do this work. Raising children is, without argument, a matter of fundamental importance for this nation. Yet, for whatever reason, our country has chosen not to devote many public resources—for example, subsidized day care—to helping parents make balanced career decisions. I think this is shortsighted. For instance, refusing to provide paid sick leave to a restaurant worker with kids means that she has to come to work sick. Not only does this expose everyone at that restaurant to the risk of illness, but it also puts great strain on her. How effective is she as a mother when she comes home after working a twelve-hour shift as a waitress? What if she gets sick, can't come to work, and loses her job and then her apartment? Even from a selfish perspective, this affects all of us. That kid—the one you don't know whose parent just lost the apartment—he's potentially your future dentist, bus driver, or teacher. What happens to him now?

These policy matters are all worthy of debate. But in the meantime, the laws that we do have to protect those with caregiver responsibilities—the FMLA, the PDA, the ADA, and so forth—need to be enforced. For your sake. For the sake of us all. That's why we do what we do.